MIGRANTS AND CITIES

Research in Migration and Ethnic Relations Series

Series Editor:
Maykel Verkuyten, ERCOMER
Utrecht University

The Research in Migration and Ethnic Relations series has been at the forefront of research in the field for ten years. The series has built an international reputation for cutting edge theoretical work, for comparative research especially on Europe and for nationally-based studies with broader relevance to international issues. Published in association with the European Research Centre on Migration and Ethnic Relations (ERCOMER), Utrecht University, it draws contributions from the best international scholars in the field, offering an interdisciplinary perspective on some of the key issues of the contemporary world.

Also in series

The Bosnian Diaspora
Integration in Transnational Communities
Edited by Marko Valenta and Sabrina P. Ramet
ISBN 978 1 4094 1252 6

Negotiating National Identities
Between Globalization, the Past and 'the Other'
Christian Karner
ISBN 978 0 7546 7638 6

Full series list at back of book

**EUROPEAN RESEARCH CENTRE
ON MIGRATION & ETHNIC RELATIONS**

Migrants and Cities
The Accommodation of Migrant Organizations in Europe

MARGIT FAUSER
Bielefeld University, Germany

Routledge
Taylor & Francis Group

LONDON AND NEW YORK

First published 2012 by Ashgate Publishing

2 Park Square, Milton Park, Abingdon, Oxon OX14 4RN
711 Third Avenue, New York, NY 10017, USA

Routledge is an imprint of the Taylor & Francis Group, an informa business

First issued in paperback 2016

British Library Cataloguing in Publication Data
Fauser, Margit, 1972-
  Migrants and cities : the accommodation of migrant
  organizations in Europe. -- (Research in migration and
  ethnic relations series)
  1. Immigrants--Cultural assimilation--Europe.
  2. Immigrants--Government policy--Europe. 3. Immigrants--
  Europe--Societies, etc. 4. Europe--Emigration and
  immigration--Government policy.
  I. Title II. Series
  305.9'06912'094-dc22

Library of Congress Cataloging-in-Publication Data
Fauser, Margit, 1972-
  Migrants and cities : the accommodation of migrant organizations in Europe / by Margit Fauser.
     p. cm. -- (Research in migration and ethnic relations series)
  Includes bibliographical references and index.
  ISBN 978-1-4094-2186-3 (hbk)
  1. Europe--Emigration and immigration--Government policy. 2. Immigrants--Europe--Societies, etc. 3. Immigrants--Societies, etc.--Government policy--Europe. I. Title.

 JV7590.F39 2011
 362.89'910576094--dc23

                                                                      2011030409

ISBN 978-1-4094-2186-3 (hbk)
ISBN 978-1-138-26852-4 (pbk)

Contents

Acknowledgements

This book is a result of empirical field work in Madrid and Barcelona and desktop reading and writing at my home institution, the Faculty of Sociology at Bielefeld University where a research and lecturing position allowed me to undertake this project.

I am grateful to my former supervisors, Professor Thomas Faist, Bielefeld University, and Professor Joaquín Arango, Universidad Complutense de Madrid who helped me start and further develop this project. Thomas Faist discussed with me many aspects of this book, provided invaluable comments on draft chapters as well as ongoing support and encouragement. For many years I have benefited from his expertise and the friendly atmosphere in the research group on Transnationalization, Development and Migration which he directs. During my visits to Madrid, Joaquín Arango was of great support in discussing with me the rapidly changing immigration situation in Spain and the equally dynamic legal reforms as well as the progress of my empirical research.

For the Spanish city cases I benefited greatly from two research stays at the Instituto Universitario Ortega y Gasset (IUOG), Madrid, and the Centro de Investigación de Relaciones Internacionales y Desarollo (CIDOB), Barcelona. Without these opportunities this study most probably would not have been possible. At both institutions I was provided with office space and other privileges, and above all with support and interest in my work. Colleagues in Madrid and Barcelona shared their professional insights into the new immigration situation in Spain and also often their more personal experiences with me. They drew my attention to recently finished studies and ongoing research and assisted me with hints and suggestions on the more practical challenges of empirical research in this special field. I am particularly indebted to Gemma Pinyol at CIDOB and Professor Joaquín Arango in Madrid for many helpful suggestions and support. The empirical field research for the Spanish city cases was supported by a grant from the German Academic Exchange Service (DAAD). A grant from the Young Researchers Fund of Bielefeld University supported my work on the book in the final stages of research and writing.

I would also like to thank the participants of several researcher seminars and colloquia at Bielefeld University for continuous discussion throughout the research process, data analysis and writing. Several friends and colleagues accompanied the writing of this book at different stages of whom I wish to mention Eva Dick, Jürgen Gerdes, He-Young Haubner, and Eveline Reisenauer for helpful comments and suggestions on several draft versions of different chapters. Special thanks also go to Peter Lenco who has carefully edited this book and to Eva Drebenstedt for providing assistance in the preparation of the manuscript.

Greatest thanks goes to all the people who were willing to share their time and perspectives with me, upon which large parts of this study are based and without which it would never have come into existence, although responsibility for interpreting and presenting their views is all mine.

Margit Fauser, Bielefeld, Germany
2011

List of Tables

List of Abbreviations

ACRS	Associació Catalana de Residents Senegalesos (Catalan Association of Senegalese Residents)
ACULCO	Asociación Socio-Cultural y Cooperación al Desarollo por Colombia e Iberoamérica (Socio-Cultural Association and Development Cooperation for Colombia and Iberoamerica)
AECID	Agencia Española de Cooperación Internacional para el Desarrollo (Spanish Agency of International Cooperation for Development)
AECUATORIE	Asociación de Ecuadorianos Radicados en España (Association of Ecuadorians living in Spain)
AEME	Asociación de Emigrantes Marroquíes en España (Association of Morrocan Emigrants in Spain)
AESCO	Asociación América España Solidaridad y Cooperación (Association America Spain Solidarity and Cooperation)
AJI	Asociación de Jovenes Inmigrantes (Assocation of Young Immigrants)
AJXIM	Asociación Juvenil por la Integración en Madrid (Youth Association for Integration in Madrid)
ATIMCA	Asociación de Trabajadores e Inmigrantes Marroquíes en Cataluña (Association of Moroccan Workers and Immigrants in Catalonia)
ATIME	Asociación de Trabajadores e Inmigrantes Marroquíes en España (Association of Moroccan Immigrant Workers in Spain)
AWO	Arbeiterwohlfahrt (Workers' Welfare Association)
BRAP	Birmingham Racial Action Programme
CCOO	Comisiones Obreras (Workers' Commission)
CDU	Christlich Demokratische Union (Christian-Democratic Party)
CRC	Community Relation Councils
CRE	Commission for Racial Equality
CPB	Centro Peruano de Barcelona (Peruvian Center of Barcelona)
DfID	Department for International Development
FAVB	Federació de Associacions de Veïns i Veïnes de Barcelona (Federation of Neighbourhood Associations of Barcelona)

FCIC	Federació de Col.lectius d'Immigrants a Catalunya (Federation of Immigrant Collectives in Catalonia)
Fedelatina	Federación de Entidades Latinoamericanas de Catalunya (Federation of Latin-American Associations in Catalonia)
IMSERSO	Instituto de Migraciones y Servicios Sociales (Institute for Migration and Social Services)
IU	Izquierda Unida (United Left)
IWA	Indian Workers' Assocation
SAIER	Servei d'atenció a immigrants estrangers i refugiats (Service for the Attention to Foreigners and Refugees)
MTAS	Ministerio de Trabajo y Asuntos Sociales (Ministry for Labour and Social Affairs)
PICA	Pla Integral del Casc Antic (Integrated Plan of the Old Town)
PP	Partido Popular (Popular Party)
PSOE	Partido Socialista Obrero Español (Spanish Socialist Workers' Party)
REMCODE	Red Euromediterranea de Cooperación al Desarrollo (Euro-Mediterranean Network for Development Cooperation)
SFC	(Birmingham) Standing Consultative Forum
UGT	Unión General de Trabajadores (General Union of Workers)
USO	Union Sindical Obrera (Workers' Union)
VOMADE-VINCIT	Voluntariado de Madres Dominicanas en España – Voluntariado Integración Colectivo Internacional de Trabajadores (Volunteers of Dominican Mothers in Spain – Volunteers Integration International Collective of Workers)

Chapter 1

Introduction

Migrants[1] have collectively organized at all times and in all places. Although migration scholarship and politicians in Europe neglected the active engagement of migrants during the first decades of post-war immigration, this attitude slowly changed throughout the 1980s (Miller 1981, *International Migration Review* 1985). Today, migrant organizations are attracting increased attention as an issue of social science research as well as in public debates as a crucial element of migrants' settlement, integration and transnationalism. In urban places and cities in particular they are considered vital elements of society and they are addressed as such by public authorities. They are thus one element in understanding the processes associated with migration and the ways societies deal with it. This book is interested in the process of accommodation of migrant organizations in European cities. It specifically asks how the city context shapes this process.

This book presents empirical case study evidence from new immigration cities in southern Europe and revises the literature on northern Europe's more established immigration localities. Research is still very scarce on the former, with most insights on migrant organization and mobilization in Europe resting on studies focusing on the latter. In analysing and contrasting both, new insights in the process of accommodation of migrant organizations can be gained. Not only can new empirical cases reveal dynamics different from those discovered by earlier studies, they may also serve to point to so far neglected factors which also shape migrant organizations. This can help to revise empirical knowledge and theoretical concepts which so far rely on the more established places. Among other aspects, migrant organizations in recent immigration cities are strongly oriented towards the receiving country, whereas processes of collective formation in other European places often displayed strong orientation toward 'homeland' issues at the point of emergence. It becomes clear throughout this study that this is shaped by very different contexts.

Scholarship on migrant organizations has put great attention on the determinants and shaping forces of migrant organization, participation and mobilization. Rather than one single theory, a number of approaches have been developed trying to explain the formation as well as the social and political action

---

1   This book will use the term migrants as a generic term for people who take up residence in another country. It will employ the terms immigrants (or emigrants) when referring to people in this specific condition of entry or stay in a country different from their place of birth or origin (or exit from this country). The same applies to policies which address these persons from that perspective.

of migrant organizations. While at the beginning, scholars paid most attention to the characteristics of the migrant community, throughout the 1990s the role of the state and its political institutions entered the focus. From this perspective it emerges that the political–institutional environment strongly shapes the formation and action of migrant organizations. Political–institutional contexts differ from place to place, which makes it necessary to focus on particular cities, not without acknowledging that influences from multiple institutional levels are playing out there. It is one of the main arguments of this book that city contexts relevant to the study of migrant organizations include local and national institutions, and that these concern integration as well as immigration regulations and policies. The other main point is that only by applying a transnational perspective that does not establish a conceptual dichotomy between migrant organizations engaging in the 'host' or 'home' country are we able to understand which contexts contribute to which processes. Against this background the book shows the different ways the processes of accommodation have taken in European cities.

The discovery of migrant organizations in European cities

Throughout history and across world regions migrants have organized in many different forms of voluntary associations. They founded mutual aid and benefit societies, first aid institutions, nationalistic political associations, cultural clubs, religious communities, advocacy groups, hometown associations and secret societies (Park, Miller 1969 [1921], Moya 2005). Such (formal) organizations are the visible sign of new collective formations and the active engagement of migrants to improve their situation and follow their interests. Early research on the dynamics and consequences of international migration which emerged at the beginning of the twentieth century in the US, in particular from the Chicago School of sociology, from the beginning considered these immigrant institutions crucial to the understanding of processes of migration and social change (Park, Miller 1969 [1921], Warner, Srole 1947).

In the study of post-war migration in Europe, migrant organizations did not appear on the research agenda until the 1980s, when migration scholars started to address migrants as political objects and subjects (*International Migration Review* 1985). Throughout the first decades of post-war migration, the dominant view insisted that migrants were rather passive and apolitical, while research concentrated on social and economic issues, in line with the ways legal frameworks generally conceptualized them (Miller 1981). When settlement was recognized, research started to problematize the existence of growing populations with limited citizenship status within European societies. Scholars began to investigate the social, civil and political rights available for migrants across Europe and to analyse how migrants mobilized on the grounds of existing rights and attempted to expand them further (Miller 1981, *International Migration Review* 1985, Rex, Joly, Wilpert 1987, Layton-Henry 1990). Additionally, their social roles and the welfare functions they fulfilled became topics of interest during this time as they were slowly becoming actors in social service delivery in many European countries (Jenkins 1988).

Today there is a new interest in migrant organizations and collective mobilization in relation to integration and participation of migrants within receiving societies (Koopmans et al. 2005, Schrover, Vermeulen 2005b; see the special issue of JEMS Schrover, Vermeulen 2005a). Newer research also exists on the transnational and origin-country related activities of migrant organizations in Europe, even though the major part of scholarship on transnational migrant organizations is still to be found in the US literature (Portes, Escobar, Walton Radford 2007, Portes, Escobar, Arana 2008). Yet, most research either concentrates on the orientations and activities directed toward the receiving or the origin side. Combining both is one of the aims of this book.

Different perspectives on the role and relevance of migrant organizations exist and this may partly explain the academic and political interest. First, the relevance of migrant organizations is a matter of dispute. Widespread assumptions sustain the limited role of migrant organizations when it comes to the expansion of the rights and recognition of newcomers in the context of reception, settlement and integration (Guiraudon 1998: 277, Penninx, Martiniello 2004: 152). No small part of the debate disputes their role and relevance altogether due to their often unclear relationship with the broader migrant community and with immigrants' integration. One reason for this is that the representativeness and membership relations of migrant organizations are often unclear. Data on membership is often difficult to get and it is also not always reliable. Therefore, it remains unclear what conclusions can be drawn from this data (Østergaard-Nielsen 2003: 23). In the cases investigated in Spanish cities that are presented later in this book, many members have a weak relationship with the public articulations of their respective organization and display rather a particular need for certain information, legal advice or job training which are offered to them in their condition as clients (for discussion and evidence see Chapter 4). Further, even under the difficult legal and social conditions which many migrants face in these places, a majority of migrants never enter into contact with any migrant organization, some have not even heard about their existence, whereas others rely on other types of organizations or public authorities, or do not receive any support at all (Díez Nicolás, Ramírez Latifa 2001). The relations between migrant organizations, their members and the broader migrant community and thus their representativeness are a contested issue in academic literature and among public authorities in their search for mediators and interlocutors *vis-à-vis* migrant groups. Migrant organizations should not be seen as representatives of certain communities per se and they do not necessarily represent larger groups in the stricter sense. In spite of these limitations, a broad literature documents the multiple functions migrant organizations fulfil for their members and beyond: the cultural and religious orientations they may give, the social services these provide, and the contributions they make for the advancement of the migrants' interests and their rights. Their engagements even include mobilizations in support of those least likely to count on the necessary resources, i.e. the irregulars (see Chapter 4; see also Laubenthal 2007).

Second, even greater discussion ranges around the 'ethnic paradox' (Park 1969, Ballis Lal 1990, Faist 1996). The implications of this discussion will be treated more extensively in Chapter 2. Here suffice it to say that the idea of the paradox refers to the fact that although migrant organizations are frequently an expression of ethnic identity different from the mainstream receiving society, they nevertheless contribute to migrants' integration into this society. Despite the fact that some authors still consider migrant organizations as markers of ethnic distinctiveness and retention, and therefore a sign of failed integration and ethnic 'ghetto' formation, most authors seem to subscribe to the 'ethnic paradox' and point out that over time the contributions of migrant organizations favour integration, although under more culturally pluralist conditions. The more pluralist perspective guides much current research on migrant organizations where their supportive character is at the centre. The existence, number and degree or forms of migrant organizations and their public activities are now frequently taken as indicators of integration and also of a favourable political environment. Accordingly, the importance of migrant organizations seems widely shared, in particular regarding local integration. 'Homeland' ties and transnational activism are frequently seen in opposition to this. The dispute has seemingly evolved into a 'transnational' version of the paradox, moving from a concern around the implications of separate ethnic identities to a critical perspective on 'homeland' ties. Different from most available studies, the approach taken in this book follows a transnational perspective, allowing potentially simultaneous agendas related to situations on the side of reception and origin to exist. Whether these enter into conflict is therefore an empirical question.

The third issue that comes to the surface in the latest interest on migration organizations is that this interest is specifically reflected in many local studies. Cities are the places where internal and international migration concentrates. The implications of migration were subject to sociological inquiry already in the early twentieth century when more and more migrants from increasingly diverse places led to great social transformations in American and European cities (Simmel 1995 [1903], Park, Burgess, McKenzie 1968 [1925]). Today again, cities are being recognized as important sites for the social and political changes caused by migration and for research on them (Auriat, Rochet 2001, Favell 2001: 390, Glick Schiller, Çağlar 2009). As in early American research (Park, Miller 1969 [1921], Warner, Srole 1947), today in Europe the latest focus on migrant organizations is increasingly connected to the local. In particular (major) cities are gaining renewed prominence in this research (Rogers, Tillie 2001, Penninx et al. 2004a). Over the past decades processes of economic globalization and political–administrative decentralization have contributed to the strengthening of the role of cities and that of local governments. These changes brought new political and administrative competences and new challenges to be handled by the cities. Local levels of government have played a major role in addressing migrant populations in the absence or reluctance of national responses in the early and today established local destinations in northern Europe (Penninx et al. 2004b: 3). In the newer destinations in the south their role seems even more pronounced (Tsuda 2006). This is at least partly related to the new forms of governance that have emerged over the past twenty years, with new non-state actors becoming part of it. Increasingly today, these newer actors also include migrant organizations. Non-state actors have become involved in local governance, consultation, decision making and social welfare implementation, although to different degrees in different places. In this situation, the formation and existence of migrant organizations in cities and localities has become an important field in the study of migration and integration. However, although most local studies are limited to the role of local institutions, the city context relevant to the accommodation of migrant organizations is not only a result of local politics. Immediate and mediated influences from higher levels of government also shape this process.

Migrant organizations are relevant actors to migrants as well as to the societies they interact with, whether in the receiving or origin country. Although their contributions for the integration of the wider migrant population have been questioned, given their often small size, the limited scope of outreach, and often scarce internal participation they have provided helpful support for migrants and have contributed to the advancement of their rights. Thus, they can be considered a vital element in modern pluralist societies and they are addressed as such by local and national public authorities. They are one important element in understanding the dynamics of migration and the ways societies deal with it. This book is interested in learning about these dynamics accompanying the formation and activities of migrant organizations and the ways societies – here the receiving society and in particular its political institutions – affect and address them.

The accommodation of migrant organizations

The majority of research on migrant organizations is guided by a perspective on the integration into the receiving society as some fixed outcome. It either discusses the role of migrant organizations for individual migrants or takes their existence and activities as signs of political and social integration. In contrast, this book is interested in the study of the process of their accommodation. In so doing, the study takes up the concept of accommodation from the Chicago School of sociology and in particular as elaborated by Robert Park. The concept of accommodation has not received great attention in the sociology and research of migration. Park himself noted that 'the voluminous literature upon immigration deals but slightly with the interesting accommodations of the newcomer to his environments' (Park, Burgess 1969 [1921]: 719). The processes of social adaptation of migrants have attracted more attention since that time, even if still not fully understood. The concept of accommodation itself though, has not acquired more attention or theoretical weight, although the term is now used with increasing frequency in social science literature and European policy documents (see, for example, European Council 2004). Consequently the concept of accommodation shall be introduced here as a guiding perspective of this book.

Robert Park and Ernest Burgess introduced the term in their 'Introduction to the Science of Sociology' as one of the basic sociological concepts (Park, Burgess 1969). In addition, Park referred to it on another occasion as one of the stages of the race-relations cycle (Park 1964). In this model, interaction between races or between the newcomers and the established society evolve from contact over conflict to accommodation and eventual assimilation. Although many scholars have taken this cycle as crucial for the understanding of Park's sociological thinking, others argue that the teleological and inevitable character of the cycle culminating in assimilation is not necessarily the key to Park's theoretical understanding of social interaction processes (Ballis Lal 1990: 5, 41–2, Kivisto 2005: 7). Accommodation may be considered but one stage in the processes initiated by social contact between different groups and individuals. More importantly, the concept describes a form of social interaction involving changes and thus not static outcomes.

Accommodation is first and foremost a social process, related to sociologically transmitted changes. It is thus distinctive from adaptation which is a result of biological transmissions (Park, Burgess 1969: 664). The socially 'acquired adjustments' bring about 'an accommodation of differences through conflict' which are the basis of social organization (Park, Burgess 1969: 664). According to Park's understanding, this implies that modern society is characterized by diversity and diverse-mindedness rather than by like-mindedness which is to be found among animals. Accommodation thus results from conflict, or in other words, from conflictual social relations. Each resolution of a conflict leads to a new accommodation and a more – although always transitory – stable situation or equilibrium. Every new conflict issues a new accommodation. Concerning personal relations, Park and Burgess note that these tend to take a hierarchical form.

Accommodation is different from assimilation insofar as it seems less coherent and also less cohesive. 'Assimilation is a process of interpenetration and fusion in which persons and groups acquire the memories, sentiments, and attitudes of other persons or groups, and, by sharing their experience and history, are incorporated with them in a common cultural life' (Park, Burgess 1969: 735). It is a slow, gradual and generally unconscious process. Accommodation, in turn, occurs more rapidly and consciously, but its results are also less stable or long lasting. Assimilation refers to a more settled situation of unity and a higher degree of social cohesion and societal integration. In contrast '[a]ccommodation may be relatively permanent, it may fall apart in conflict or resolve itself by assimilation. Only when assimilation occurs is the latent antagonism inherent in accommodation "wholly dissolved"' (Ballis Lal 1990: 44). It should be noted though, that assimilation refers to a process based on unity, not on uniformity or homogeneity. Diversity is central to Park's understanding of modern society, with assimilation describing the general frame of societal incorporation, including individualism and ethnic distinctiveness.

Such distinctiveness is then not so much an expression of ethnic groups in an essentialist understanding, but rather part of cosmopolitan dispositions involving shared traditions and diverging individual opinions (see Kivisto 2005: 8–9). 'The unity thus achieved is not necessarily or even normally like-mindedness' (Park, Burgess 1969: 737). Park was concerned with the degree of unity necessary for an inclusive society as a basis for a political community of democratic institutions.

This perspective brings Park and his colleagues close to the later emerging cultural pluralist paradigm, as Barbara Ballis Lal (1990) points out. At the same time, the survival of distinctive ethnic characteristics seems relatively unlikely in the long run, when cooperation continues and more and more common experiences are acquired by all members of the society. Rather, 'the remaking of the mainstream' seems to characterize this approach (Alba, Nee 2003: in particular Chapter 2). Since this is a matter of ongoing dispute and the degree of distinctiveness or homogeneity associated with assimilation is difficult to determine with precision, and moreover assimilation today seems to suggest uniformity or even coercion, one may argue that accommodation is a more appropriate perspective for modern societies as 'composed of groups accommodated, but not fully assimilated' (Park, Burgess 1969: 667).

In addition, assimilation is more strongly related to and occurs more easily within primary contacts, whereas accommodation builds upon secondary group contacts. This is what makes it particularly relevant in relation to migrant organizations.[2] In fact, the authors themselves state: 'One of the most important factors in the process [of accommodation] [...] is the immigrant community which serves as a mediating agency between the familiar and the strange' (Park, Burgess 1969: 719). Here, the text makes explicit reference to another study of the immigrant communities and institutions including migrant organizations within the Carnegie Corporation programme of the 'Americanization Study', which Robert Park conducted together with William Thomas and Herbert Miller (Park, Burgess 1969: 719, Park, Miller 1969). Migrant organizations are not only mediators for the broader migrant communities. They can themselves be considered an accommodation. In this sense, Barbara Ballis Lal (1990: 107) argues

---

2   Park did also refer to assimilation in secondary groups. In fact, he was particularly concerned with the 'Racial Assimilation in Secondary Groups', as the title of his *American Journal of Sociology* article from 1914 shows. However, therein lies the fundamental problem: neither Black Americans nor Asian immigrants such as the Japanese were given the opportunity to assimilate. Where the 'Negro' was in close contact with the family which he or she served as a slave or servant, assimilation occurred. Where relationships were more distant or later became so after abolition of slavery, it failed. The increasing solidarity, self-consciousness and organizing among the Black community which took place in the following years then 'must be regarded as a response and "accommodation" to changing internal and external relations of the race' (Park 1914: 618). Finally, once a race has achieved its moral independency in this way, 'assimilation will continue', providing the necessary bonds for loyalty within one state. Loyalty, however, is only likely 'insofar as the state incorporates, as an integral part of its organization, [these people]' (Park 1914: 623).

that Park's thinking about immigrant institutions includes their consideration as adaptive mechanisms since these are located in American cities and influenced and to a certain degree produced by this situation. They are 'the products of the immigrants' effort to adapt their heritages to American conditions' (Park, Miller 1969: 120). By so doing, immigrant institutions are not only supporting individual and group accommodation and potentially assimilation (or integration) into the greater society, they constitute an adaptation to the new environment. Therefore, migrant organizations are a means and an expression of accommodation. Although both aspects are related, this study is particularly interested in the latter, considering them an adaptation or accommodation to the environment. What shapes the processes of accommodation of migrant organizations? Park himself does not offer a comprehensive framework for an analysis of contextual determinants in this respect. Although he puts considerable emphasis on the efforts and the character of the immigrant community in the comparison of different communities in the Americanization study, he nonetheless refers to 'opportunity structures' in his writings (Ballis Lal 1990: 93). These were predominantly structured by the economy and the labour market conditions offering opportunities to newcomers to improve their lives. 'This optimistic prognosis was shattered by the Great Depression of the 1930s when the promise of social mobility as a result of individual effort was contradicted by the realization of life chances which had more to do with international economic markets and political events outside individual control' (Ballis Lal 1990: 93). This situation is further aggravated by xenophobia and racism which Park and his colleagues highlighted as inhibiting forces to assimilation (Ballis Lal 1990: 94–5). In relation to the state Park and Burgess also note that 'coercive policies' as they had observed in relation to efforts of denationalization in Europe, that is, suppression of cultural minorities in European nation-building processes, failed. In contrast, more indirectly providing opportunities for participation is more likely to contribute to accommodation and eventually assimilation (Park, Burgess 1969: 740).

Different from the times and places Park was dealing with, the role of the state has become more particularly prominent in migration research in Europe throughout the last two decades. A broad literature has developed on the environment for migrants' accommodation in terms of state institutions. The analytical framework proposed in the next chapter links up to the approaches dealing with the role and shaping forces of the political–institutional context. As this study is interested in the process of accommodation, it looks at the political institutional contexts and the ways these shape the formation of migrant organizations and their activities and struggles in relevant fields of action and contention.

In comparison to integration or assimilation approaches, accommodation has one additional advantage in that it does not establish a theoretical opposition between migrants' engagements in the situation in the 'host' or the 'home' country. It allows for observing processes of collective formation and social and political action initiated with the arrival and potential settlement of migrants, whether this is directed toward the improvement of migrants' rights and interests in relation to the receiving country or to the political, economic or social situation in the country of origin, or to both. So far, most research has concentrated on one side or the other.

In sum, this study applies the concept of accommodation for three reasons. First, it points to a process rather than to a particular outcome. Second, it places emphasis on the role of the environment in which this process occurs. In this respect, the study concentrates on political–institutional contexts. Third, accommodation is not exclusively directed towards integration (or assimilation) into the receiving country, but may also involve engagement with the places of origin. Consequently the concept is open for a transnational perspective.

One remark is necessary before proceeding further. Accommodation has become an established term in academia as well as in policy guidelines of some European countries and on the level of the European Union (European Council 2004). Here, the term is used to point out the mutual interaction between the receiving society and migrants and to the changing nature of society as a whole. Most often this implies a normative sense and to a lesser extent a theoretical concept (Zapata-Barrero 2004, Zapata-Barrero, Adamuz García, Martínez Luna 2002). This book uses the concept of accommodation as an analytical tool, not as a normative claim or assumption.

Research strategy and methodology

In the following chapters this book deals with migrant organizations in places of recent and established immigration in Europe. In its empirical part it presents primary research on migrant organizations in the two major Spanish cities, Barcelona and Madrid, and contrasts these with existing research on German and Dutch cities, more concretely Berlin and Amsterdam, and from British local cases. The aim of this proceeding is to contribute new insights into local dynamics, similarities and differences of migrants' collective formation within and across countries in Europe.

The empirical analysis uses a framework, presented in more detail in Chapter 2, that considers multiple institutional levels as constitutive for the city context. This framework comes out of the dialogue between theoretical approaches and the qualitative and more inductive primary research conducted in Barcelona and Madrid. Explanations and insights on the accommodation of migrant organizations, to date based on the northern European contexts of today's more established immigration, only partly resembled what this research found in the two new immigration cities. This is a result not so much of the difference in timing, but mainly because earlier migrations have been affected by different (political) conditions. In order to capture these processes a framework has been elaborated which partly differs from existing explanations in the field. This in turn seems helpful in order to better understand not only the accommodation in recent immigration places, but also brings to the fore more systematically some aspects which can be observed in the established immigration cities. Most importantly this concerns the role of the immigration regime. Conditions of entry, stay and work for the early post-war migrants in European cities were very different from those that affect today's newcomers in the recent immigration cities. This is one important factor that influences the diverging processes of accommodation.

Contrasting city contexts

Comparative methods are well established in migration research. This has meant either to select on the basis of ethnicity and to compare various ethnic groups in one place, city or country (convergent comparison), or to make a selection based on structural constraints and opportunities of contexts and compare one ethnic group across these (divergent comparison) (Green 1991). These two ways of comparison reflect the main approaches in the study of migrant organizations. These are either concerned with the role of ethnic community characteristics or with that of political opportunity structures. Since the main question of this book is how specific city contexts shape migrant organizations, it contrasts different cities and can thus be considered divergent. At the same time, however, rather than taking one (ethnic or national) group as the element to be explained, the interest lays in the process of migrant organizing as such, and not that of a particular group (Green 1991). Accordingly, migrant organizations in the primary research were selected from different nationality backgrounds (see below); the same strategy is used in the revision of existing literature, at least to the extent this is possible (for instance the majority of literature on migrant organizations in Germany stems from research on Turks, and this specifically applies to Berlin).

Concerning contrasts of institutional contexts, the bulk of existing research that offers insights into local variations does so on the basis of comparisons across countries. Most commonly, studies investigate, for example, a French city as compared to a British one (Moore 2001, Garbaye 2000), a French and a Dutch city (Bousetta 1997) or compare the German and the Dutch capitals (Koopmans, Berger 2004). This research often uses local cases to analyse national differences. Only very few studies offer a comparison of selected cities in one country (Ireland 1994, Caponio 2005, Koopmans 2004). This research can show that even within one national setting, local governments differ in their responses to the challenges of diversity and in the interaction between authorities and migrants and their organizations.

Moreover, comparativists have argued in favour of within-country comparison for the significant local differences these may reveal resulting from diverse economic, cultural and political factors – an argument that has been developed with regards to Spain specifically (Linz, de Miguel 1966). In the face of recent decentralization and broader economic and political transformations that allow for more local and regional divergence, scholars in comparative politics have once more argued for comparing sub-national units (Synder 2001). In addition, in the critique of methodological nationalism, prominently reflected in migration studies, limitations in the understanding of the diverse processes of migration and related social change are attributed to the sole focus on the national state as an institution and territory. This calls for putting more emphasis on scales below and beyond the nation state in the study of political institutions responding to migration and in relation to migrants' agency (Wimmer, Glick Schiller 2002). In line with these arguments and findings, this book makes use of city contrast in order to advance the understanding of migrant organization and their accommodation and to reveal the relevant elements shaping them.

Hence, the structure of the study presented here uses three different levels for contrast. First, it looks at differences (but also similarities) within one country (the Barcelona and Madrid cases); second, it concentrates on differences between cities across countries in established immigration places; third, it contrasts both results from recent and established places with one another. To achieve this, one main part of the study and presentation uses mainly primary data from Barcelona and Madrid and the institutional contexts playing out there. Here, similarities and differences emerge from contrasting both city contexts. The other main part revises existing literature using comparative research and single case studies of individual cities. This serves to point to differences across established European immigration cities due to varying institutional contexts. Less prominently reflected in the literature are similarities. A comparison of Berlin and Amsterdam, for instance, has found fairly similar patterns and agendas – although not overall numbers – among migrant organizations in the two cities (Vermeulen 2006). That study, as many others, attributes the observed similarities to the characteristics of the immigrant group, based on the comparison of one national group in different contexts. However, some similarities emerge from the background of shared characteristics of relatively stable guest worker immigration regimes. Thus, the fact that these organizations emerged from migrants who were guest-workers rather than the fact that they were Turks contributed to similar types and activities of the organizations. The role of the immigration regime becomes particularly discernible when contrasting this with the findings from new immigration places. Here, the high incidence and characteristics of irregularity among many migrants has led to the formation of different types of organizations.

Research design for the Spanish city cases

The first main part of the empirical study relies on the analysis of migrant organizations in the recent immigration cities of Barcelona and Madrid. It is based on qualitative empirical research and most data was collected in two longer field stages in 2006 and one shorter field trip in 2007. Further desktop and internet research on available documents and digital material has accompanied data collection. The core material is composed of around 45 interviews conducted with representatives from migrant organizations, public administration primarily from the local level, but also from national and regional agencies as well as with representatives from trade unions and non-governmental organizations (see Appendix 2 on the visited institutions). Most migrant organizations as well as some other interviewees were visited twice, one time in the first stage and another time in the second stage of field research. These repeated visits often included the possibility to talk to different persons from one organization and thus to learn about the perspectives of various persons active in the organization. Further material includes annual reports, flyers, press releases and web-site contents by the migrant organizations as well as similar material from public authorities. Two sampling strategies characterize this research. First, in each of the two cities five migrant organizations were selected for in-depth research. This sampling follows the intent to reflect variation in nationality and peak of inflows from particular countries which can be observed in statistical data on annual inflows and growth of resident populations. Second, after the first coding and analysis of the collected data three fields of action and contention have been chosen for further in-depth research since these proved to be particularly insightful as regards the characteristics of the accommodation process in the new immigration cities. With this proceeding it was possible to reveal locally different accommodation processes emerging from local political-institutional contexts as well as from the differential influences of national policies in the different cities (for a more detailed description see Appendix 1 on methodology).

A few words on the use of existing literature on northern European city cases

The second main part of the empirical study in this book makes use of existing studies on migrant organizations in northern European cities. In addition, it uses other secondary literature on the relatively well documented elements of the political-institutional contexts which compose the explanatory framework proposed in this book. In relation to the migrant organization a number of insightful comparative research and case studies exist which include or concentrate on Berlin, Amsterdam and/or some British localities (generally those which developed an explicit multicultural approach in the 1980s). These studies have been undertaken from different theoretical perspectives. Available research often accounts for one of the elements proposed for the analytical framework of this book. Drawing on these different perspectives and their empirical insights allows for seeing some of the combined effects of the different elements which have so far not received systematic attention.

Structure of the book

Different perspectives and approaches have pointed to a number of different elements of the political-institutional context relevant to the accommodation of migrant organizations. Chapter 2 offers a theoretical discussion and introduces the analytical framework and related key concepts of this study in three main respects. The chapter starts with a more detailed discussion of the 'ethnic (now transnational) paradox' already referred to and points to the implications the different perspectives have for the research on migrant organizations. In contrasting existing perspectives, this part introduces the transnational approach taken in this book. Often, migrants' engagement in integration and existing transnational orientations are conceptualized in opposition, while here the aim is to avoid (implicit) dichotomies. Although recent transnational migration research has revived the discussion around the relationship between integration and ethnicity and 'homeland' attachments, very little research considers the possibility of dual agendas of migrant organizations. The transnational perspective taken in this study does not oppose engagements for the political, economic or social situation in the origin country to those directed at the improvement of migrants' rights and interests in the receiving country or city. It is interested in learning about the different aspects of the process of accommodation and the contexts contributing to them.

The second section of Chapter 2 concentrates on the role of cities in relation to migration and migrant organizations and introduces the perspective on the city context as composed of influences from multiple political–institutional levels. For a long time, migration research has primarily concentrated on the nation state as its unit of analysis and, as a consequence, on national institutions. More recent research focuses on cities and local levels of government. Local levels are closest to newly arriving migrants and settling populations. They have often reacted to migratory inflows relative early. Most importantly, the transfers of authority and competence in the last decades have broadened the space of local action for public authorities. This leads to the fact that different cities provide different conditions for migrants and migrant organizations. In this respect recent research highlights the great variety of local responses to migration across and within countries. This points to the need to investigate migrant organizations in specific cities if we are to understand the processes of their accommodation. Still, national-level institutions also influence local actors. The bulk of research, however, either concentrates on the national level or, more recently, on local institutions. This study argues for the systematic analysis of the interplay of political institutions on multiple levels which play out in the city context.

The third and main section of the chapter goes into the literature on explanatory approaches in the study of migrant organizations. Different strands of theory have used partly different conceptual elements and operationalizations of the political–institutional contexts and opportunities. The framework applied in the empirical parts of this book combines four of those elements. It considers first, the approach and attitude of powerful actors, most importantly the government, on migrants' reception and integration and their organizations; second, the existing institutional patterns of state/society relations; third, the fact that these stem from multiple institutional levels (national and local); and finally, the immigration regime and the conditions of entry, stay and work it establishes represents the last element and the one which has been greatly neglected by existing research.

The following three chapters constitute the empirical part of the book. These cover examples from Spanish, German, Dutch and British city cases.

The empirical part gives more space to the Spanish cases which are dealt with in two chapters, since literature on political regulations, most notably on local levels, and on migrant organizations is still scarce for this country. The German, Dutch and British city cases are dealt with in one chapter. Here insights can be gained by contrasting across these cases and with the Spanish ones. Chapter 3 analyses the political–institutional contexts playing out in Spanish cities, of which Barcelona and Madrid were selected for in-depth study. The institutions of immigration and in particular the ways in which these contribute to and deal with irregularity, that is the absence of legal residence and work authorization among many migrants, is particularly relevant to the contexts in question. Various procedures and instruments contribute to the existence and maintenance of irregular statuses, while at the same time various procedures allow for ways to address and change this status, but also imply high fall-back rates. This situation is accompanied by a relative absence of state measures in the reception of the newcomers and their further integration. At the same time, relatively early on the state started to offer economic support and participatory structures for migrant organizations, most of which were in fact located in Madrid. On the local level, responses to the growing migrant populations can be observed in Barcelona and Madrid from early on. The cities strongly differ, though, including the ways in which they address migrant organizations. For instance, while Barcelona opened participatory channels in the mid-1990s, Madrid only established an immigration council as late as 2006. These differing contexts have meant very different conditions for newly emerging migrant organizations in both cities. Furthermore, the analysis in Chapter 3 includes newer local public policies promoting migrant organizations' transnational activities which emerge around the by now global debate on development–migration linkages, and are facilitated through Spain's decentralized development cooperation. These initiatives strongly contribute to transnational projects on the agendas of migrant organizations.

Chapter 4 shows how migrant organizations in Barcelona and Madrid are shaped by these contexts. It is divided into two parts of which the first analyses the formation and particularities of a selected number of migrant organizations from different national backgrounds. The second part concentrates on the activities in three fields of action and contention. Hence, the chapter describes their emergence and the common turning point that characterizes their formation in both cities. This turn is defined by the growing numbers of often irregular migrant inflows and the scant state support they receive. In this situation, the migrant organizations were primarily concerned with providing support to the newcomers, advising them in the application and renewal of work and residence permission, and other legal and social questions. At a relatively early point in time, this situation was augmented by access to public funding from national and/or local level governments as well as the formal participation in consultative councils. This, however, differs strongly in the two cities. Most of the Barcelona-based organizations investigated have not received large amounts of funding, but are nonetheless represented in the municipal immigration council. In Madrid, by contrast, some of the organizations based in the capital are supported by local and national authorities with both contexts mutually reinforcing in terms of recognition, public funding, and participation.

As regards migrant organizations' activities and struggles in relevant fields of action and contention, the analysis considers social and political rights in the receiving places as well as transnational activities for situations abroad. Since the degree and the conditions of inclusion into subsidies and participation differ in the two cities, the intensities and forms of actions in these fields also differ. Further, the chapter describes notable overlaps of the fields of action. Political voting rights and claims for regularization have been articulated together in many instances. Based on the concept of 'citizenship of residence', regular and irregular statuses are often not clearly distinguished. Moreover, claims presented in formal participatory channels, informal meetings and demonstrations have fluid boundaries with the delivery of services which deal with the same topics, that is, contributing to the regularization of migrants' statuses and the improvement of their living conditions and rights. In addition, the chapter documents the increasing involvement in transnational projects among these actors. The analysis puts particular emphasis on transnational development cooperation, since this is strongly promoted by institutions in the receiving context.

Chapter 5 brings together existing literature on migrant organizing in local places in Germany, the Netherlands and the UK. Here as well differences in policies from country to country and from city to city contribute to the different characteristics of migrant organizations. Germany, for instance, is characterized by a rather restrictive attitude towards migrants and migrant organizations as well as the lack of state support to the latter on the national level. The city of Berlin, in contrast, has been more open to migrant organizations since the early 1980s and has thereby shaped their numerical growth and their activities. In the Netherlands, multicultural or ethnic minority policies both from the national and the Amsterdam city levels have strengthened a wide spectrum of organizations where interest articulation is high on the agendas in line with the role attributed to them. The UK displays a generally more localized picture of migrant organizations, which are also more strongly integrated in welfare policies and non-state actor service delivery. Existing studies also reveal a number of similarities among migrant organizations in northern European cities. Most frequently these are related to group factors and community characteristics. However, some similarities in policies, most strongly at the early stage of guest worker and post-colonial migration, are also responsible for similar patterns among migrant organizations. These came out of the immigration regimes and the conditions of migration, as well as of the relative ignorance on the side of public authorities which migrant organizations encountered at the beginning in northern Europe, especially in the German and Dutch capital and less so in British localities. Relative security in labour market and social realms, expectations of return and few (public) resources first led to cultural and 'homeland'-oriented associations, especially in Berlin and Amsterdam. Over time, greater concerns with migrants' situation in the receiving society evolved, and here differences became more pronounced across local contexts. Nonetheless, some similarities remain, which become particularly visible in contrast to the situation in recent immigration localities. Generally, a decline in origin country-oriented activities over time has been observed in most places. So far, transnational ties have often been considered as opposed to engagements with receiving societies, and few studies have systematically analysed transnational activities or the possibility of simultaneous agendas. More recently, empirical studies reveal the existence of transnationalism and in addition document its compatibility with the will to and efforts towards integration into receiving society among some migrant organizations. Differences across European localities in the degree of transnationalism are again related to different policy approaches. Supportive approaches on migrant organizations and migrants' rights are linked to less extensive transnational agendas. However, given the emerging debates on migration–development linkages and related policies in particular on local levels all over Europe, migrant organizations in some places may also strengthen their transnational work, at this stage only few indications exist in this respect, though.

The conclusion of this book contrasts the findings from the recent and the more established immigration localities and discusses the question whether there is a 'transnational paradox'. It points to the different ways the accommodation of migrant organizations in European cities has taken concerning their formation, their evolution as well as their local and transnational activities and struggles.

Chapter 2

Approaching the Research on Migrant Organizations in Cities

This chapter offers a theoretical discussion that introduces the relevant perspectives and elements for the study of migrant organizations and their accommodation. Specifically, it addresses three key issues that seem necessary in order to approach the question of the accommodation of migrant organizations in European cities. First, the chapter reflects on the frequently voiced concerns in this research as well as in public debate around the relationship between integration into the receiving society and the persistence of distinct ethnic identities and transnational orientations toward the 'home'-country. This relationship is frequently considered paradoxical and it is generally assumed that this paradox would – under favourable conditions – progressively lead from ethnic identification and transnational activities in relation to the culture and society of origin toward integration into the mainstream of the receiving society. From an original focus on ethnicity the debate has turned into a transnational version of the paradox. While ethnic diversity is today often seen as less problematic, it is expected that an evolution from 'home' to 'host' country-related activities occurs. The simultaneous existence of receiving and origin-side-oriented agendas is rather rejected as a long-term feature. On the one hand, their co-existence does not seem very likely in the eye of many scholars. On the other hand, to many people it is also normatively not a welcomed option. However, this relationship is not necessarily, and in fact very seldom, the object of analysis in the research on migrant organizations. As a consequence, simultaneous engagements have often been rejected, ignored or downplayed, but they are hardly addressed in empirical studies. This book suggests a transnational perspective on the process of accommodation. It analyses the formation, persistence and evolution, as well as the activities and claims of migrant organizations whether related to receiving or origin countries. In so doing, it shows how receiving cities' contexts can shape both.

Thus, second, the chapter addresses the city as a context that has become a prominent site for accommodation for a number of reasons. One important reason is the emergence of new structures of local governance across Europe, which promoted decentralization, the transfer of authority from higher to lower levels of government, and non-state actors' participation in implementation, consultation and decision-making. This has opened more manoeuvring space for cities, and the latter have responded differently to migrants and their organizations. Political and administrative decentralization have, however, not decoupled local levels and cities from national state regulations. Rather have they changed the interrelationship between multiple levels of government and brought about new structures of governance, including that of migration. It will be important to consider the city context as composed of multiple levels in this book.

The third and main part of the chapter then discusses the analytical elements related to the role of the political–institutional contexts and opportunities within receiving states and cities. In this respect the study combines four elements: a) the approach and attitudes of powerful actors toward immigration, migrants and their organizations; b) the existing institutional arrangements in state/society relations; c) the consideration of multiple institutional levels that affect the city context, whereas most other research has been limited to one level – generally national or local; and d) the immigration regime which has hardly received systematic attention in the research on migrant organizations. It is argued here that those institutions related to the immigration regime and the resulting conditions of arrival, that is, entry, stay and work are part and parcel of the understanding of the formation and activities of migrant organizations. With these elements this books offers a comprehensive analytical framework for the study of the accommodation of migrant organizations. The empirical section (Chapters 3–5) shows that this approach can lead to new insights and to a reconsideration of existing knowledge on migrant organizations' formation and activities across European cities.

From ethnic to transnational paradox

Most research to date on migrant organizations has investigated their numbers in a particular city or country and sometimes from a particular nationality, and then looked at the organizational density of this specific group. It has also analysed the process of their formation and persistence, as well as the types and activities, and the claims advanced, together with the forms and intensity of their mobilization. Whereas the cross-cutting question is whether these engagements are related to the 'home' or 'host' country, in the research on migrant organizations studies have most often concentrated on either one. Those studies that are interested in migrants' integration concentrate on policies and situations in the society of reception and the orientation and action of migrant organizations toward it. Transnational agendas by and large are ignored, downplayed or rejected in these studies. In contrast, transnational migration studies are still less prominent and have so far exclusively accounted for cross-border activities in hometowns and countries. Few exceptions exist which systematically take into account action toward both the reception and origin side (Østergaard-Nielsen 2003, Portes, Escobar, Arana 2008).

In the research interested in the role of migrant organizations for integration, three positions can be broadly distinguished. Some authors argue that migrant organizations have hardly been relevant to immigrants' integration and the improvement of their living conditions and rights (Guiraudon 1998: 277). Others consider them a sign of failed integration and an element of ghetto formation, ethnic closure and parallel societies. This perspective maintains that the participation of migrants in their 'own' organizations contributes to the preservation of their ethnic identities and thus symbolizes a separation from the receiving society (Breton 1964).

Most of the time, though, migrant organizations are seen as a mediating force for migrants' integration into mainstream society. In this sense, migrant organizations are the expression of an ethnic (or ethnicity) paradox, as Barbara Lal Ballis (1990 in particular Chapter 5) summarized Robert Park's perspective. Most scholarship on migrant organizations today seems to subscribe to the idea of their role as mediators and considers them an important contribution to migrants' integration. As stated above, in the meantime, more controversial than ethnic identification are potential transnational engagements and activities toward situations abroad.

The 'ethnic paradox' refers to the idea that immigrants' participation in separate ethnic institutions helps their integration since it provides them with necessary resources and is able to serve as a bridge to the existing dominant institutions of the receiving society (Park, Miller 1969 [1921], Ballis Lal 1990, for a discussion see Faist 1996). Immigrant institutions in this respect help to meet practical needs, link past experiences to new ones, support self-esteem and social status, and prevent deviances through maintaining social control. In this sense migrant organizations and networks provide resources otherwise not available to migrants but which may be necessary to their economic success, linguistic adaptation, social orientation, psychological support and interest articulation. Migrant organizations are then crucial for the progress of integration and eventual assimilation into the receiving society. In their early study on migrant communities in the United States and their cultural heritages, Park and Miller state that:

> [t]he present immigrant organizations represent a separateness of the immigrant groups from America, but these organizations exist precisely because they enable the immigrants to overcome this separateness. They are signs, not of the perpetuation of immigrants groups here, but of their assimilation. (Park, Miller 1969 [1921]: 306–307)

Similarly, research in Europe during the 1980s has viewed this paradox opposing ethnic identity and increasing integration as a question of time. This predominant perspective also holds that migrant organizations were to evolve from 'home' country attachments to 'host' country inclinations since they 'are inevitably, over time, drawn into closer contact with the institutions and authorities of the country of settlement' (Layton-Henry 1990b: 102). In this process interests and concerns would re-direct from those related to the origin country to that of the receiving country. Accordingly, it has been argued that the value of the contribution of migrant organizations largely depends on whether an organization focuses on the culture, politics and society of the country of origin or whether it is more concerned with conditions on the side of reception. Only in the latter case would migrant organizations effectively be able to promote migrants' collective and individual integration. Where migrant organizations deal with political issues concerning the country of origin, in turn, no positive effects are expected (Schöneberg 1985). Although the implications of migrant organizations are still subject to discussion, scholarship in the field, as well as the public debate, share the rather pluralist perspective expressed by Park, and consider migrant organizations a contribution and sign of integration – as long as the efforts are directed to the receiving society and the integration therein. Where origin country attachments and cross-border activities predominate, they are taken as a counter-part to receiving side orientations working to their detriment.

Thus, the discussion has now shifted from the ethnic to the transnational paradox, not least due to the emergence of a transnational perspective or a 'transnational lens' in migration research that revived the discussion. In their field-defining publication, Basch, Glick Schiller and Szanton Blanc define transnationalism as

> the processes by which immigrants forge and sustain multi-stranded social relations that link together their societies of origin and settlement. (...) An essential element of transnationalism is the multiplicity of involvements that transmigrants sustain in both home and host societies. (Glick Schiller, Basch, Blanc-Szanton 1994: 7)

Crucially, research from a transnational perspective points out that attachments to the society of origin persist whereas the gradual evolution of exclusive receiving country inclination is not an automatic process. Such attachments may continue to exist over longer periods of time, sometimes lasting several generations. At the same time these do not necessarily withstand progressive integration, but may be an indication of different ways of integration – or accommodation, the concept suggested in this book. This has given way to a broad discussion on whether and how transnational ties are empirically compatible with migrants' integration into the receiving society and how this can be reconciled with integration or assimilation theories (Morawska 2003, Kivisto 2005). This discussion generally shows that transnational orientations can hinder or limit integration as much as it can create support and favourable conditions to this end (Faist 2000: 318). Often, transnational migration scholarship has emphasized the possibility of simultaneous engagements, but so far little research has investigated this possibility (Portes, Escobar, Walton Radford 2007: 244).

The majority of transnational studies focus on the individual, family and household levels. Most of the available studies on transnational migrant organizations, collective cross-border efforts and hometown associations limit their focus to the transnational engagements oriented toward political and socio-economic changes in migrants' 'home'-countries and towns (Levitt 2001, Goldring 2002, Smith 2003, Orozco, Lapointe 2004, Smith, Bakker 2005). Some new studies, though, look at the interrelationship of transnationally oriented organizations with migrants' integration (Portes, Escobar, Walton Radford 2007, Portes, Escobar, Arana 2008). Here, studies investigate the individual dispositions for collective engagement and analyse the socio-economic profile and political interest of the members and representatives of these organizations. These show that the better-educated, longer-established migrants are more likely to engage in transnational organizations (Portes 2001: 188, Guarnizo, Portes, Haller 2003, Portes, Escobar, Walton Radford 2007).

On the collective level of migrant organizations the potentially existing dual and simultaneous agendas directed at the country of origin *and* settlement is only starting to become a subject of research. One first quantitative survey undertaken in three US cities reveals that transnational migrant organizations are almost as involved in activities with the local society and politics as those exclusively focused on the context of settlement (Portes, Escobar, Arana 2008). Experiences and skills, exchange with institutions, and resources acquired in transnational activities have contributed to bring such organizations and their leaders into closer contact with local, and sometimes also national, issues and authorities in the place of reception (Smith 2007). A number of studies provide indications that migrant organizations today include transnational activities along with other activities such as the cultural festivities or the delivery of services for local communities (Koopmans, Statham 2003, Østergaard-Nielsen 2003, Waldrauch, Sohler 2004, Cordero-Guzmán 2005, Pries, Sezgin 2010). This includes the observation that aspects of integration and migrants' rights are also tackled transnationally. Migrants address the governments and institutions of their countries of origin as mediators *vis-à-vis* the institutions of the country of reception for the improvement of their living conditions. This has been shown to be the case for Turkish organizations in Germany (Østergaard-Nielsen 2003). Although this is an interesting finding, research has hardly followed this track. This book follows the argument that these 'transnational immigrant politics' may constitute an important dimension on the agendas of migrant organizations in established immigration places. For new immigration cities, the primary research presented here shows comparable efforts of migrant organizations, although conditions differ. As a consequence, transnational activities related to migration and integration also cover very different issues compared to those identified in Germany. One of the empirical findings is that migrant organizations from Spanish cities are active in their countries of origin where they provide information for emigration, arrival and future integration in those cities.

Such developments are also related to the role of the state, for which this book shares a particular interest. In relation to transnational engagements, much attention has been paid to the interventions by migrants' sending states. Many emigration countries have indeed invested great efforts to remain in touch with their fellow citizens. They have lowered transaction costs for remittance sending and financial investment, extended dual citizenship and introduced absentee voting rights. They have changed their symbolic attitude by appreciating migrants' contributions whereas previously these had not received much attention and were often looked down upon (Smith 2003, Itzigsohn 2000).

Concerning the role of the receiving state and society for migrants' transnationalism, scholars have identified the discriminatory attitudes in the social environment and restrictive approaches of the political institutions as strong influences on the 'adaptive strategies' of migrants. 'Reactive ethnicity' and intense transnational practices characterize these strategies (Portes 1999: 465, Koopmans, Statham 2003). Here, migrants respond to limited institutional opportunities for integration by turning their back on the receiving society, relying on transnational solutions and resources. Some scholars argue that in this way they are advancing their integration, even in a hostile environment and under adverse conditions (Portes 1999, Landolt 2008).

A different role of receiving-side institutions can be seen in open, supportive and in particular multicultural policies. These may also offer opportunities for migrants' transnational engagement and border-crossing attachments. In this sense, 'multicultural policies of the countries of settlement are conducive to upholding immigrants' transnational ties. (…) Put otherwise, not only repressive policies and discrimination advance immigrant transnationalization but also the opposite, windows for multicultural rights and activities' (Faist 2000: 214). The empirical findings cited above support this assessment in that they show the successful integration of those involved in transnational activities, a process that is likely to flourish under favourable political conditions. To which degree multicultural approaches provide more positive conditions for migrants' integration is a matter of contestation, though. Further, it is a main argument of this book that various elements, located at multiple political-institutional levels, exercise influence on migrant organizations. Therefore these processes are likely to be more complex than the assumption of the progressive dissolution of the paradox as a result of the approach on integration suggests. In addition, there is a new institutional environment emerging in many receiving places as regards migrants' transnationalism. Against the background of the by now global migration-development debate, many public authorities on various levels of government and international agencies across Europe and beyond have started to actively promote migrants as transnational agents of development (De Haas 2006, Faist, Fauser 2011). The analysis presented in Chapter 3 shows that this is particularly strong in the Spanish cases. Here policies promoting migrants' development engagement are closely interwoven with integration policies. These initiatives create new environments for transnational activities and shape processes of accommodation (see Chapter 4).

Hence, this study follows a transnational perspective. It considers the possibility of potentially simultaneous and multiple linkages and practices of people and migrants, and, in this case, specifically of migrant organizations. This is reflected in the concept of accommodation. This concept focuses on the processes initiated upon the arrival and potential settlement of migrants at a new place, independently from the direction these activities take. Accordingly, the empirical investigation that this book presents considers the formation and activities of migrant organizations, whether directed towards reception or origin countries and societies. It thereby shows how receiving city contexts can contribute to both.

The city context

Sociological inquiry since its early days has had a particular interest in the relationships between the social and economic transformations of cities and migration, focusing on changing individual lives, group interactions and transforming local societies (Park, Burgess, McKenzie 1968 [1925], Simmel 1995 [1903]). Today, international migration, growing diversity as well as economic, social and political changes that affect cities and city life have put new emphasis on their relevance. Against this background, researchers interested in migration address the local with increasing interest. Cities are (re)discovered as 'arenas of accelerated social transformations' confronted with many new diversities in terms of the ethnic, cultural and socio-economic backgrounds of people, and in particular the newly arriving international migrants settling there (Auriat, Rochet 2001: ix, Favell 2001). Cities, thus, constitute relevant places and contexts for migrants' social and political integration and they are also the locations of migrants' transnationalism (Smith, Guarnizo 1999, Portes 2000: 166–8, Smith 2001). Particular localities and cities thus need to be analysed as significant contexts for the processes of accommodation (Glick Schiller, Çağlar 2009).

Cities are today the prime targets of internal as well as international migrations. Most migrants settle in cities and urban areas where jobs, social networks and other opportunities tend to be available. In the older, established immigration cities of north-western Europe, the foreign resident and immigrant population grew steadily in the post-war period and constitutes between one-tenth to one-third of the local population in many places, often much more (Alexander 2004: 58). In Amsterdam, immigrants and their children make up around 47 per cent of the city's population (Penninx et al. 2004b: 4). In Berlin the foreign population constitutes 13.2 per cent of all residents, and amounts to an estimated 25 per cent when taking into account the broader category of immigrants, i.e. including those born as Germans and those naturalized of migration background (Ohliger, Raiser 2005). In contrast, in cities of more recent immigration in southern Europe, the migrant population has increased dramatically only over the last ten to twenty years. In this short period, the foreign population has already risen to 15 per cent and more in many southern European cities. Barcelona and Madrid's foreign populations reached 17 per cent in 2008, whereas in the mid-1990s the share was less than 2 per cent (see Chapter 3). In addition to these often quickly expanding numbers of foreign residents, cities are today also more strongly characterized by 'super-diversity' (Vertovec 2006). Cultural, religious, and national backgrounds are more varied than in previous phases of migration and settlement. Moreover, migration inflows have also become more diverse in terms of socio-economic and residence status. Cities now also often subscribe to this diversification. London's official declarations highlight it's aspiration to host 'the world with 179 nationalities present in the city' (Vertovec 2006: 1). And even the mayor of such a young immigration city as Madrid proudly announced local diversity with its 180 nationalities (*Europa Press*, 18 March 2005).

It is also true that the local level is most directly confronted with migratory inflows, settlement and increasing diversity. Local governments more immediately face the needs of the newly arriving people, groups and communities, as well as potential conflicts than other political–administrative levels. Newcomers bring with them specific needs and characteristics not always easily met by existing institutions. Among these are often a different language, culture and religion, accompanied by specific or increasing demands concerning welfare services, housing, labour markets or schools and education. Growing segregation due to concentrations of migrants in certain neighbourhoods further challenges local policies. Migrants' integration is generally expected to be provided on the local level. All over Europe, local governments have generally been the first to react to migrants' arrival and settlement (Penninx et al. 2004b: 4). The reaction of local governments in southern Europe seems even more pronounced in face of the relatively reluctant national institutions (Agrela, Dietz 2006, Pájares 2006, Tsuda 2006). Participation in politics is also most often a local affair, be it through municipal voting rights which today exist in many European countries (Waldrauch 2005) or through consultative councils and other participatory channels (Andersen 1990).

Ongoing economic globalization has further increased the prominent role of cities, turning some of the major metropolises into world or global cities (Friedmann, Wolff 1982, Sassen 1991). Growing economic interdependence and global competition place new pressures on the local authorities, and innovations in technology, communication and transport reshape the economic environment for local competitiveness. This environment often causes fundamental changes to local labour markets, attracting new waves of (labour) migrants. Small-scale and informal economies have expanded in the last decades drawing from all economic sectors in many cities. This trend is accompanied by increasing migratory inflows attracted by (informal) work in these localities.

Economic pressure and political–administrative reform by central governments from above as well as demands for more autonomy and participation, from local levels of government and civil society from below, have brought decentralization in decision making and in policy implementation (Andrew, Goldsmith 1998). Responsibilities have been conveyed to local levels in particular in social policy and welfare services, including public assistance to migrants (García 2006: 746). This is also related to privatization and the contracting out in the public sector on both national and local levels, further changing the conditions for local governments (Goldsmith 1992, Andrew, Goldsmith 1998, Brenner 1999, García 2006). The emerging structures of local governance include new practices and a plurality of new actors in the implementation and provision of social services as well as in decision-making processes and consultation. These changes have opened important venues for the local incorporation of migrant organizations in otherwise rather different places such as Spanish and German cities as will be shown in Chapters 4 and 5. Emerging new structures have also changed the interrelation of political–institutional levels and have brought new complex situations (Andrew, Goldsmith 1998: 106, García 2006: 746). In southern Europe where non-state actor involvement in social welfare is often historically stronger than in northern Europe, this has further expanded in the last two decades (Rodríguez Cabrero, Codorniú 1997). In addition, in southern Europe these processes are connected to post-dictatorial democratization and have often also led to new forms of local participation (Walliser 2001, Navarro Yáñez 2004). Naturally, whereas more federalized countries like Germany or Spain allow for more room for local policies, more centralized states like France give a narrower frame for local activities. Notwithstanding existing differences, since in many European countries decentralization shifted competences down from the central to the local level, this frame is widening almost everywhere. This contributes to considerable local variations in the ways cities deal with migration and increasing diversity across and within countries.

This transfer in competences concerning migration from central to local government has often increased the latter's authority, though not always their resources. In France, for instance, the use of the 'housing certificate' issued by the city hall in the application for family reunification caused great controversy in the early 1990s (Lahav 1998, Lahav, Guiraudon 2000). French mayors used various strategies to keep numbers of applicants low. Some refused to distribute the required forms or simply neglected their delivery and the press reported that 50 per cent of the municipalities demanded papers not legally required (Guiraudon, Lahav 2000). By 'shifting down' competences, local governments became part of the framework of restriction and control of immigration of the central government. Local powers, however, may not only use their competences as a means of restriction. Municipalities have also used their space of action to promote migrants' integration. The city of Berlin, for example, accounted for a quarter of all discretionary naturalizations in Germany in some years (Alexander 2004: 65, Thränhardt 2008). Another example is the active use of municipal registration for regular and in particular irregular migrants which many Spanish cities and towns pursue, notwithstanding certain contestation. Since the legal reforms of 2000, local registration has been central for the access to basic social services and education, and thus local governments' activism has contributed to the improvement of the living conditions and integration of (irregular) migrants (see Chapter 3).

Cities are also regarded as sites of today's transnationalism. Transnational social processes from below are complementing transnational flows of economic capital, technology and information from above. Individual migrants, groups, communities and migrant organizations often maintain close relationships to the places where they and their families originate. Integration and membership in the local realm is considered more easily compatible with transnational attachments since it does not infer nor have to solve the relationship with national membership and nationality (Bauböck 2003). Local authorities are thus more likely to tolerate or recognize transnational attachments. In addition, local governments have decentralized instruments at their disposal as regards international cooperation and development aid, which in some places has now opened new opportunities for local migrant communities to strengthen their role as transnational actors, and to contribute to development 'back home' (Faist, Fauser 2011, Fauser 2011). In Spain in particular, such policies promoted with the policy concept of co-development have greater influence on the accommodation of migrant organizations, and similar initiatives, although seemingly less prominent, also exist in some more established immigration countries as will be shown in the chapters to come.

Hence, the city context offers an important focus on the accommodation of migrant organizations. Often debates concentrate on local economic and labour market conditions favouring or hindering successful integration. Here, the analysis concentrates on political–institutional structures and their effects on migrant organizations, stemming from local- and national-level authorities. It is the aim of the next section to lay out in greater detail the explanatory elements of these institutional contexts.

Explanatory elements in the research on migrant organizations

The more recent rediscovery of migrant collective formation and action has given way to many insightful studies and important theoretical considerations. Even so, until now there exists no predominant theory to explain the phenomenon. Rather, research tends to follow either of two broader perspectives in asking what stimulates and shapes migrant organizations. On the one hand, scholars have looked at the characteristics of the migrant communities, namely the cultural, religious, political and organizational features and traditions related to the migrant community and the country of origin. On the other hand, particularly since the 1990s, migration scholarship has investigated the opportunities provided by the receiving state. The first perspective is founded on the observation that different national or ethnic groups show different forms and intensities of associations in the process of arrival and settlement at a new place. Accordingly, this perspective has often used convergent comparisons of various groups in one country or city (Green 1991; see Chapter 1 on methodology). It has revealed that the Turks, Moroccans and Surinamese organize differently in the Netherlands (Fennema, Tillie 1999) as do the Spanish, Italians, Greeks and Turks in Germany (Puskeppeleit, Thränhardt 1990), or the Moroccans as compared to the Senegalese in Spain (Ancin 2004). The explanations for such differences are given on the basis of characteristics such as the cultural backgrounds of migrants as well as the cultural distance to the respective receiving society. Also considered are ethnic resources and social capital, organizational traditions prior to migration as well as the pattern of migration, in particular the size and volume of one particular group at a given point in time (see most prominently Raymond Breton's 1964, and recently Schrover, Vermeulen 2005a). Some limitations of this approach include that cultural differences as such hardly provide a basis for broad generalization. An extensive historical and cross-country literature review (Moya 2005) shows that first, a group needs to perceive itself as different from others. Second 'it does not follow logically, and the evidence does not support, that the greater the real or perceived difference is the easier it will be for them to develop their own institutions' (Moya 2005: 840). Hence, the concentration on the migrant community and the pre-migratory experiences cannot account for differences in the formation of migrant actors across time and space, or in other words, within different contexts.

Different contexts provide different opportunities that result in different ways of accommodation. This is best addressed by divergent comparison across places (Green 1991, see also Chapter 1 on methodology). From this perspective, considerable differences in the patterns of mobilization and organization by migrants in Germany, the Netherlands and Great Britain can be observed (Koopmans, Statham 2003). Migrants sharing the same national background organize differently in different countries, like the Turks, for example, a group that displays very different organizational patterns in Netherlands as compared to the UK or Germany (Soysal 1994). Cross- and, although scarce, within-country comparison of local cases also shows that collective political participation of Moroccans is very different in Lille from that in Utrecht (Bousetta 1997), and that across German cities, many differences in the public engagement of migrants exist (Koopmans 2004). These variations are a result of the differences in the political–institutional contexts provided in each country and city.

Furthermore, it seems logical that when the same nationality group is investigated across different places in Europe, differences are attributed to the political contexts while similarities are related to group and community characteristics. This is, for instance, one of the conclusions drawn from a comparative study on migrant organizations in Berlin and Amsterdam that reveals surprisingly similar types and activities among Turkish migrant organizations in the two cities (Vermeulen 2006: Chapter 4). At least partly, however, similarities also reflect some comparable features across these northern European national and local contexts. Throughout the first decades of post-war immigration, governments all over Europe showed relative reluctance, and scarce integration efforts towards migrants and their organizations. Other features, related to comparable schemes of guest worker recruitment and sometimes post-colonial migrations also provided similarly stabile entry, work and residence regimes. These similarities in the contexts of the more established immigration places in northern Europe are one of the main issues of Chapter 5. These, in turn, can explain some similarities in the accommodation of migrant organizations across these countries and cities. In the recent immigration destinations of today, conditions of immigration are rather different – less stable and more weakly regulated. As a consequence, these different immigration contexts also contribute to different forms of action among migrant organizations there. Thus, rather than looking at group factors in the following the analysis is interested in the particularities of the political institutional contexts as explanatory elements for accommodation. This is related to the methodological approach which is based on data from various national or ethnic groups in order to see such contextual implications, whereas most research compares one (national) group across contexts. The inclusion of diverse nationalities can be done more exhaustively on the basis of the primary data presented in Chapters 3 and 4 on the southern European cities, while existing material on more established immigration contexts used in Chapter 5 allows such a perspective in more limited ways. Still, contrasting both experiences makes the impact of contexts particularly discernible.

Concepts of political–institutional opportunities

Theoretical approaches which focus on political–institutional opportunity structures have become very prominent in the study of migrant organizations over the past years. Various research streams offer different versions of how to conceptualize institutional structures and they apply these in somewhat different ways. Most work is available from studies using concepts which originally stem from social movement and resource mobilization theory (McAdam, McCarthy, Zald 1996, Tarrow 1996) and these studies are interested in how political opportunity structures shape migrants' mobilization (Ireland 1994, Koopmans, Statham 2000, Koopmans et al. 2005). Some studies also originate in neo-institutional sociology and concentrate on the established, organized patterns of state–society relations and the ways these structure the incorporation and formation of new migrant actors (Soysal 1994). Some of the available studies have concentrated on one institutional aspect, for example citizenship legislation to define the relevant institutional contexts. Others have used a broad range of features:

> The political opportunity structure considered here includes the immigrants' legal situation; their social and political rights; and host-society citizenship laws, naturalization procedures, and policies (and nonpolicies) in such areas as education, housing, the labour market and social assistance that shape conditions and immigrants' response. Furthermore, indigenous trade unions, political parties, and religious and humanitarian 'solidarity groups', have acted as institutional gatekeepers, controlling access to the avenues of political participation available to the immigrants. (Ireland 1994: 10)

The analysis presented here also uses a broader range of elements but makes a systematic distinction between them.

The general approach and attitude of powerful groups and in particular that of the government towards migrants and their organizations can be considered crucial since these 'influence the opportunities immigrants have for setting up organisations' (Schrover, Vermeulen 2005b: 828). Where migrants are seen as transient or temporary residents, organizational activities may be either forbidden or strongly constrained, and therefore these are less likely to exist in great numbers. In other places, migrants are regarded as new citizens and their participation and organization is encouraged and supported. Here one would expect them to be more numerous and more resourceful. Typologies of integration approaches distinguish at least four types of relationships between the attitude towards migrants' integration and the related policy responses: a transient perspective on migrants' stay is reflected in non-policies since integration is not envisaged; the assimilationist approach which advocates the one-sided adaptation of new immigrants to the receiving society; the ethnic pluralist or multiculturalist approach which tolerates and even promotes cultural diversity; and more recently the intercultural approach which puts more emphasis on social cohesion, conviviality and dialogue between cultures, groups and individuals (Castles 1995, Alexander 2003, Koopmans, Statham 2003). Newer diversity approaches seem to add a further perspective here in that they are generally less focused on groups and more on multiple individual characteristics (Faist 2009).

The ways in which policies promote migrants' integration may, however, be different from the ways their organizing is perceived. Comparative analysis between the processes of migrants' participation and mobilization in France and Switzerland shows that state assistance to migrants and the responses to migrant organizations can follow different paths (Ireland 1994). In France the relatively inclusive welfare programmes for migrants reduced the need for self-provision by means of the ethnic or migrant community itself. In combination with the strong control on political activities and constraints on migrant organizations, this discouraged associationism among migrants at the beginning. Later on migrants followed the more confrontational examples of the class-based activism into which they were channelled, rather than developing strong ethnic identity discourses. In contrast, the reluctance of Swiss welfare institutions to specifically work with migrants was one factor leading to a stronger incidence of ethnic community organizations, supported by the consulates of the migrants' origin countries. At the same time, ethnic organizing was allowed, but restrictive labour policies and a strong focus on rotation and temporariness of migration also dampened activism. This led to the existence of a variety of migrant organizations which upheld 'homeland'-oriented relationships there (Ireland 1994: 248–50). Thus, broad public (welfare) assistance to newcomers does not necessarily go along with the recognition and funding for newly emerging migrant actors. Absence of state attendance, in turn, also does not automatically preclude tolerance or even support to migrant organizations. In addition, conditions and requirements for public support may favour some actors over others, whether these are migrants or other non-state actors.

Furthermore, there is also no automatic relationship between a certain approach and attitude and one set of policies. Similar attitudes may translate into different policies and instruments, while different attitudes can lead to similar instruments. One related aspect here is that state funding may support as well as divide the field of actors, whether migrant or non-migrant, by favouring particular groups over others. A number of studies show that it makes a great difference to whom and under which conditions and requirements authorities provide financial and symbolic support (Bloemraad 2005, Caponio 2005, Vermeulen 2005). A comparison of Italian cities shows that different local governments' attitudes can go hand in hand with similar policies on migrant organizations. Although the cities of Milan, Bologna and Naples were governed by different political parties which displayed divergent attitudes on migrants and their organizations and thus were likely to offer different opportunities to migrant organizations, the results of the study proved this expectation wrong.

Authorities in all three cities were strikingly similar in the concentration of funding on Italian (welfare) organizations rather than on migrant associations (Caponio 2005). Researchers on the Spanish context have observed a similar picture. Most public resources and influence is focussed on indigenous Spanish, pro-migrant organizations. This has been continuously criticized by migrant organizations' leaders (Martín Pérez 2004a). Nonetheless, there are also many local differences in the degree and forms of migrant organizations' participation in policy consultation and implementation. The comparative analysis of Barcelona and Madrid presented in this book illustrates that similar approaches and attitudes articulated in the two cities go along with very different instruments as regards collective migrant organizations. While in Barcelona the consultative council for immigration was set up in 1997, in Madrid a similar council was not created until 2006. This difference can be explained by the existing local organization of state/non-state relationships in each of the cities, as this is the pattern upon which new actors are addressed. Thus, the approach of political actors and governments towards migration and the integration of migrants does not necessarily translate into one specific and uniform set of policies and instruments. Different attitudes can be accompanied by similar policies on migrant organizations, while a similar approach can relate to very different policy instruments.

One important reason for this difference can be found in the existence of institutional templates. The role of existing institutional arrangements strongly shapes state responses in different realms. For instance, one of the conclusions drawn from the comparative city project Multicultural Policies and Modes of Citizenship in European Cities (MCMP) was that the observed differences in the realm of education were related to the institutional set-up previous to migration. This led to very different practices across European cities, even among those grounding their attitude in multiculturalism (Penninx, Martiniello 2004: 151). Such differences are also reflected in a comprehensive overview of possibilities of local responses to migration which gives an impressive account on the many different measures and instruments summarized under one approach on integration, whether these are working with an assimilationist, multiculturalist or intercultural understanding (Alexander 2003, 2004).

Resources and channels of participation open to migrant organizations are thus shaped by established state–society relations. These create templates for interest organization and the involvement in policy formulation and implementation of non-state actors (Soysal 1994, Ireland 1994: 259). The relationship between the state as political system or polity and society and non-state actors follows different patterns in European nation states (Soysal 1994) – and to a certain extent, this also applies to cities within one nation state. The organization of this specific pattern of incorporation of members of society into the polity is the ground upon which new actors are addressed. Thus, when the states that are today more established immigration destinations encountered the incorporation of post-war migrants as a new issue area, they drew upon existing institutional repertoires and resources (Soysal 1994: 79). Similarly, migrant organizations, in turn, define their goals, strategies, functions and level of operation in relation to the existing policies and resources of the host state. They advance demands and set agendas *vis-à-vis* state policy and discourses in order to seize institutional opportunities and further their claims. In that sense, the expression and organization of migrant collective identity are formed by the institutionalised forms of the state's incorporation regime. (Soysal 1994: 85)

Therefore it will be relevant for the purpose of this book to take into account the role of existing state/non-state actor relationships. In particular, whether social actors are involved in the delivery of social services or in structures of political consultation, and whether these are centralized at the national governmental level or more decentralized, opens or closes venues for migrant organizations. In this respect, institutional templates are not only exclusive to the national context. They are locally specific and hence characterize the local governance model in place. Different traditions in local democracy can have great implications on the involvement of migrant organizations and individual migrants. The analysis presented in Chapter 3 shows that the differences between Barcelona and Madrid in the ways local authorities have addressed migrant organizations are due to different institutional set-ups in matters of local democracy and citizen participation.

Multiple institutional levels

In the study of political institutions and opportunity structures and their implications for migrant organizations most attention is paid to the national state (Soysal 1994, Koopmans, Statham 2000, Koopmans et al. 2005). Studies specifically interested in cities now also constitute a dynamic research field (Rex, Joly, Wilpert 1987, Ireland 1994, Bousetta 1997, Rogers, Tillie 2001, Penninx et al. 2004a). A number of local studies have taken the city as the place where national institutions effect policy outcomes and have investigated how national institutions work in the local context (Bousetta 1997, Moore 2001). Here, it has been pointed out that national approaches can not sufficiently or not exclusively explain local situations. Some authors argue that local differences are variations within a particular national context and thus point to the greater explanatory value of national approaches (Koopmans 2004, Bloemraad 2005), while others put more emphasis on cross-country comparison showing that existing local differences in dealing with migration and ethnic diversity cannot always be explained by different national approaches on integration. Among other factors, authors have pointed to the informal practices of local authorities as well as to their differing orientations from those of the national government (Ireland 1994, Moore 2001). Moreover, the still scarce studies using within-country comparisons reveal the many differences in one and the same national context, varying according to the room for manoeuvre, discretionary power and the decision-making competences available to local governments (Ireland 1994,

Koopmans 2004, Caponio 2005). Generally, research has either concentrated on national or local contexts. Consideration of both levels has sometimes meant looking at them separately (Ireland 1994, Koopmans 2004, Caponio 2005). Migration scholars have practically ignored the interplay of different political-institutional levels which play out in the city context.

From the side of urban studies, authors advocate that current economic restructuring and the emergence of new forms of governance require investigations into the multilevel and multi-scalar relationship connecting cities with national governments (see for instance Brenner 1999, García 2006). Similarly, migration researchers have stressed that various governmental levels need to be integrated into the analysis. Interestingly this argument is presented by authors specifically dealing with migrant actors in the new immigration cities of southern Europe (Marques, Santos 2001, Morén-Alegret 2001, Agrela, Dietz 2006). These authors maintain that:

> Local political structures and dynamics do not sufficiently account for the reshaping of political opportunity structures for immigrants and ethnic minorities. The city level analysis has to be opened to higher level processes if we are to understand the – often unintended – consequences of local policies. Conversely, local level policies influence the ways in which participation opportunities created at higher levels are appropriated, namely by the selection of local actors. (Marques, Santos 2001: 144)

Higher level policies have direct and indirect impacts on the local level. A study on a smaller municipality in the Lisbon Metropolitan Area (Marques, Santos 2001), for instance, shows how the regularization programmes introduced from the national government led to unprecedented mobilizations and new local coalitions among migrant organizations, non-governmental organization, Catholic associations and others voicing severe criticism on the poor preparation and implementation of the programme. Moreover, state-level policies have not only immediate implications for local actors, they are also mediated through the local government. In that same study, this becomes discernible with the Special Re-Housing Programme. Where the local authorities had previously rejected the idea of the specific representation of migrants through a council, the ways in which this programme was implemented meant a *de facto* recognition of the particularities of migrants' and their ethnic representation. The primary research presented in this book shows similar processes of direct and mediated effects of national policies in cities. For instance, subsidies from the Spanish central government level almost exclusively benefited (local) actors in the capital Madrid, at least until recent changes. This is in turn amplified by their representation in the national-level migration consultation council. In addition, within-country comparison also shows how differently cities responded to migrant organizing in that they also implement national-level programmes very differently. Newer funds from the central government destined to local administrations in Spain are partly used to subsidize non-state actors in addressing the reception and integration of migrants. The sums and methods of distribution to local actors are very different from place to place. Whereas Barcelona dedicated between 300,000 and 400,000 euros to these projects, Madrid's subsidies range between 1.3 and almost 4 million euros. At the same time, Barcelona benefits more migrant organizations with these funds, but with smaller amounts of money, whereas in Madrid, greater sums are distributed among fewer actors. This creates fundamentally different conditions for migrant actors in the two cities.

In the relationship between political institutions and migrant organizations, other non-state actors also play a role. These can work as interlocutors, gatekeepers or competitors. Some authors have considered the gatekeepers as part of the institutional channels and opportunities (Ireland 1994, Landolt 2008), while others position them as affected by this structure (Giugni, Passy 2004). However, non-state actors may be considered both at the same time. Gatekeepers can work as facilitators and are affected by the political approaches and policies reigning in the field of migration. The emergence of new forms of local governance that implies a shift of authority to the local level and partly also to non-state actors requires going beyond clear-cut, top-down perspectives. Rather, dynamic and highly complex situations make it difficult to consider context and actors as static categories. This is most pronounced where non-state actors play an important role in the governance of migration, which often cross-cut central, regional and local government levels (Agrela, Dietz 2006).

> This becomes clearer if we consider the multiplicity of agents working at local levels (neighbourhood, Catholic or national and international non-governmental organisations, to name but a few), all of which engage in autonomous horizontal relations with each other and with the neighbourhood, as well as in vertical relations with municipal, national or even international actors. (Marques, Santos 2004: 108)

In many cities across Europe non-state actors have received support from different state levels in order to assist migrants, and they are called on for participation and consultation in the representation of certain groups or based upon the experience they have acquired on migrants' situations and needs, often prior to state institution. In Germany, for instance, for many decades only the major welfare organizations received funding for attending to migrants' needs, leaving little room for smaller initiatives and migrant organizations. This has changed over the last years and service provision has become more decentralized. In the United Kingdom or Spain smaller organizations are part of predominantly local structures of welfare services. This has included migrant organizations at a relatively early point of increasing international migration in both countries. At the same time, non-state actors have also supported or channelled migrant organizations. In the recent immigration context of Spanish cities this is particularly interesting. There, neighbourhood organizations, trade unions and other social (movement) actors encourage migrant organizations and often provide support, for example, in the form of office space for migrant organizations, which in turn is funded by public authorities. This was the case with a number of organizations investigated in the course of the research on which this book draws (see in particular Chapter 4). In addition, migrant organizations themselves have not only received but also have given support to new actors. The major Moroccan migrant organization in Spain Atime was founded in Madrid at the end of the 1980s with support in from the trade union UGT. Atime, in turn, supported Peruvian organizing and the set up of ARI Peru (Veredas Muñoz 2001: 18). All these organizations are competitors for attention and funding by public authorities on different governmental levels.

The immigration regime

Political institutions matter as they provide social assistance to migrants upon arrival and potential settlement, focus resources on their integration and respond to migrant organizations' formation and activities. These institutions are located in the realm of what is classically considered integration policies, as distinguished from immigration policies (Hammar 1985). The majority of studies have limited their analysis to the context emerging from their specific approach on integration and the policies of integration as explanatory features for the formation as well as the social and political activities of migrant organizations. However, the immigration regime and the ways it structures conditions of entry, stay and work also shape the process of accommodation. Very few studies have systematically taken this into account. Where authors have considered the legal status of migrants and policies on immigration control, these are mostly taken as one element of open or restrictive national approaches on the issue of migration as a whole. But as these regulations influence the conditions of inflows, they affect the resources and needs migrants develop in a particular situation. This also shapes migrant organizations, their formation, their activities and the claims they advance.

This idea is reflected in the concept of modes of incorporation and the context of reception defined therein (Portes, Böröcz 1989, Guarnizo, Portes, Haller 2003, Landolt 2008). According to this definition, the context of reception includes the conditions of entry, the related legal status and the question whether this is accompanied by state assistance. These factors contribute to the patterns of settlement and the formation of migrant organizations, and they shape migrants' transnational activism (Portes, Escobar, Walton Radford 2007, Landolt 2008). Whether immigrants are accepted as legal labour migrants or lawful refugees, or whether they live their lives undocumented or irregularly has important implications for the resources available to them. Further, whether any of these statuses is connected to state support or welfare assistance by private organizations or whether these have to be provided by means of the ethnic or migrant community itself plays a greater role for migrant organizations' formation.

Availability or lack of resources are often attributed to the respective communities as characteristic of a certain ethnic migrant group in a given place and at a particular point in time (most prominently Breton 1964). But even different groups in the same country may share some characteristics as they are an effect of the immigration regime and the similar situations and conditions these immigrants encounter in terms of entry, stay and work, independently of their national, ethnic or cultural origins. Where guest workers migrated within recruitment schemes that secured them a stable, although temporary, legal status as well as inclusion into welfare systems, accompanied by specific state or (state-funded) welfare organizations' assistance, migrants started to organize around origin country politics, culture and leisure activities. This characterizes the majority of migrant organizations in Germany throughout the first decades of guest worker immigration (Puskeppeleit, Thränhardt 1990). More recent situations in new immigrant Spain strongly differ from this. Greater parts of arriving migrants are confronted with irregularity and a lack of secure status, accompanied by scarce state assistance. There, migrant organizations emerged over time, in parallel with non-governmental organizations and financially supported by different governmental levels and embedded in the particular Spanish structures of welfare governance. One of the main results this book allows to observe is the role of the immigration regime. This emerges when contrasting accommodation processes in established and recent immigration places.

Toward a framework for the study of accommodation

In the following chapters this book will focus on how the city context composed of multiple institutional levels shapes and influences the processes of accommodation of migrant organizations. That is, the analysis is interested in the process of migrant organizations' formation and their activities and claims, rather than on their outcomes, for example concerning the integration of migrants. To this end the analysis follows three main perspectives. First, it starts from a transnational perspective in that it accounts for both the receiving- and origin-side orientations and activities of migrant organizations. Frequently, the study of migrant actors has regarded these engagements working to the detriment of each other. Dependent on (favourable) state policies, migrant organizations are expected to evolve from origin to receiving side orientations. Migration scholarship has frequently argued that adverse conditions and restrictive state approaches on migrants offering limited opportunities to newcomers and settling populations (indirectly) work in favour of origin country attachments. It is one of the contentions of this book that migrant organizations may maintain simultaneous agendas related to issues on the receiving and origin side. This is all the more likely where government approaches and policies recognize and promote the transnationalization of (local) migrant organizations. This is what the analysis of the Spanish city cases reveals. Second, the analysis focuses on the city context. It acknowledges the renewed importance of cities for diverse social processes, including that of migration. Global economic restructuring, policy reform and decentralization from above together with claims for greater autonomy and participation from below have changed the conditions for local government in the last decades. Everywhere local governments and authorities, along with other non-state actors, have responded to new migrant populations in their cities. These responses differ within and across countries and thus local situations for migrants and their organizations vary greatly. At the same time, neither cities and local governments, nor local actors and processes are shaped by local policies alone. There are immediate and mediated higher level policies at work as well.

Third, the political institutional contexts and the opportunities these provide are crucial in shaping migrant organizations' accommodation. In this respect, the analysis takes up insights from a number of existing approaches and combines four elements. The first element is the approach and attitudes toward migrant integration and their organizations in that these determine the opportunities, venues, resources and constraints to them. Here it is important to note that one approach does not translate into one uniform set of policies. These have to be scrutinized carefully. In particular, the policies dealing with the reception and integration of migrants and those addressing migrant organizations do not necessarily follow the same logic. Therefore, the second element concerns the existing institutional patterns of state–society relations. In this respect the existing organization of state/non-state actors' relationships is important because these constitute the patterns upon which venues for the participation of migrant organizations are opened. In addition, gatekeepers and other third actors can also play a role as supporters and competitors for migrant organizations. These can constitute opportunities to the latter as much as both are affected by the political opportunities in place. The third element pays attention to the various levels of government and their influence in the city context. In this book particular attention is paid to both local and national levels and their interplay. Lastly, different from the bulk of existing studies on migrant organizations, not only are the contexts of integration considered relevant. The immigration regime regulating the conditions of entry and arrival, stay and work forms an integral part of the analysis here.

Chapter 3

The Dynamics of Recent Immigration and Policy Responses in Spanish City Contexts

The previous chapter argued that the city context is influenced by multiple political institutional levels and that together these shape the accommodation of migrant organizations. This chapter now provides an analysis of the situation in two city contexts of recent immigration, Barcelona and Madrid. It looks at the Spanish immigration regime, the national policies on migrants and their organizations, and the respective local institutional features within these two major Spanish cities. The next chapter then moves on to an analysis of migrant organizations in the two city contexts and shows how the latter shape the former.

Today, Spanish cities and localities are among the new places of immigration in Europe. Unexpected by authorities and society, Spain slowly became an immigration country from the early 1990s onwards (Cornelius 1994, Izquierdo Escribano 1996, Arango 2000). In 1980 there were 182,000 foreign citizens living in Spain, in 1990 these were almost 277,000. A sharp increase occurred toward the end of the 1990s and by the year 2000 official statistics showed 895,720 legal foreign residents. Since then, a dynamic increase has occurred every following year and in 2008 the foreign resident population consists of more than 4.4 million people (OPI 2004, 2008). In parallel, political efforts responding to the growing inflows were rather incremental and became more dynamic toward the end of the 1990s. Consensus exists among observers that immigration measures were lagging behind changing realities, and that the central governments' political reforms concentrated more on immigration control than on the reception or integration of migrants for many years (Blanco 2001, Agrela, Dietz 2006, Aja 2006). The first comprehensive integration plan was issued in 2007 for the 2007–2010 administration. Existing responses to new immigration at local levels by various actors and authorities are accorded a crucial role in this overall setting.

The governance of migration in Spain is therefore characterized by a certain national–local divide. Whereas the central state is seen as the regulator of control and of the conditions of access to the territory and to work and stay, the local levels are regarded as the managers of integration (Blanco 2001, Agrela, Dietz 2006: 206, Pájares 2006) – a perspective common to other recent immigration locales in southern Europe as well (Marques, Santos 2001, Koff 2006: 178, Tsuda 2006: 6). The evolution of policies and instruments dealing with migrant inflows and their integration in Spain has been characterized as a process *de abajo hacia arriba* (Ramos et al. 1998: 8) or 'bottom up' originating from sub-national government levels and non-governmental actors. This is largely the result of decentralization which has been ongoing for several decades. In parallel to local governments' efforts, and often even before, non-governmental organizations, trade unions, church-based groups and solidarity associations have responded to the needs of migrants. In this situation also many migrant organizations emerged as will be demonstrated in next chapter.

This chapter shows that notwithstanding the emphasis on control, irregular migration has remained a specific feature of immigration to Spain. A great range of legal and administrative measures deal with the issue of (ir)regularity. One of the main findings in the analysis of migrant organizations presented in the next chapter is the importance the institutions dealing with irregularity have for the need for migrants to form collectively, and for the ways migrant organizations act. Hence, section two of this chapter is dedicated to the immigration regime (after briefly describing the situation and dynamics of international migration relating to the two Spanish cities in focus in a first section). The legal provisions around (ir)regularity constitute a crucial feature of this context, signalling both the ways in which irregularity emerges and the means by which it is handled and attended to. This situation is accompanied by a relative absence of specific social policies and state intervention addressing newcomers at the central government level. At the same time, the overall negligence on the part of the central government was soon paralleled by the state recognition of the role of migrant organizations, together with that of other non-state actors. This includes the establishment of a national-level consultative council on the integration of foreign immigrants in the mid-1990s as well economic support for non-state actors' social initiatives. The last few years have also seen financial schemes for the support of local reception and integration granted to local authorities. Parts of these funds are also dedicated to migrant and immigrant-support organizations. These latter issues, concerning the reception and integration of immigrants and their organizations, are the subject of the third section. Section four offers an analysis of the responses by local public authorities in Barcelona and Madrid. One main insight here is that although the two cities share a similar approach on migrant integration, they developed partly different measures for the reception and integration of migrants, and the venues open to migrant organizations also differ. This is mainly an effect of the established models of local governance and specifically the local state/non-state actor relationships in each of the cities, as will become clear. As argued in Chapter 2, the approach and attitudes towards migrants and their integration interact with the existing institutional patterns of the organization of state–society relations. These structure the pattern upon which new migrant actors are incorporated (see also Soysal 1994).

In this overall contextual setting emerging from multiple levels of government, three issues merit particular attention due to their reflection in the activities and claims presented by migrant organizations. The first issue refers to irregularity which is a main topic that motivates and accompanies processes of formation and leads to manifold actions among migrant organizations. The second one concerns political participation and in particular voting rights. Local voting rights for (non-communitarian) migrants have become an important topic for the national government in the last years. Some local governments, including Barcelona, as well as migrant organizations have claimed voting rights for many years already. The third issue refers to migrants' transnationalism. At the interface of development cooperation and migration policies new perspectives are currently emerging which actively involve national and more prominently local level agencies. These are based on the policy concept of co-development which intends to promote transnational engagement of migrant communities and their organizations. Co-development as a policy is, thus, a further element which shapes the activities of migrant organizations already. These issues cross-cut the multiple levels of government and are addressed at different stages of the chapter. Chapter 4 shows how the interplay of the elements described in the following shape migrant organizations. It will analyse how migrants form their organizations and how these in turn act out their concerns and claims within specific city contexts.

The dynamics of new immigration

In 2008, 4.4 million foreigners were living in Spain, almost 6 million when taking all locally registered foreign-born persons into account (González-Enríquez 2009: 4). This international migration concentrates mainly in four autonomous communities. These are Catalonia, Madrid, Andalusia and the Community of Valencia where 67 per cent of all foreign migrants live (OPI 2008). 18 per cent of all foreigners live in the cities of Barcelona and Madrid, which are also the two localities with the highest absolute numbers of migrants in Spain.

Migration scholarship has put much emphasis on Spain's transition from a country of emigration to one of immigration (Cornelius 1994, Izquierdo Escribano 1996, Arango 2000,). This perspective is also articulated by the most recent integration plan of the central government (MTAS 2007). Yet, from the perspective of the cities of Barcelona and Madrid the changes in the dynamics of migration make for a different picture. Both cities have attracted internal migration from the poorer and more rural regions in Spain, mostly from Andalusia, Extremadura, Galicia and Castile (Morén-Alegret 2002a: 68, Ayuntamiento de Madrid 2005a) since the 1950s when both cities were economically expanding, modernizing, and prospering places. From 1950 to 1980 Barcelona's population grew by a third to 1.7 million, while in Madrid the population doubled to 3.1 million (data from INE 2008). To what degree the cities' migration histories influence local responses to new international migration is difficult to say, but previous experiences may contribute to more sensibility and comprehension. References in official documents support this impression. Barcelona and Madrid both subscribe to this perspective in their current integration policies and their respective documents.

Prior to the 1990s, foreigners in Spain were often European retirees who settled in the coastal regions and on the Spanish islands. In the cities also lived post-graduate students, mainly from Latin America, as well as political refugees fleeing South American dictatorships and political repression in the Middle East. The first labour migrants were often Moroccan male workers and soon the first female migrants came from the Philippines, the Dominican Republic and later on from other Latin American countries, seeking for jobs in domestic services. Still, in the mid-1990s foreign residents in Barcelona and Madrid made for less than 2 per cent of the local population. By the year 2000 their share had grown to 3.5 per cent and after that the turn-of-the-millennium statistics display sharp increases. In 2004 the figure reached 13 and 14 per cent, and over 17 per cent in 2008 (see Table 3.1).[1]

Table 3.1   Foreign population in Barcelona and Madrid (1996–2008)

	1996	2000	2004	2008
Barcelona				
Total number of registered foreigners	29,354	53,428	202,489	280,817
% of total of inhabitants	1.9	3.5	12.8	17.3
Madrid				
Total number of registered foreigners	53,593	156,504	444,172	566,392
% of total of inhabitants	1.8	3.5	14.0	17.3

Source: for Barcelona: Ajuntament de Barcelona, Departament d' Estadística. Ajuntament de Barcelona, Padró municipal d'habitantes (various years); 1996, 2000 as of 1 March; 2004, 2008 as of 1 January; for Madrid: Ayuntamiento de Madrid, Dirección General de Estadística, Padrón Municipal de habitantes (various years), as of 1 July.

In addition to dynamic rises in numbers, the composition of the migrant population also changes very dynamically. Stock numbers in general hardly decline, although there are now some changes with the financial and economic crises in Spain. Over the years many small groups grew rapidly, while at a certain point they were outnumbered by other, more quickly growing nationality groups. A quarter of the foreign residents in Barcelona (25 per cent) and Madrid (24.2 per cent) are citizens of the European Union, 21 and 15 per cent respectively when considering the EU-15 only. The great majority of foreigners come from

---

1   This data reflects registration at the municipalities. On the one hand it gives a fairly close account of the foreign population because it includes the majority of migrants in irregular conditions due to specific legal regulations. The reform of the foreigners' law LO 4/2000 granted access to basic health care to all those registered with any municipality in Spain. It further upheld that the local registry was not an instrument to control a person's legal status. This led to a considerable increase in registrations. On the other hand, due to a number of further legal and administrative changes registration has augmented since the year 2000 while de-registration in the last years occurs due to clearance of files and the requirement to annual renewal.

non-European and also from non-Western countries. The top ten non-EU origin countries of migrants in both cities in 2008 include Ecuador, Bolivia, Peru, Morocco, Colombia, the Dominican Republic, Brazil and China. In Barcelona Pakistan and Argentina are also among the top ten, while Paraguayans constitute a major group only in Madrid (see Appendix 3). Today, the largest migrant group in both cities, the Ecuadorians, illustrates the tremendous dynamics: In 1996, 200 Ecuadorians lived in Barcelona and slightly over 1,000 in Madrid. Today, there are more than 22,000 Ecuadorian citizens in Barcelona and almost 98,000 in Madrid. Other new migrant groups are also strongly growing, including sub-Saharan Africans, and more recently migrants from the new EU accession countries are arriving, mainly from Romania and to a lesser extent from Bulgaria. Since this is a very recent development and reflects partly different conditions (these migrants became European citizens on 1 January 2007), this study puts the most emphasis on non-EU migrants.

The Spanish immigration regime and the role of irregularity

Policy responses to new international migration in Spain evolved slowly (Arango 2000, Cornelius 2004). Legal and administrative reforms subsequently introduced new instruments and revised existing ones. Throughout all phases, legal reforms, their official justification and the accompanying debates in Spain have put emphasis on the control of immigration as well as on the integration of immigrants, although the former has received more prominence than the latter (Blanco 2001, Aparicio, Tornos 2003 Agrela, Dietz 2006). Still, since irregularity has remained a characterizing feature of this migration and public integration measures were greatly lacking until recently, some authors conclude that immigration policy did not substantially advance in either direction throughout the first decades (Calavita 1998).

Four phases of Spanish migration policies

The control of inflows and the combat of irregular migration and the integration of migrants have received different attention in the various phases of immigration policies, partly related to alterations of the party in government at any given time. Before going into more detail as regards the policies on immigration and irregularity, it seems necessary to give a brief overview of major policies and their changes which can be distinguished along four phases (see Table 3.2).

The first phase started with the Law on the Rights and Liberties of Foreigners in Spain (LO 7/1985), approved in 1985 under the Socialist government (1982–1996), at a time when still comparatively small numbers of migrants lived and worked there. It introduced conditions for work and stay, including a new visa, focused on a clear distinction between legal and illegal statuses, and granted the rights of assembly, association, and trade union affiliation to foreigners. Work permits

Table 3.2   Four phases of Spanish immigration and integration policy

	Immigration	Integration
1985–1992	1985 First foreigners' law 1986 Implementation rules 1986 Regularization 1991 Regularization	1990 Government report on integration, and parliamentary proposal
1993–2000	1993 Contingent system 1996 New implementation rules 1996 Regularization 2000 New Foreigner Law 2000 Regularization	1994 Plan for the Social Integration of Immigrants 1995 Forum for the Social Integration of Immigrants
2000–2004	2000 Reform of foreigner's law, incl. end of contingents as 'disguised regularization' 2001 Re-opened regularization 2003 Reforms of foreigners' law	2001 Programma GRECO 2001 Curtailing of competences of Forum for Integration
2004–	2004 New implementation rules 2005 Regularization	2005 Strategic Plan for Citizenship and Integration 2005 First budget for sub-national integration measures 2006 Expansion of competences of Forum for Integration

were mostly granted for a very short duration (Calavita 1998), aspects related to integration or settlement were not a topic, and permanent residency was also not regulated (Gortázar 2002: 5). The law received great criticism for being vague and unspecific (Kreienbrink 2004: Chapter 2.4).

In the second phase, over the decade of the 1990s, efforts increased both on control and on integration. This included several regularization programmes to confront existing irregularity, the introduction of an entry visa requirement for countries with high numbers of irregulars in the country starting with Morocco, the Dominican Republic and Peru, and the establishment of a quota system (*contingentes*) for the recruitment of foreign workers in 1993. Contrary to its proclamation, the contingents worked *de facto* as a mechanism of regularization until the year 2000. In parallel, a first integration plan was approved which also introduced the Forum for the Social Integration of Foreign Immigrants. Further legal reforms improved administrative procedures and introduced a permanent residence status and the right to family reunification in 1996. At the end of the decade, a new foreigners' law (LO 4/2000) continued the still relatively liberal approach on irregularity, and relativized the distinction between legal and irregular as regards the entitlement to certain rights. Among the most important changes was the introduction of municipal registration (*empadronamiento*) for access to social rights, in particular health care, independent from the residence status (Gortázar 2002). The change to the conservative Popular Party (PP) (1996–2000 and 2000–2004) in this period did not alter the general course.

The re-election of the PP in the year 2000, which brought them a majority government, introduced a third phase with marked differences, especially as regards the previous one. A more restrictive approach on irregular migration became a central topic of the Spanish government and immediately after the election a new legal reform changed 60 of the 70 articles of the foreigner's law (Santolaya 2006: 131). Among other effects, this ended the previous regularization practice of the contingent system. However, important rights related to the *empadronamiento* remained, although some restrictions here also occurred. Major protests arose around the reform because of its restrictive course, and strong street protest, accompanied by the occupation of public buildings and churches, demanded a new regularization programme. In the end, the government saw itself forced to implement a new follow-up programme to the one opened in their previous mandate a year before. Further restrictive legal reforms went into force in 2003 (LO 11/2003 and LO 14/2003) and the government signed a number of agreements for the re-admission of irregulars and for the regulation of labour migration with relevant origin countries (Pájares 2004: 57, Ette, Fauser 2005). In the realm of integration policies, the Programma GRECO from 2001 to 2004 disappointed many expectations since it did not substantially advance the situation of foreign migrants in the country.

Again, with the change in government in the year 2004 and the Socialist party taking over the government, a different course began. Intentions focused on a more comprehensive and profiled migration policy. In 2004, new implementation rules to the immigration law came into force, and a regularization programme followed in 2005. The new Plan on Citizenship and Integration is considered more strongly committed to the integration of migrants as previous initiatives and introduces new measures and resources for this goal. At the same, contracting from abroad as well as combating irregularity accompany this course, and labour market inspections have increased (Finotelli 2008).

The institutions of irregularity

One, if not the, most distinctive feature of new international migration to Spain, as well as in other southern European countries, is the high number of irregular migrants. Here, irregularity is generally considered the rule rather than the exception. Scholars have described this situation as 'institutionalized irregularity' (Santos 1993: 111, Calavita 1998: 552, Cornelius 2004: 393). This has two important consequences which contribute to the fact that irregularity is high on the agenda of migrant organizations, reflected in the processes of their formation and their activities and claims. First, the share of irregular migrants has always been high, and second, a major part of today's legal migrants have been affected by it. Irregularity is a common experience among extra-communitarian migrants in

Spain. At any given point in time rates of irregularity are high and still today these are considerable. Recent studies reveal shares of irregular migrants of 40 to 50 per cent of the total foreign population (Pájares 2004, González-Enríquez 2009). In the early 1990s and in specific sectors of the economy, irregularity was even between 80 and 90 per cent (Solé 1997: 26, Calavita 1998: 553). For instance, a study carried out in Barcelona and Madrid throughout the year 1990 concluded that 10 per cent of the migrants working in domestic services, predominantly women, had a stable contract, whereas 80 per cent had no contract at all (Solé 1997: 13). In general, applications in the regularization programmes are usually highest from those groups which most recently arrived in the country and had entered the labour market at first informally (Pájares 2004: 14–15, Finotelli 2008: 88–9). For many years, this situation meant that 'almost all regularized and settled migrants have been irregular at some point' (Pumares Fernández et al. 2001: 109, translation MF). Even after the year 2000, around 50 per cent of Moroccans and Senegalese in Spain had been illegal at least once (see CIS-study by Joaquín Arango cited in: Aparicio, Tornos 2003: 215). Today, the share of irregulars has declined due to stronger controls, such as visa requirements and labour market inspections, the latest regularization programme from 2005, as well as the accession of Romania and Bulgaria to the European Union (González-Enríquez 2009: 23).

The following five aspects are useful for understanding the way that the institutions of irregularity in Spain function in that they account for its existence and the mechanisms which exist in dealing with the situation. These have relevant implications for the lives of migrants and they shape the accommodation of migrant organizations. First, it has been relatively easy for immigrants to find jobs in the expanding informal economy. Second, obtaining work and residence permission for formal employment is often difficult for both employers and employees. Third, the application and renewal of legal statuses is confronted with a slow bureaucracy and scarce resources on the side of the administration. Fourth, there are various mechanisms which allow for regularization. These, however, also have their difficulties which in turn contribute to certain insecurity as well as to further irregularity. Finally, legal changes have improved conditions and social rights for irregular migrants over time. As a result entry into the labour market is often irregular, but obtaining a legal work and residence status is possible over time, though this may also be followed by a fall-back into irregularity (Cabellos Espiérrez, Roig Molés 2006).

These aspects have important implications which shall be discussed in more detail in the following. First, 'immigrants have found it relatively easy to find work' (Baldwin-Edwards 1999: 4) in Spain. A study from 2000 carried out in the five major immigration regions showed that 83 per cent of the interviewees arrived without a work permit and started to search for a job after arrival (Díez Nicolás, Ramírez Latifa 2001). Most frequently, migrants arrive as tourist and overstay their permission, while unauthorized border-crossing is less prevalent, in particular since efforts to control the Spanish border and territory have been enhanced (Pájares 2004: 7, Ette, Fauser 2005, González-Enríquez 2009). The kind of work migrants encounter is often located in the informal economy which has grown in parallel to international migration at an estimated rate of 5 per cent between 1980 and 2000 and amounts to 20 to 23 per cent of the Spanish GDP (Baldwin-Edwards 1999: 5, Pájares 2004: 26). While an informal economy has traditionally existed in Spain, it further expanded across all economic sectors in the past decades. Some industrial branches (e.g. textile, clothing and shoe industries) or domestic services predominantly rely on informal work, while others are internally segmented and cover both formal and informal work, even within one single firm (Calavita 1998: 535, Martínez Veiga 1999, Pájares 2004: 26).

Second, the two instruments intended to regulate legal labour market incorporation and the stay of foreign migrants are considered 'notoriously ineffective' (González-Enríquez 2009: 13, Comisiones Obreras 2003). These regulations neither respond to the labour market needs nor to the inflows of migrants comprehensively. Both instruments were in principle oriented toward contracting from abroad. Until 2001 the first instrument, the general regime, permitted individual contracting by an employer conditional upon the certification by the National Employment Institute that this was in accordance with the domestic employment situation. Since this is a very costly procedure for many employers it never functioned. Since 2004 there is an established 'catalogue of jobs difficult to cover' based on information provided by the provinces, trade unions, employers' organizations and state employment services. However, small scale enterprises where migrants most frequently find jobs are not well represented in the process of determining the eligible sectors. As a consequence, labour market demand exists beyond the coverage of the general regime. In addition, the requirement of contracting from abroad is often not easily met. Particularly in those sectors where demand for a foreign workforce is high, employers have little means to recruit in another country and are often reluctant to make an offer to a person whom they do not know. As a consequence, most migrants find employment after their entry into the country (Pájares 2004: 55, González-Enríquez 2009). The second instrument, the contingent system introduced in 1993, was also meant to coordinate labour market demand and confront irregularity. Although also directed toward contracting from abroad, in fact 90 per cent of the applications within the contingents were presented by people who had already been in Spain (Gortázar 2002: 3, Comisiones Obreras 2003: 32, Pumares 2003: 55). Applicants had often already worked irregularly for the same employer who then signed the necessary pre-contract (Pumares Fernández et al. 2001: 107). Not surprisingly then, no contingents were established in those years when extraordinary regularizations took place (Comisiones Obreras 2003). Through this system until 1999 around 133,000 migrants could regularize their status (Finotelli 2008: 84). The reformed foreigners' law LO 8/2000 put an end to this practice of 'disguised regularization' (Comisiones Obreras 2003: 32, Pumares 2003: 57). Preferential treatment was now to be given to migrants within the bilateral agreements that had been signed with a number of countries such as Colombia, the Dominican Republic, Ecuador, and Morocco. At this stage the degree to which these agreements really work are unclear since commissions and mechanisms for the selection of workers abroad are only slowly being set up (Pájares 2004: 57).

The third aspect that has implications for the existence of irregularity is the complicated legislation and administrative practices which make access to and the maintenance of a legal status difficult. One of the consequences is that 'the boundaries between legal and illegal populations are porous and in constant flux, as people routinely move in and out of legal status' (Calavita 1998: 531). A first difficulty is the short duration of many of the work and residence permits. These are often granted for only one or two years (Calavita 1998, Rodríguez Cabrero 2003: 294, González-Enríquez 2009: 14). This implies that the maintenance of a legal status of work and residence depends on subsequent and frequent renewal. This shortness brings further difficulties because the renewal of permission depends on remaining in the same job or economic sector, depending on the type of permit. This, however, reflects a paradoxical situation: on the one hand, access to a regular status is based predominantly on labour market segments of high instability, while on the other hand its maintenance depends on considerable stable employment (Cabellos Espiérrez, Roig Molés 2006: 119). Other difficulties concern the application procedure itself which is generally described as slow, non-transparent and complicated, involving contradictory procedures and requirements. This is mainly due to the relatively scarce personnel and limited financial means on the side of the administration. Many 'bureaucratic absurdities' (Reyneri 2001: 26) are reported in this respect. Often, it seems unclear which papers to present to whom and in which order. Migrants have received their permits the day it expired (Calavita 1998: 522–3) or with dates for residence and work permission which did not coincide. In addition, due to delays of several months, migrants cannot always rely on a job offer or even a pre-contract, because in the meantime, the employer had dealt with the vacancy in other ways. As a response to critiques voiced by employers and employees both of whom see their interests hampered by this situation, the LO 4/2000 introduced the criterion of 'positive administrative silence' in the case of renewal. Whenever six months had passed from the date of application and the administration had not yet issued the renewed authorization, this was made equivalent to renewal. However, due to the overload of administrations in many places, this rule was often not applied because not even the application procedure could be fulfilled (Cabellos Espiérrez, Roig Molés 2006: 121). In addition, the validity of the permissions in the end depends on the employer paying social security. Not infrequently a work permission never enters into force because the employer has failed to pay to the social security.

Fourth, in this situation of high rates of irregularity, a number of instruments developed to address this situation and to offer channels of regularization. The most important legal instruments for regularization in terms of people affected are exceptional regularization programmes. Since the early days of Spanish immigration, six such programs have been issued (1985/86, 1991, 1996, 2000, 2001, and 2005), and 1.2 million foreigners legalized their status within these programmes (Finotelli 2008: 85, González-Enríquez 2009: 11, see also Table 3.3). Most reforms of the foreigners' law were accompanied by a regularization programme. These

Table 3.3   Regularization programmes in Spain

Regularization programme	Number of applications	Number of persons regularized
1985/86	44,000	23,000
1991	110,000	98,000
1996	23,972	15,061
2000	247,598	163,913
2001	351,269	223,425
2005	690,679	578,375

Source: For 1986–2001, Giménez Romero 2006: 107; and for 2005, Observatorio Madrid 2005: 14 and Finotelli 2008: 86.

were generally intended to improve the situation of those migrants already in the country and to restrict and control further immigration with the new legislation. Generally, these programmes were announced to be singular and unique events. In some instances, strong mobilizations demanded the (re)opening of regularizations, in particular in 1990/1991 and 2000/2001 (Chapter 4 offers a more detailed analysis of these protest actions).

Although many migrants were able to regularize their status through these programmes, they are also not without problems. Critics always addressed the non-transparent procedures and the poor implementation. Often the papers to be presented for the application were not clearly indicated in the underlying rules. Some of the programmes were dedicated to particular groups, some included family members, and others rejected asylum seekers and refugees. In addition, sometimes the conditions changed during the on-going process. In this respect, the 2000/2001 programmes have been considered a 'sequence of processes' (Arango, Suarez 2000 cit. by Finotelli 2008: 85). The same applies to earlier programmes which were open for limited periods of time for a limited group of migrants and subsequently became more open in the face of public protest (Cornelius 1994: 353–4). In spite of the fact that considerable numbers of migrants achieved their regularization through these programmes, for many this was of short duration and fall-back rates into irregularity were high. Frequently regularized migrants became irregular when their permission expired. Only one-third of the applicants were still holding a regular status after three years in the first regularization campaign in 1985. After the 1991 campaign, which had given only a one-year work permit, only 64 per cent were still legal two years after (Calavita 1998: 550, Reyneri 2001: 26). With the 2005 campaign fall-back rates seem to be lower, primarily because renewal was made automatic. Eighty per cent of the regularized migrants were still in a job covered by social security after the first year (Finotelli 2008: 86). The 2005 'normalization programme', as the regularization was called this time, is generally considered an improvement due to a more comprehensive preparation and implementation. Preparation included an intensive dialogue between the government and the social actors which aimed at avoiding the difficulties of previous programmes. The conditions and necessary documents were more clearly explained in the regulations and the campaign counted on higher administrative resources. Among other measures, the government installed 725 information offices throughout the country. The institutions serving as information points included trade union offices, non-governmental organizations as well as migrant organizations which allowed for the broad outreach of information and assistance to migrants.

Beyond these programmes for collective regularization, individual regularization is also possible within the provision of 'exceptional regularization based on *arraigo*' (rootedness). After several modifications this mechanism allows for regularization based on social, labour-related and humanitarian grounds. After two years of continued residence including at least one year of work, or after three years of residence and the proof of both a signed work contract and strong family ties, a temporal residence permission can be granted by the authorities (Gortázar 2002, Santolaya 2006: 139). Since 2005 municipalities are responsible of issuing a report on the confirmation of the *arraigo social* (social rootedness).

Finally, the ways dealing with irregularity over time also include the expansion of social rights to irregulars, in particular through the role attributed to the *empadronamiento*, the municipal registration. This has been interpreted as the central element in the emergence of 'an integration model based on the local administration' (Rodríguez i Villaescusa 2003: 59). In the mid-1990s the Spanish Federation of Municipalities (FEMP) had still voiced its criticism of the tension between the legal requirement of local registration for any inhabitant and the government which demanded that irregular migrants should not be registered (FEMP 1995: 24). In 1997 a governmental resolution then clarified that the municipal registries should not control for the legal status of residents (see Rodríguez i Villaescusa 2003: 60). Finally, the reform of the foreigners' law in 2000 (LO 4/2000) related municipal registration to the access to certain welfare services, in particular to healthcare and indirectly to education. It also made the municipal registry a legitimate proof for potential future regularization in exceptional programmes and within the provisions on *arraigo*. Further legal reforms of a more restrictive stance did not alter this. Some modifications through the LO 14/2003 may partly endanger the *de facto* role of the *empadronamiento* as a source for rights, though. The law established the renovation of the municipal registration every two years for anyone without permanent residency. It furthermore now allows for potential access of the police to the registry which may reduce the likelihood of irregulars registering. Only in very few cases of criminal investigation has this occurred so far, and which in any case would have been possible prior to the reform (Santolaya 2006: 135, see also Gortázar 2002).

Municipal registration is not only a right but also an obligation for the localities and the persons concerned. It is further an instrument of statistical use since it reflects – relatively closely – the real number of people living in a municipality so that characteristics of the local population such as age and gender can be determined. Finally, and perhaps most importantly, municipalities have an economic interest to reflect the real number of inhabitants in the registration because this is the basis of attribution for the central government's budget (Rodríguez i Villaescusa 2003: 59–60). At least since the late 1990s municipalities started to actively promote municipal registration of irregular migrants. In the meantime, in the midst of an on-going economic crisis, some smaller municipalities announced they would put an end to these practices. This has not yet been reported from the major cities.

National (non)policies towards migrants and their organizations

While control of immigration and irregularity has received considerable attention in Spain, interventions by the central state in relation to reception and integration are considered minimal, with concepts lacking definition and concrete measures missing (Blanco 2001, Aparicio, Tornos 2003, Agrela, Dietz 2006). However, at least since the mid-1990s the absence of more comprehensive instruments and resources is nonetheless accompanied by a relatively liberal attitude toward migrants, their rights and participation. This has also included the recognition of migrant organizations by the state. In addition, one element addressed early in migration policies was development cooperation. Today, these policies make explicit references to the recognition of migrants' transnational ties and migrants' financial and social contributions to the development of their 'home'-towns and countries. This includes an attitude that articulates a positive relationship between integration into Spanish society and transnational engagement with the society of origin. Respective efforts to promote this positive relationship on the national level are currently emerging, though such perspectives are still more strongly articulated from local levels (see below).

The (non-)policies of reception and integration

The Spanish policy approach on migration in the beginning, primarily in the 1985 foreigners' law, displays a rather restrictive character. It focused on limiting further immigration and irregular migration specifically, and offered no perspective on settlement, permanent residency or integration (Kreienbrink 2004: Chapter 2.4). In spite of the reference to the term 'integration' in the preamble, the law did not regulate any measures in this respect. And although the equality of the rights of foreigners was articulated prominently, the law did not entirely follow this declaration. To the contrary, some political rights were severely restricted with public assembly, for instance, requiring the permission of the authorities, although this was declared unconstitutional by the constitutional court a few years later (Aja, Díez 2005). In general, the first law is characterized by 'considering immigrants implicitly as only workers and neglecting other personal aspects' (Aparicio, Tornos 2003: 229).

The course changed during the early 1990s when government efforts started to address migrants more positively, although concepts remained vague and measures limited. A report from 1990 and a parliamentary proposal in the following year specifically addressed the situation of migrants in Spain and their integration (Blanco 2001: 211). This document was meant to guide further migration initiatives based on three pillars: the integration of migrants, control of inflows and borders, and support to developing countries. It gave way to the first Plan for the Social Integration of Immigrants, approved in 1994 (MAS 1994). In its introduction, the plan highlights a positive attitude towards immigration and explicitly delimits the Spanish approach against European discussions of the time led by established immigration countries which put negative aspects at the centre of attention. In line with this attitude, the integration plan states that 'it is necessary to articulate a policy of immigration which, without abandoning the aspects related to limitation and control of flows, emphasizes the need to underline the aspects concerning the integration of immigrants and development cooperation' (MAS 1994: 6). One of the instruments which emerged from this plan was the Forum for the Social Integration of Immigrants which represents different levels of authorities, non-state actors as well as migrant organizations (Blanco 2001, Gortázar 2002, Kreienbrink 2004: Chapter 3.3). The plan articulates an open, positive and liberal understanding of international migrants and their rights (Aparicio, Tornos 2003: 232). Although full political participation is reserved to Spanish nationals, the plan articulates a perspective on citizenship and points to relevant rights in equal conditions to nationals such as trade union affiliation and assembly. Great relevance is given to the formation of migrant organizations. Nevertheless, in none of the realms did the plan clearly define further measures (Pájares 2006: 371). In addition, no budget was put aside to achieve the goals formulated there (Calavita 1998: 547). The second plan, the Programma GRECO, intended to guide policies from 2001 to 2004, was formulated as a 'global program for the regulation and coordination in matters of foreigners and immigration in Spain' (MIN 2001). The GRECO programme is based on four basic guidelines: a global and coordinated approach on immigration as a necessary and positive phenomenon; the integration of migrants and their families who are actively contributing to the economic growth of the country; the regulation of flows; and the maintenance of the refugee protection system. However, it too failed to fulfil expectations mainly because it did not formulate any particular policy (Blanco 2001: 216–18). It was also not accompanied by a budget. At the same time, the municipalities which already carried out many of the daily services for the reception and integration of migrants were not provided any specific support (Pájares 2006: 371).

With the Strategic Plan for Citizenship and Integration, approved in 2007, integration policy is recognized as more comprehensive. For the first time there is a dedicated budget of around 2 billion euros for the four years of its administration, 2007 to 2010 (MTAS 2007). The plan is articulated through an understanding of integration as a bi-directional process of mutual adaptation by migrants and the Spanish majority society. To this end, it follows three strategic principles: equality and non-discrimination, citizenship, and interculturality. Although these principles were already reflected in the first integration plan, they are more clearly articulated in this third version. Equality supports the idea that migrants shall enjoy the same rights and duties as the native (*autochton*) population. In this respect, the combating of discrimination is considered necessary because social mobility is understood to be crucial for *convivencia* (conviviality or 'living together'). By interculturality the plan refers to the recognition of cultural diversity and the necessity of mutual respect between immigrants and Spanish society. The principle of citizenship puts great emphasis on civic and active dimensions and on 'citizenship in the city', while access to Spanish national citizenship is not a major topic. It is noteworthy that reforms of the nationality law in the last years were concerned with emigrant Spaniards and their decedents abroad, and not with foreign immigrants (Rubio-Marin 2006).

The focus on (local) citizenship and participation is also expressed in parliamentary debates of the last years and recent government efforts that aim at advancing local voting rights for (non-communitarian) migrants. This claim had been an important topic on the agendas of migrant organizations, social actors and some municipalities for many years already (see Chapter 4, Local struggles for voting rights). The Spanish constitution (*CE*, Art. 13.2) in principal allows foreigners to vote at the municipal level conditional upon reciprocity agreements which grant Spanish citizens the same rights in the respective other country. So far, only European citizens and, due to the existence of such an agreement, Norwegians had the right to vote in municipal elections (Méndez 2005: 126). The foreigners' law from 2000 emphasized the need to advance matters of local voting rights to non-EU foreigners. Since 2006 the issue has gained greater prominence in the central parliament and government and the new Strategic Plan for Citizenship and Integration from 2007 also affirms the need to advance the local electoral participation of migrants. Since then, the government has signed agreements of reciprocity with origin countries of migrants living in Spain. The next municipal election in May 2011 will allow citizens from certain countries to participate. This includes nine countries, of which six are Latin American, plus Norway, New Zealand and Iceland. Major migrant groups such as the Moroccans and the Chinese will be excluded from electoral participation, however.

'Normalization' has expressed the ways in which migrants shall be addressed in Spain ever since the immigration debates entered the public forum. In principal, attendance to and rights for migrants should be channelled through the existing legal frameworks and the mainstream institutions and services. This goes hand in hand with the idea that specific instruments shall serve particular needs of migrants where they are disadvantaged in their *de facto* access to these institutions. Accordingly, specific measures directed at immigrants are limited. In practice, state measures generally concentrate on information about existing regulations and rights (Aparicio, Tornos 2003: 236). The attitude on the non-preferential treatment of migrants is in line with a more general perspective of avoiding special treatment of particular groups in Spain and providing equal access to state assistance for all citizens (Aparicio, Tornos 2003: 234). This reflects the main characteristics of the Spanish welfare state model. It is generally employment based and channels most benefits through contributory schemes. Beyond that it is characterized by relatively limited state intervention, few resources for housing, the prevention of social exclusion and general welfare benefits. Different social groups are not meant to receive separate treatment. This relates to a greater role of the family and kinship networks, but also voluntary, non-state organizations (Rodríguez Cabrero, Codorniú 1997, Andreotti et al. 2001, Danese 2001). In this situation, the access of migrants to the existing schemes – often provided by municipalities – together with state subsidies for the social projects offered through non-state actors are of importance. This also leads to the situation that few specific measures are set up to address or support migrant organizations, which generally receive no specific funding on an ethnic basis. Despite this, they are eligible for existing and expanding subsidies for social services and particular measures for migrants.

Generally, social services are organized through the National Institute for Social Services, renamed the Instituto de Migraciones y Servicios Sociales (IMSERSO) in 1997, which forms part of the structure of the Ministry for Labour and Social Affairs (MTAS). In the second half of the 1990s the subventions for service delivery to migrants granted by IMSERSO augmented (López Sala 2005: 305). These funds subsidize services for the reception of migrants, their educational and cultural integration, labour market insertion, as well as their adaptation, social integration and participation (MTAS 2003: 314). Subsidies for non-state actors considerably expanded again from 2004 onwards (MTAS 2007: 14) as well. The newer policy guidelines recognize the role of non-state actors and that of local governments for migrants' reception and integration. In 2005 local governments for the first time received specific funding for the 'support of reception and integration of immigrants' and for educational efforts, which is partly handed on to non-state actors and migrant organizations. The Fondo de Apoyo a la Acogida e Integración de Inmigrantes y al Refuerzo Educativo counted on 120 million euros in the year 2005 and 182 million euros the following year (MTAS 2007: 143). In 2009 its budget was 200 million euros (MTIN 2009). 50 per cent of these funds support the municipalities.

Migrant transnationalism and development

In addition to the evolving integration policies, the socio-economic situation in the countries of origin of migrants has been a reference point for the early guidelines of Spanish migration policies. The first integration plan of the national government of 1994 mentioned development cooperation as one of its basic pillars. According to this perspective, development cooperation should contribute to the improvement of living conditions and thus reduce migratory pressure. In the course of time, the linkages between migration and development have gained greater prominence in Spain, paralleled by a Europe-wide and global discourse on the issue. This implies the recognition of migrants' transnational contributions to socio-economic and human development of the place of their origin (Faist, Fauser 2011). In line with this, the migration policy Programma GRECO of 2000 made reference to the originally French concept of 'co-development' with a focus on migrants' return and reintegration, the channelling of savings into productive investment, as well as micro-credits and technical assistance for migrants' origin countries. Since then, notwithstanding a certain vagueness, the policy concept of co-development has received great attention from many different actors in Spain (Casas Álvarez 2000, Pacheco Medrano 2003, Giménez Romero et al. 2006). The latest Strategic Plan for Citizenship and Integration from 2007 further details new instruments and offers a more elaborate understanding of co-development. The objectives refer to the promotion of development in source regions of international migration to Spain, support to non-state actors engaging in this area, and the prevention of 'human de-capitalization' (brain drain), including support for voluntary return. In this respect, national level policies also put emphasis on the need to involve local governments and actors on 'both sides' into this transnational endeavour. To this end the plan's budget dedicated 57 million euros to an array of projects for the period 2007–2010, distributed through the Spanish development agency AECID and the Ministry of Labour and Social Affairs. These are, however, very recent developments and started when the field research on migrant organizations, on which the analysis presented here predominantly relies, had already ended. Therefore, few implications of this new course have yet been observed. It is to be expected that the national-level recognition and promotion of migrants' transnationalism will have further implications in the nearer future. So far initiatives from the local levels have been more important. The existence of decentralized development cooperation and its emergence in tandem with the increase in international migration has given way to local initiatives of co-development, and their effects on the accommodation of migrant organizations of local and transnational scope can already be observed. Again, these are locally very different (see below for the local initiatives in Barcelona and Madrid, as well as Chapter 4 for their impact on migrant organizations, Transnational development cooperation; see also Fauser 2011, Østergaard-Nielsen 2011).

Recognition and resources for migrant organizations

The central government recognized the role of migrant organizations for social and political participation at a relatively early point in the increasing migration to the country, although migrant organizing was also restricted at the beginning. Thus, this section addresses the four main aspects that are particularly relevant in relation to the accommodation of migrant organizations: the right to association, the forum for the social integration of immigrants, its *de facto* openness for dialogue, and the existence of subsidies, mainly in relation to social services.

First of all, the Spanish foreigners' law from 1985 already granted the rights of assembly, association, trade union affiliation, strike, and petition to foreigners

(LO 7/1985, Art. 7 and Art. 8). In different phases, legislation conditioned these rights upon a legal status and some other requirements, which were subsequently declared unconstitutional by the constitutional court (Aja, Díez 2005, Tribunal Constitucional 2007).

The idea that migrants should participate and also form collective organizations was also expressed in the early phases of migration policy-making in Spain, as reflected in the integration plan from 1994 for instance. From early on the formulation and implementation of immigration policies also involved dialogue with social actors. Throughout the summer of the year 1995 representatives of three migrant organizations were invited to the seat of government, Moncloa Palace. This included ATIME and VOMADE (Veredas Muñoz 2003: 218), two of the migrant organizations that are part of the Madrid sample of the research presented here. Some weeks later, the Forum for the Social Integration of Immigrants came into existence.

According to its regulations the integration forum shall fulfil the following functions: a) facilitate communication and exchange between immigrants and the society of reception, b) formulate proposals and recommendations for the promotion of social integration, c) receive information from the different departments of the public administration, d) achieve and channel the recommendations of the social actors, e) promote studies and projects, and f) maintain contacts at the international, regional and local levels. Its first regulation stated that legal changes in matters of migration had to be presented to the forum prior to their approval. This was modified in 2001, but the new regulation in 2005 has reintroduced it. The integration forum is composed of a tripartite representation of the responsible public authorities, trade unions and non-governmental actors and migrant organizations, each represented by eight members, ten since 2006. The selection criteria for the representation of migrant organizations refer to the congruence of the goals of the organization with the objective to achieve migrants' integration, the territorial scope of the activities, and experience in carrying out integration programmes. Here, any state subsidies received in the previous three years are taken into account. In addition, ethnicity or national origin matters in that member organizations should reflect the most important migrant groups in Spain (RD 367/2001 and RD 3/2006, both Art. 9). As a consequence, member organizations are professional service-providers which seek to represent particular national groups. At the same time, they generally offer services to the broader migrant community, independent of nationality. These two somewhat diverging orientations are reflected in a distinction between ethnic/national roots and immigrant services that migrant organizations employ as the analysis presented in the next chapter shows.

Over time, the role and openness of the integration forum for dialogue has changed. Regarding its first mandate in the years 1995–1998, members point to its success. In these years, the forum established an internal ad hoc commission for the regularization programme carried out in 1996, made proposals for legal reforms, and elaborated a proposal for a new integration plan together with the national social service agency IMSERSO (Martín Pérez 2004a: 131, López Sala 2005: 308). In the period 2000 to 2004, that is, the second conservative mandate, dialogue was more limited. A new regulation (Real Decreto 367/2001, 4 April 2001) restricted the competences of the forum, excluded the previous obligation to discuss relevant legal proposals, and moved the institution from the Ministry of Social Affairs and Labour to the Interior Ministry. It also put in the Ministry's hands the nomination of the forum's president. In these years, the role of the integration forum was rather limited. The reports available from this period hardly contain clear standpoints and rather reflect a summary of discussed topics (Foro 2002, 2003). Little dialogue with migrant organizations and other social actors took place and strong conflicts and mass mobilization occurred in the streets (see Chapter 4). Again, with the change of the ruling party in 2004, the new Socialist government intensified the dialogue with social actors. The social dialogue which accompanied the preparation of new implementation rules to the foreigners' law included 4,000 contributions from autonomous communities, cities, experts and non-governmental actors, and it also involved the integration forum. The migrant organizations' members of the forum expressed their satisfaction with the negotiations around the implementation rules of the immigration legislation, and gave their consent to the final version. The state secretary for immigration, in turn, highlighted the importance of this approval by 'the organ representing the migrants' (*El País*, 16 November 2004). A new regulation to the forum from 2006 aims explicitly at strengthening its role and, among other things, allows for the preparation of reports at the forum's own initiative. It also re-introduced the need to present migration-related legal reforms to the forum, and elevated the number of its members from 24 to 30, maintaining the tripartite structure of public administration, social actors and migrant organizations.

Very interestingly, although the need to support migrant organizations is officially recognized, there is generally no particular funding to organizations based on ethnicity or other group-based criteria. Nonetheless, migrant organizations are eligible for state subsidies with equal conditions to other non-state actors. Most important here are subsidies in the realm of social services for migrants. Yet, a comprehensive overview of the subsidies that have supported migrant organizations in Spain is impossible due to the diverse public sources.

Important parts of these subsidies were originally channelled through IMSERSO and today are among the functions of the directorate general for migrants' integration. These funds considerably expanded in the second half of the 1990s (López Sala 2005) and again after 2004. The criteria required for these subsidies refer to the territorial and social scope of activities, the capacity and characteristics of the organization such as the date of establishment, management capacity and experience, the annual budget, and the financial mechanisms. These types of criteria contribute to the fact that those organizations previously granted subsidies are more likely to receive further funding in the future (Veredas Muñoz 2003: 214, López Sala 2005). These conditions are difficult to meet for emerging and inexperienced migrant organizations competing with established non-state

actors. With the generally more profiled policies on migrants since 2004, a
new line of subsidies for immigrants' integration came into existence (Orden
TAS/1783/2006, 2 June 2006). In 2004 the government's budget for immigrants'
reception and integration was 3.5 million euros rising to 8.2 million euros in
the year 2006 (MTAS 2007: 147). In addition, a number of Spanish ministries
such as those dealing with education, women and youth have also supported
migrant organizations for individual projects. The empirical research on migrant
organizations presented in the following chapter additionally reveals that some
migrant organizations were also granted subsidies in the realm of development
cooperation from the Spanish development agency AECID for projects in
countries of origin. Further subsidies also exist through established support
for social projects and volunteering based on income taxes. The reception of
immigrants as well as support for their return and reintegration into origin
countries have acquired high priority within this scheme (MTAS 2007: 149).

Between 1995 and 2005 at least, a strong overlap between migrant organization
members of the integration forum and the recipients of IMSERSO subsidies
existed, affecting mainly Madrid-based organizations (Veredas Muñoz 2003:
214). For instance, the IMSERSO subsidies funded 47 projects in the year 2000.
Thirty-six took place in Madrid or were granted to Madrid-based organizations.
In 2001, this applied to 43 out of 53 projects. In most other regions, no project
was financed by IMSERSO; only five were financed in Barcelona, and two in
Murcia. The majority of the subsidized migrant organizations were and are
members of the integration forum and the list of beneficiaries in all programmes
of the funds related to measures dealing with immigration mentions the same
seven migrant organizations (MTAS 2003).[2]

In this respect, it is also important to note that in the mid-1990s migrant
organizations hardly met the experience criterion that was officially required
for receiving state subsidies as well as for membership in the integration forum.
Thus, it is likely that the selection of the first beneficiaries was rather based on
existing relationships with the governing Socialist Party and the trade union
UGT, in turn close to the socialists (Veredas Muñoz 2003). This implied that
the first members of the integration forum were exclusively Madrid-based
organizations, with the exception of the Barcelona-based organization Ibn
Batuta. In the meantime, its president has entered the Catalan regional parliament
as the first deputy of Moroccan decent for the Socialist Party. At the time the
integration forum came into existence, these organizations did not represent a
nation-wide representation of migrants, particular nationalities or groups. They
were local organizations in Madrid as in-depth research presented in the next
chapter shows, though many of them have opened branches in other regions of
the country in the meantime. Thus, as one element, the differential impact of

---

2   These organizations are ACULCO, ATIME, VOMADE, AESCO, AICODE,
Asociación Socio Cultural Ibn Batuta and Asociación de Chinos en España. The first four
are part of the Madrid sample of the field research presented in the next chapter.

national policies in local contexts has shaped migrant organizations according to the place where they emerged.

Local responses in Barcelona and Madrid

The previous sections have referred to the Spanish immigration regime and the national policies on migrants and their organizations. These are crucial elements that form part of the multiple levels that constitute the context for the processes of accommodation of migrant organizations in Barcelona and Madrid. The following analysis now concentrates on the third element of these city contexts, the local responses to migration and migrant organizations. Local levels are responsible for social service delivery in Spain to a great degree, and in the absence of more specific central state programmes responses to new international migration have strongly relied on sub-national authorities from the beginning. Many local authorities started to adapt their public services accordingly in an effort to facilitate access to mainstream measures and to establish specific instruments for first reception, judicial advisory, translation and other services. These evolved from more spontaneous reactions at the beginning into comprehensive policies (Carrillo, Delgado 1998, Ramos et al. 1998, Agrela, Dietz 2006: 217–18, Pájares 2006). Today, integration plans exist in many of Spain's big cities and smaller localities (Aragón Medina et al. 2009). This also applies to Barcelona and Madrid. Many new aspects were incorporated within municipal mainstream services and led to the elevation of these budgets. At the same time, in many cities and localities various municipal departments have developed particular measures for specific topics or groups like women or young people. As a consequence, knowledge and consequently comparison of the intensity and financial volume of social measures dedicated to migrants in individual cities is practically impossible.

The policies addressing the reception and integration of migrants in cities are also connected to the field of development cooperation and now also refer to migrants' transnational engagements with their places of origin. This has to do with the fact that decentralized development cooperation has existed in Spain since the early 1990s. As a response to the '0.7 per cent' protest campaigns which demanded the fulfilment of UN declarations to spend 0.7 per cent of public budgets on development cooperation, many regional and local governments in Spain institutionalized international cooperation (Ruiz Jiménez 2006). This is also to say that new municipal departments and funding lines for local development cooperation emerged in parallel with increasing international migration to the cities. In Barcelona and Madrid this has led to a situation in which the municipal departments and programmes which had been set up to deal with development cooperation soon took up international migration as a new issue area. Today, in line with the global and European debate on the migration and development nexus, co-development policies promote the involvement of migrant communities and organizations in the development of their places of origin. The recognition of migrants' transnational ties and the positive relationship with local integration became a shared perspective. The measures, the financial volume and the content of the programmes of co-development, however, differ.

Similar to the national level, channels for participation and funding for migrant organizations evolved at the local level, but these also take different forms from place to place. In this respect, the existing state/non-state actors' relationship greatly influences the degree and forms of migrant organizations' participation in policy making and implementation (Soysal 1994; see Chapter 2 of this book).

Although most research, whether concentrating on national or local levels, establishes a relationship between, on the one hand, the government's approach and attitude on migrants' integration and, on the other hand, the respective policies and resulting opportunities – which can be more liberal and thus more encouraging, or more restrictive and therefore rather inhibiting for migrants to organize collectively – the following analysis shows that attitudes do not explain the differences here. To the contrary, articulated attitudes on integration in the two cities are relatively similar. Differences can be explained by the diverging pre-existing models of local governance. The decentralization that has delegated competences and resources to local levels and contributed to a greater room for manoeuvre for local governments (Ramos et al. 1998) has also led to diverging models of local governance. Barcelona and Madrid stand out as strongly different in the ways in which local governments have pursued their model. Thus, before presenting the cases of Barcelona and Madrid as regards their policies on migrants and migrant organizations, the following section describes the governance models in place based on secondary literature and primary research carried out within the framework of the study on migrant organizations. Available research is more extensive on Barcelona than on Madrid. This imbalance indicates the differences in their governance models with Barcelona symbolizing the paradigmatic case of progressive local democracy in (southern) Europe (Walliser 2001: 298). Madrid, in turn, is not known for greater efforts on citizenry participation before 2003. This translates into a different treatment of migrant organizations and participation, notwithstanding similar attitudes.

Models of local governance

As in other parts of Europe, political and administrative decentralization occurred in Spain over the last two to three decades as a consequence of new economic policies, state modernization and supranational integration from above, as well as in response to demands from below from sub-national levels and local governments as well as non-state actors. The emerging models of governance, thus, also incorporated non-state actors in policy implementation, consultation and decision-making (Andrew, Goldsmith 1998, Ramos et al. 1998, Brenner 1999, García 2006). In the realm of migration, this has meant the inclusion of church-based groups, trade unions, neighbourhood associations, and other non-governmental organizations, solidarity and human rights groups and, more recently, migrant organizations into the system of service provision, consultation and decision-making in many Spanish localities (Casey 1998, Danese 2001, Agrela, Dietz 2006) as well as in other parts of southern Europe (Marques, Santos 2001, Petronoti 2001, Caponio 2005). Thereby the Spanish welfare model and its traditionally strong state/ voluntary sector relationships was 'turning into a more open and decentralized model, which combines forms of private contracting, the externalization of certain services and the promotion of different forms of citizenry participation' (Sarasa, Guiu 2001: 125 translation MF; see also Walliser 2001). Furthermore, in Spain decentralization is also related to post-dictatorial democratization. Political parties from the left together with strong social mobilization of a particularly urban character pushed for many political and administrative reforms in this respect (Walliser 2001, Navarro Yáñez 2004). Although this is a common trend, there are also great differences between municipalities. Today more than two thirds of the Spanish municipalities count on regulations determined by citizen participation (Navarro Yáñez 2004). This has applied to Barcelona since the mid-1980s, while Madrid issued a first regulation in 2003. Hence, '[w]hile in Barcelona citizen participation and political and administrative decentralization were a priority for the new democratic governments, no such initiatives were launched in Madrid' (Bruquetas Callejo, Fuentes Moreno, Walliser Martinez 2000: 142, Brugué, Goma, Subirats 2001).[3]

Barcelona introduced the first consultative (sectorial) councils as a form of collective participation in 1985. Today the city counts on 21 of these councils dealing with relevant urban issues such as consumption, youth, women – and since 1997 – immigration. In Madrid early attempts from the 1980s onward were more strongly characterized by conflicts with the urban social movements, and

---

3   Even though in both cities the Socialist Party won the first local elections after democractic transition in Barcelona, the Catalan Socialists in coalition with other leftist parties promoted local democracy and participation, whereas the Madrid Socialists did not. In 1991, the conservative party took over in Madrid and has remained in power ever since. At the same time, differences between Barcelona and Madrid throughout the 1990s and after cannot be explained by different party configurations alone. Differences in decentralization and participation policies have also existed between the city of Madrid and the Autonomous Community of Madrid in times when they were both governed by the same party, the conservative Partido Popular. Whereas on the regional level the conservative government had actively promoted social actors' engagement, on the local level the same party made few attempts. Accordingly, the different approaches to local democracy and citizenry participation cannot be explained by the colour of the governing party, but rather by different policy styles (Bruquetas Callejo, Fuentes Moreno, Walliser Martinez 2000: 158–9). In 2003 greater parts of the previous regional governments' political and administrative team, and most importantly its president, entered the local government of Madrid. This has brought a more proactive course to the city in matters of participation, including the realm of immigration. Nonetheless, the differences from Barcelona are still notable.

the model of participation initiated predominantly focused on control by the local government (Bruquetas Callejo, Fuentes Moreno, Walliser Martinez 2000). It was not until 2003 that the local parliament approved the first regulation on citizen participation and defined the channels of consultation (Ayuntamiento de Madrid 2004). The Foro Madrid for Social and Intercultural Dialogue and Convivality followed as one of the first sectorial councils in 2006. Still, the electoral procedures and composition differ from the Barcelona council and leave more control in the hands of the authorities as will be explained below.

The general associative fabric in the two cities is related to diverging policy approaches (Bruquetas Callejo, Fuentes Moreno, Walliser Martinez 2000). A comparative study reveals that Barcelona is rather characterized by a web of organizations working on many different issues which are also interrelated. Initiatives often not only focus on immediate demands, but also on more social dimensions and aim to promote the broader participation of other individuals and collectives. Madrid, in turn, displays a type of organization that originated in the urban struggles of the 1970s which is more focused on mobilization in character and shows weaker relationships among social actors and towards the authorities. In both cities, the specific model of state/non-state actors' relationships has provided an important foil upon which authorities also incorporated emerging migrant organizations. This has led to considerable differences in their social and political participation, notwithstanding similar attitudes on immigration and early social responses to it on the side of the local authorities in both places.

Barcelona: incorporating migrants into local democracy

Barcelona reacted relatively early to the initially slow-growing number of migrants who arrived there at the end of 1980s. Municipal social services started to address the newcomers and have adjusted to changing situations over time. In the second half of the 1990s, the city opened channels of participation in order to incorporate migrants into local democracy. In subsequent integration plans the official understanding on migrants and their integration has been described with the concept of interculturality. This has meant the recognition of migrant organizations, as well as their access to formal participation and more or less scarce financial support. The Fondo de Apoyo which was introduced by the central government in 2005 has now contributed to the more systematic incorporation of migrant organizations into local social service delivery. At the same time, migrants' transnational engagements are only starting to become an issue of the municipality in Barcelona. Another local agency, the Fons Català de Cooperaciò al Desenvolupament, has been promoting migrant organizations into development cooperation since the mid-1990s.

Principles and policies of intercultural integration

Local responses to newly arriving international migrants in Barcelona started to develop around the turn to the decade of the 1990s, when the number of arrivals was still relatively low. In 1989 the Working Group on Refugees and Foreigners was constituted within the existing Municipal Council on Social Welfare. Upon its suggestion, the municipality created the Service for the Attention to Foreigners and Refugees (SAIER) in 1991. SAIER collaborates with non-state actors, including trade unions and the Red Cross, and is funded by the municipality.[4] It gives advice on legal issues, labour market insertion and the like, and in the last few years it offers Catalan language courses. Other services and programmes followed throughout the 1990s, predominantly focusing on assistance to newcomers, education and health care (Zapata-Barrero 2002). Over the last years services and resources by SAIER have been expanded so that 25,000 people seek its services every year (Aragón Medina et al. 2009: 112).

In parallel to services of the municipality, many other initiatives emerged from non-state actors. Among the most important is the Centre d'Informació per Treballadors Estrangers (CITE) organized by the trade union Comisiones Obreras (CCOO) for the provision of information on juridical, social and labour issues, founded in 1986.[5] A similar initiative came into existence in 1993 with the Association of Mutual Help of Immigrants in Catalonia (AMIC) of the trade union Unión General de Trabajadores (UGT). Since 2005 the city coordinates and supports activities by non-state actors supporting migrants' reception and integration with the so called *xarxes d'acollida* (networks of reception). To this end, the municipality introduced a new funding line and initiated several working groups and held meetings for the exchange of experiences and knowledge among the manifold actors involved. This was possible through financial resources from central government's Fondo de Apoyo, of which Barcelona received three million Euros, complemented by another million from the regional government (Ajuntament de Barcelona 2006).

In parallel to local welfare services the dimensions of migrants' rights and anti-discrimination constituted an important realm of local activities (Morén-Alegret 2002a: 61). In 1991 a commissioner for civil rights was nominated and later on became institutionalized as one of the municipalities' departments in 1995. To this department belong the Centre Interreligioso de Barcelona and the Oficina per a la No Discriminació (OND). Although the OND deals with any kind of discrimination, migrants accounted for 42.5 per cent of its cases in 2005, for example; other concerns include women and sexual orientation (Ajuntament de Barcelona, OND 2006).

The attitude toward migrants' integration on the side of local authorities in Barcelona is not only reflected in these and other measures, it is also articulated

---

4   At the beginning these were the immigration departments of one of the big trade unions, CCOO-CITE, Red Cross, the city's legal college and two non-governmental organizations originally dedicated to support refugees (Comissió Catalana d'Ajuda al Refugiat and Associació Catalana de Solidaritat i Ajuda als refugiats); in 1998 UGT-AMIC, the immigrant department of the other big trade unions also became part of the initiative.

5   In the 1990s, CCOO started a strategy to spread the CITE offices over the Catalan territory and today CITE exist in all over Spain.

in local integration plans. A first plan was issued in 1997 with the Pla Municipal per la Interculturalitat (Municipal Plan for Interculturality) (Zapata-Barrero 2002). In 2002, the local parliament approved a new Pla d'Immigració. Here, as well as in other documents and conversations held in the course of this research, interculturality describes the integration model (Interview transcript, no. 26; Ajuntament de Barcelona 1997).

Interculturality is explicitly meant as a critique of multicultural as well as (coercive) assimilationist policies towards migrants. Here, as in Madrid, country examples known for either one concept – Britain and France, respectively – are used to delineate the city's approach. The understanding of interculturality is based on equality of rights and opportunities for all citizens (*tots els ciutadans i les ciutadanes de Barcelona*) independent of their origin, gender, religion or socio-economic condition. In many instances, official documents and other statements by local authorities and policy-makers include irregular migrants explicitly as part of the local citizenry, especially when referring to social participation. Accordingly, *empadronament actiu*, the active promotion of municipal registration for regular and especially for irregular migrants is one of the means for real access to local social services in line with the legislation (LO 4/2000). Cultural diversity is also recognized as a matter of individual rights rather than those of collectives. In addition, emphasis is put on the acknowledgement of the existing culture and norms, which includes the promotion 'of the knowledge and respect for the culture and language and symbols of the city and the [Catalan] nation' (Ajuntament de Barcelona 2002: 89). This is embedded in a situation where the current 'immigration wave is very different to those of the 20th century, as it brings new cultures which are very distant to ours' (then mayor Joan Clos, cited in: Ajuntament de Barcelona 2002: 71). One expression of this attitude is the Festa de la Diversitat which took place annually throughout the 1990s with municipal support. Today, more emphasis is put on the incorporation of migrant cultures into existing local events, neighbourhood festivities, and within the local cultural centres.

As on the national level, normalization is a guiding perspective and is often opposed to 'ghettoization' in interviews and documents.

> [Normalization here means to] attend to people within the framework of existing services without creating parallel structures. However, normality must be applied with special care to different needs and the diverse situations of each person who wants to integrate in Barcelona's society. The policies of normalization imply: guarantee the access of all citizens to the municipal services. (Pla d'Immigració; Ajuntament de Barcelona 2002: 89)

Participation plays an important role in the city's policies on immigrants. The Carta Municipal from 1998 recognized local voting rights of migrants and their participation in local referenda (Ajuntament de Barcelona 1998). Public officials from Barcelona have repeated this position over the years on different occasions.

In the year 2000 the local parliament approved a motion which demanded further advancements from the Spanish Parliament in this issue (Ajuntament de Barcelona 2004). This is also expressed through the media and other public announcements (see for instance *El País*, 15 January 2000). Over the years, Barcelona's politicians continued to publicly voice themselves in favour of local voting rights, as illustrated by a more recent newspaper article of the then mayor Joan Clos of the Catalan Socialist Party (PSC):

> The voting right of immigrants is an indispensable piece in the shorter and middle term in order to achieve the real social integration of immigrants. Integration advances on the basis of equality of rights and obligations, in this sense, the right to vote, is the highest expression of citizenship. (Joan Clos cited in *Cinco Días*, 18–19 June 2005)

Local policies on transnational development cooperation

The attitude expressed by Barcelona's local authorities and political and social actors regarding new international migration have never claimed that migrants' involvement into local affairs should substitute their interest and ties with their localities of origin. The municipal programme Barcelona Sòlidaria has also funded some public events by migrant organizations on the situation in their origin countries such as the 'Jornades culturals colombianes' or 'Jornades àrabs'. And the municipal development guidelines 2005 to 2008 pay attention to migration and refer to migrants' origin places as priority regions for the city's cooperation projects. Nevertheless, the now relatively prominent term and concept of co-development was not a reference point at the time when field research for the study presented here took place. The latest local integration plan from 2008, however, now makes reference to the concept, but its influence is beyond the phase investigated here (Ajuntament de Barcelona 2008).

So far, more active around the concept of co-development in Barcelona is the local development consortium Fons Català de Cooperació al Desenvolupament. This agency started to work along the lines of co-development in 1996 in order to 'connect the organizations of immigrants with the projects in decentralized international cooperation' (Fons Català, website). This includes the activation of migrant groups and local actors, capacity building for migrants, the inclusion of the communities of origin in projects, and the creation of networks. Fons Català defines its approach on co-development the following way:

> It is about involving immigrants in the cooperation with their communities of origin and to raise awareness in the society of reception about the deep causes of current migrations. The involvement of immigrant communities in this process means a commitment to collaborative management of the problems of development. (Fons Català website)

The combat of the root causes of migration and rural exodus in Africa are articulated as primary goals of co-development projects. To this end, those projects involve

> the Catalan municipalities where the migrants reside, as well as other local actors in the transnational development project. On those grounds, the progressive individual and collective integration of migrants into the local society shall also be facilitated. (Fons Català website)

Since this agency intensively collaborates with smaller Catalan municipalities, only a limited number of Barcelona-based organizations have been involved in their co-development projects. In addition, their focus has so far been exclusively on Africa. This has contributed to a situation in which transnationalism exists on the agenda of migrant organizations, but so far this has translated into very few cross-border projects.

Local policies on migrant organizations

As stated above, participation has been part of the city's outlook on migration from an early point on. At first, civil society's participation in the realm of migration was covered by the Working Group on Refugees and Foreigners which emerged within the existing Municipal Council on Social Welfare. The working group included representatives of political parties, trade unions, employers, non-governmental organizations like the Red Cross or Caritas, experts from various universities, and personnel of various municipal departments. Contacts with representatives of migrant groups and organizations were rare and informal. They were invited only occasionally to the meetings (Morén-Alegret 2002a).

In 1997 the Consell Municipal d'Immigració was established. In line with other experiences in various realms of urban politics, the responsible functionary at that time explained the emergence of the immigration council in an interview the following way:

> The council of these immigrated persons is first a similar process as the other participatory councils which we have in the municipality (*ajuntament*). In the municipality some years ago we created the consultative council for eldery people and the council for women in Barcelona. We thought that it might be interesting to do the same thing with the immigrated persons of foreign origin. (cited by Morén-Alegret 2002a: 58–9; translation MF)

Moreover, the installation of the immigration council took place in the context of Barcelona's participation in the European Local Integration/Partnership Action (LIA). Together with other members of the Eurocities network, Barcelona formed part of the project for '[p]romoting the participation of migrants and ethnic minorities in local political life'. Since Madrid participated in the same programme, but developed very different instruments, this again illustrates how differently both cities address migrant organizations following their existing model of local governance and non-state actor participation therein.

The municipal immigration council is meant to serve as an organ of consultation and participation in order to contribute to 'a plural and integrated city' (Ajuntament de Barcelona 1997). Its goals are the promotion of full citizenship of all immigrated persons 'without exceptions and exclusions and independent from the administrative situation' as the regulation states, in other words including people in irregular conditions. Members of the council include the mayor and a first vice-president from the municipality, representatives of the political parties in the local parliament, technical personnel of the municipality, experts in matters of migration and representatives from migrant organizations, as well as a few non-state actors, in particular the trade unions and the local federation of neighbourhood associations. Upon its foundation, the council included 16 migrant organizations; at present there are 32. The regulation itself as well as other official declarations express a need to include all local migrant communities (*col.lectius*) in the council. The majority representation of migrants in the council differs from other comparable councils on local, regional and national levels in Spain. The national level integration forum as well as the Foro Madrid, for instance, uses a clearer mixed structure of political, social, and migrant actors.

A certain ambivalence on its function accompanies the council. On the one side the idea is 'to keep it a temporary solution with a longer view of achieving direct participation and voting rights' (LIA 1999) for migrants. On the other side it is seen as a necessary although transitory mechanism toward individual and collective 'normalization' as expressed by clearly procedural perspectives:

> Obviously the debate in the background is that the associations of immigrants should integrate with the associations of the city. We would like this. But, of course, *at the moment*, immigration to our city is strong; we are *now* at 16 per cent of the population. *The reality* tells us that it makes sense that immigrant associations exist, it's a natural posture, and they have a function as a bridge, they have a very important function, in the process of reception, in attendance. It is all *in steps*. (…) But these are processes of *evolution*. I see it like this. I don't know, but maybe *in five years* the council does not exist *anymore*. Fantastic! (Interview transcript, no. 23; emphasis MF)

Some migrant organizations are already incorporated into other municipal councils such as the council on women and the council on associations, for instance. In various conversations, public officials in the city portray this way of normalization as the ideal means of engaging migrant organizations. Further discussions and some first efforts also exist to bring migrant organizations within and outside the council more strongly into dialogue and exchange with other local social actors.

In line with the general approach, this recognition of migrant organizations has not been accompanied by any particular economic support. Over many years, migrant organizations have received little financial support from the city with most of them receiving none at all (Morén-Alegret 2001: 71). Some subsidies and other kinds of support were granted to migrant organizations supporting individual organizations, smaller projects and cultural activities from time to time (Zapata-Barrero 2002: Table, 84–8, Morén-Alegret 2002b: 144). Looking at the different funding lines on citizenry participation, social welfare, culture or solidarity and cooperation, very few migrant organizations received grants. For instance, in the realm of culture, of the 330 projects which received support, six where presented by organizations of migrant background (Fauser 2008). The situation changed in

Table 3.4   City of Barcelona, subsidies for 'immigration'

Year	Budget (€)	Number of financed projects	(by migrant organizations)
2005	83,985	29	13
2006	330,000	48	9
2007	397,500	59	14

Source: Ajuntament de Barcelona, Subvencions 2005, 2006, 2007.

2005 when subsidies for the delivery of services increased and the city introduced new guidelines and the *xarxas d'acollida* (networks for reception).

In parallel to the increase of the central governments' funding, the municipal budget for multiplied by five between 2005 and 2007. Fourteen out of 59 projects which received funding in the year 2007 in the line 'immigration' were carried out by migrant organizations, while the majority of projects came from non-migrant support organizations as well as neighbourhood organizations. On average, projects received 5,700 euros. The highest sum granted in this budget was 22,000 euros for a project for migrants' reception presented by a migrant organization. While the number of migrant organizations in the immigration council has been growing over the years, so far migrant organizations have not received greater economic support. Recipients of the newer subsidies are now predominantly those which are also member of the municipal immigration council.

Madrid: Promoting intercultural dialogue for the city of tomorrow

Similar to Barcelona, social services in Madrid started to address the slowly growing numbers of newcomers in the early 1990s. An articulated concept came relatively late with the Plan Madrid de Convivencia Social e Intercultural in 2005, but many instruments developed earlier. Also similar to Barcelona, the attitude toward immigration and migrants displayed by Madrid's authorities can be described by the term interculturality. Different from the Catalan capital, however, emphasis is on dialogue and mediation as a means for daily *convivencia* (conviviality) for a peaceful and integrated 'city of tomorrow' rather than on political participation and representation by migrant organizations. Further differences exist in the more pronounced recognition of transnational development engagements of migrant organizations, including their economic support.

Principles and policies of conviviality and integration

In the 1990s Madrid's social services saw themselves confronted with the increasing demands of newly arriving and settling migrants which they answered within the existing facilities and programmes. These included mainly information, advisory and economic support in such matters as housing and schooling. At the same time, since as early as 1991 the department of social services began to subsidize projects for the reception and integration of migrants presented by non-state actors, including neighbourhood associations, non-governmental organizations, Catholic groups and others. Since 1995 the city has granted these subsidies within the local development cooperation budget along with projects in developing countries, a parallelism which will receive more attention below. In addition to the support of projects by other local actors, the municipality initiated a number of intervention projects in order to improve integration, enable intercultural dialogue and tolerance, and eliminate mistrust in the second half of the 1990s (Ayuntamiento de Madrid 1997). To this end, these projects addressed both the immigrants and the *autochthon* population, and worked collaboratively with non-governmental organizations and district associations. They established *mesas de coordinación* (round tables for coordination) in order to mediate in various city districts where conflicts arose between newcomers and settled populations around the use of public space, or where increases in social demands on public institutions had led to tensions. In the beginning these intervention projects received financial support from the central government and were continued within the European Local Integration/ Partnership Action (LIA) with finance from the European Commission.

Different from Barcelona's approach within LIA, Madrid's efforts focused on the improvement of the access of migrants to existing social services and on interchange and dialogue following from 'the necessity to participate in the daily construction of society in order to form part of it and accordingly to be integrated into it' (Ayuntamiento de Madrid 2005a: 16). To achieve this, the city developed the Service on Social Intercultural Mediation (SEMSI) as a mechanism between municipal social services and the immigrant population, at first concentrated on a number of districts with a high share of immigrant population. Over the years as municipal competences expanded due to legal reforms, among them the great importance attributed to municipal registration, the municipal budget for immigration rose, SEMSI extended to other districts, and different departments initiated other projects addressing particular groups such as Romanian gypsies or unaccompanied minors.

At the same time, the promotion of participation for migrants and their organizations was an officially declared goal, in particular in the LIA programme, though migrant organization participation has been low. A crucial problem that the city identified in this period was that 'the city has good partnerships with NGOs and voluntary sector. [However, a]ssociations of migrants are weak and therefore participation is hindered' (LIA 1999). Notwithstanding this, by that time the city council had already studied the possibility of setting up a council of immigrants. The installation of a consultative integration council did not materialize before 2006, though. In this phase, local voting rights were not an issue on the local agenda either, and retrospectively public officials stated that this would have been 'utopian' to think of (Interview transcript, no. 52).

The general attitude on migrants articulated by local policies has been officially laid out with the 'Plan Madrid de Convivencia Social e Intercultural' in the year 2006. Although introducing many topics more prominently, the Plan Madrid does not deviate from the previous path taken. It is 'not only a plan for the integration of immigrants, but a plan which involves the construction of the society *madrileña*' (Ayuntamiento de Madrid 2005a: 51). As is the case in Barcelona, it is also articulated in terms of interculturality, and similarly, in official documents and conversations held in this research, the integration model is explicitly confined in relation to other known concepts:

> We studied the French assimilationist models. The systems of co-existence in Britain, peaceful co-existence, but separated. And we choose a different model for Madrid, one that possibly takes the best of each of the models. (Interview transcript, no. 19)

This involves the recognition of cultural diversity and change resulting from new international migration. It further advocates social justice based upon equality independently from such factors as origin, sex, age, and religion.

In terms of implementation, normalization embraces the access of 'all *Madrileños*' to municipal services, accompanied by measures specifically designed to meet migrants' needs and particular situations. The main instruments mentioned in the plan are the adaptation of existing services, the increasing of financial support in order to respond to more people and to the specific needs of migrants – in terms of language or legal status for instance – as well as intercultural training of public officials. In addition, specific measures for migrants' special needs were to be further developed. Other measures introduced with the plan relate to intercultural education, mediation, anti-discrimination and the combat of xenophobia and racism, labour market insertion as well as co-development, and participatory channels specifically intended to promote intercultural dialogue. Before moving on to the participation of migrant organizations in consultation and service delivery, the next section addresses the role of migrants' transnational engagements in relation to co-development, since it is connected to the local approach on integration and here further resources are provided for migrant organizations.

Local policies on transnational development cooperation

Migrants' transnational ties and especially their engagements with the development of their places of origin are explicitly recognized in Madrid's policy on migrants. Co-development is one of the goals articulated in the Plan Madrid. As early as the second half of the 1990s the linkages between migration and development and the involvement of migrant communities and organizations in development cooperation have been on the local agenda already (see Tables 3.5 and 3.6 below on the distribution of subsidies). Until the year 2004 projects addressing migrants in the city were funded from the local development budget. During this time some projects by migrant organizations in their origin countries already received economic support here as well. Since 1999 the annual reports make explicit reference to the term co-development. In the year 2004 subsidies were finally separated into development cooperation, co-development, and reception and integration. With reference to this institutional linkage of the instruments for migrants' reception and development, interlocutors from the municipality interviewed in the course of this research declared that the evolution of the concept co-development was something 'natural' (Interview transcript, no. 54).

The primary objective of co-development is defined in the Plan Madrid thus: 'to relate the migrant communities to the social and economic development of their countries of origin, given their incorporation into the local society of Madrid and their contributions to the development of our city' (Ayuntamiento de Madrid 2005a: 141). This approach includes the prioritization of the development cooperation in the most important emigration regions of migrants in Madrid. The topics addressed by co-development projects are organized along the migration cycle, as for instance explained in the development cooperation plan 2005–2008 (Ayuntamiento de Madrid 2005b: 84–5):

1. Strengthening the 'rootedness' in the region and the canalization of migratory flows to Spain: Assistance and information for emigrants, accompaniment of legal migration, prevention of irregular migration, vocational training, capacity building and job opportunities.
2. Economic activities involving the development potential of migrants: productive and commercial projects, fair trade and remittances.
3. Return and reintegration: Assisted return, preparation of re-integration and vocational training in Madrid and after returning.

This perspective implies that migrants, but also potential migrants as well as family members have a role to play in these projects. Furthermore, key to the linkage between migrants and development are not only migrant organizations. Other non-governmental (development) organizations are also eligible for funding within this scheme and have also received the major part of these funds. Nonetheless, the respective funding schemes express a special encouragement for applications from consortiums with migrant organizations. Public officials point out that the participation of a migrant organization or work with a migrant community is essential to be successful in their calls for tender.

Local policies on migrant organizations

For the first time, the Plan Madrid institutionalized participatory channels in matters of migration in the city. Nonetheless, the city does count on earlier experiences in the co-implementation of particular projects and round tables in the districts. So far, the dialogue with migrant organizations has mostly been either weak or informal. For instance, within the LIA project, the good relationships with NGOs were highlighted, while migrant organizations were considered weak and their participation hindered (see citation above). In this sense, the project sees its achievements in having contributed to the strengthening of contacts among the former and the latter (LIA 1999). However, although there were some contacts with migrant organizations, the *mesa de coordinación institucional*, the decision-making round table of the project, did not include migrant representation (Gil 1998). The limited involvement of migrant organizations is also documented by a survey conducted by the Migration Observatory Madrid on the participatory experiences in the city in matters of immigration. It shows that three-quarters of these experiences took place without the participation of migrant organizations (Observatorio Madrid 2005).

The consultation processes preceding the elaboration of the Plan Madrid and its instruments display similar characteristics as to the rather limited involvement of migrant organizations. In 2003 and 2004, the city called two social fora in order to discuss the guidelines of the plan with civil society actors. Social actors contributed more than 200 suggestions which were taken into consideration for the further elaboration of the plan. Participants of these two fora came from neighbourhood associations, trade unions, employers' organizations, non-governmental organizations as well as migrant organizations. This was followed, among other initiatives, by a consultation process on the related participatory channels in 2005. The list of participants in this process included political parties, employers, trade unions, neighbourhood associations, and two Islamic organizations, but no migrant organization in the stricter sense (Observatorio Madrid 2005).

The Plan Madrid institutionalized two new channels: the Foro Madrid de Diálogo y Convivencia and the Mesas de Diálogo y Convivencia Distritales. The first elections to both institutions took place in autumn 2006. The Foro Madrid is a so-called sectorial council, similar to the municipal council in Barcelona, and is meant to enhance participation and advise municipal activities. This type of council is new in Madrid and the underlying participatory regulation was approved in May 2004 (Ayuntamiento de Madrid 2004). The immigration council, then, was one of the first of those councils to be established. Concerning the composition and mode of election of Madrid's council, considerable differences exist compared to the one in Barcelona. It gives less weight to migrant organizations' participation and puts more emphasis on a mixed character and structure. Its members consist of representatives of public authorities from the local, regional and national level, from the political parties, trade unions, the municipal neighbourhood associations' federation, parents' organizations, as well as a speaker from each of the 21 district councils and twenty representatives of social organizations. Among these twenty social organizations are ten migrant organizations. All organizations are elected among the registered electoral entities. Fulfilling some basic requirements, any organization in the city of Madrid can register to participate in this electoral process and present a candidate. The electoral procedure is a mixture of voting among the registered organizations and the credits distributed by the electoral commission. This commission is composed of public officials from the municipality. The criteria it applies refer to the goals of the entity in relation to those of the forum, the representative character of the organization as measured by membership size (reflecting ethnic and national diversity of migrants in the city), experience (for example, age, territorial distribution, social services carried out in the last two years), and the organizational capacity (measured by economic management and permanent staff).

In addition to the forum at the city level, the Mesas Distritales are meant to provide an instrument for participation and interaction on the level of the city's 21 districts. They are composed of local authorities, social organizations and individuals. Six out the 19 organizations and ten out of the 16 individual persons are reserved for migrants' participation. The organizations and individuals are elected within each district on the basis of the local registration, including any person registered there over 16 years of age. The election is free, secret and direct.

Thus, both channels of participation in Madrid are of mixed character and incorporate migrant representatives as well as other social and political actors. This implies that migrant organizations have less weight since these bodies do not only represent these but also other local actors. Their election is moreover mediated through the municipal electoral commission, and the overall intention focuses primarily on dialogue, daily needs and potential conflicts. What is more, concerning the Foro Madrid, requirements for participation include experience in the provision of services. This proceeding has contributed to the representation of six migrant organizations in the Madrid forum which are also represented at the national-level forum.

Concerning financial support, Madrid does not count on specific funding lines for migrant organizations as has been shown for the Spanish national level and the local level in Barcelona. Still, between 1995 and 2003 the development cooperation budget financed projects for the reception of migrants in Madrid in parallel to projects in developing countries. In 2004, following the re-organization of the administration, these budgets were separated. Since then specific subsidies are dedicated to integration and reception, development cooperation and also

Table 3.5   City of Madrid, subsidies for 'cooperation/immigration' – 1

	Number of projects (by migrant organizations)			
	1995–2003	2004	2005	2006
Cooperation, projects in Madrid	355 (23)	–	–	–
Cooperation, projects in Developing Countries	783 (8)	–	–	–
Immigration	–	59 (9)	76 (3)	56 (6)
Development	–	69*	56*	45 (1)
Co-development	–	6 (0)	7 (1)	7 (0)

Source: Ayuntamiento de Madrid, Memoria de Cooperación al Desarrollo 2003; Memoria de Actividades del Ejercicio (various years); *no accounts for individual projects.

Table 3.6   City of Madrid, subsidies for 'cooperation/immigration' – 2

	Budget (in €)		
	Immigration	Development cooperation*	Co-development**
2004	1,342,060	16,665,033	1,165,712
2005	3,927,930	12,043,141	1,541,829
2006	1,174,322	18,731,196	1,777,100

Source: Ayuntamiento de Madrid, Memoria de Cooperación al Desarrollo and Actividades del Ejercicio (various years); *the budget for development cooperation includes cooperation projects, education for development and awareness rising, emergency aid and co-development; **co-development is part of the development cooperation budget.

co-development projects. The topics of the projects in relation to immigration cover first reception, legal advisory, labour market insertion, second generation, awareness building, and social integration and participation.

The low number of projects carried out by migrant organizations compared to other non-state actors is noteworthy in all the funding lines displayed in Table 3.5. The majority of projects are carried out by other social organizations such as neighbourhood organizations, charitable associations, and pro-migrant entities as well as non-governmental development organizations, depending on the character of the projects. In the following analysis of the migrant organizations it becomes clear that there is a concentration on a few migrant organizations in all these lines of subsidies. This concentration partly overlaps with formal representation and economic support from the national-level government. This has strengthened a small number of migrant organizations as local and national actors and it contributed to their transnationalization through development funds. Looking at the sums provided in the cooperation and immigration budgets, some additional differences from Barcelona become visible. Regular funding has been in place since 1995. In the last years between 1.3 million and almost 4 million euros supported initiatives by non-state actors in the realm of the reception and integration of migrants. On average this means between 20,000 and 50,000 euros per project. Most projects in fact range between 10,000 and 50,000 euros.

Chapter summary

This chapter has presented an analysis of the multiple institutional levels that affect the city contexts of Barcelona and Madrid. Therefore, the analysis has not only concentrated on the local responses to migration and migrant organizations, but has looked at national-level political institutions as well. It further pointed to the mediated effects of the latter through the former, through new central governmental funding to local authorities, for instance. It also found important immediate influences of national policies in the city which also differ from place to place. Among other aspects, the central governments' recognition of migrant organization has translated into the preferential treatment of a limited number of Madrid-based migrant organizations. On both national and local government levels the approach on migrants' integration is articulated through the concept of interculturality. The ways in which migrant organizations are addressed, however, not only emerge from this approach as the major part of scholarship in the field suggests. It interplays with the existing institutionalized forms of state/ non-state actor relationships in relation to policy formulation, consultation and implementation. Here, specifically local differences emerge due to diverging established models of local governance. As an additional element, which also differs from other explanatory frameworks interested in the forces shaping migrant organizations, in this book the immigration regime is identified as an important influence on the formation and activities of migrant organizations and so is accorded more attention. Furthermore, scholarship on migrant organizations has generally pointed out that transnational- and 'homeland'- oriented engagement, ties and activities of migrants would lessen with progressive integration under the condition of favourable and active integration policies. In contrast, the investigated cases document the official recognition of transnational engagements and their promotion within frameworks of development cooperation as another element which is explicitly related to migrants' integration in newer political programmes. Before moving on further with the analysis of the accommodation processes of migrant organizations in the two cities in focus, the following gives a summary of the main aspects addressed in the chapter.

Both Barcelona and Madrid are recent immigration cities which have been experiencing very rapid and dynamic increases in their foreign resident population for the last two decades. Controls of migratory flows as well as the integration of new international migrants have stood high in the official proclamations of the Spanish government. Nevertheless, irregular migration has persisted and there was little advancement in relation to integration for many years.

The high incidence of irregularity has been and remains one of the most significant features of recent international migration to Spain. Migrants have frequently found jobs in an ever expanding informal economy. The instruments of the immigration regime that intend to regulate the labour market access of migrants were found to be of limited success, and slow, non-transparent and complicated administrative procedures have often further hindered the access and maintenance of legal status. At the same time, there exist mechanisms to confront this situation and change legal statuses over time through extraordinary regularization programmes and other mechanisms. In this context, numerous social as well as legal and bureaucratic needs and problems exist, which greatly differ from the early post-war migratory flows regulated through guest-worker agreements or for those who came as post-colonial subjects. Individually, this means that a great number of migrants have been affected by irregularity at some point of their migration – depending on the point in time and the economic sector where they found work, between 40 and 80 per cent of all migrants. At the same time, it is possible for migrants to leave the status of irregularity; but also to fall back into this status again. Nevertheless, many have managed to maintain a legal status over time. Collectively and structurally, irregularity remains the most striking feature of the Spanish immigration regime. Social rights for irregulars have been improving and municipal registration allows for access to relevant social services and education. In this setting, the formation of migrant organizations was and partly still is influenced by conditions of irregularity, and protest on (ir)regularity remains a perennial feature on their agendas, although forms and degree of contention have varied over time as the next chapter shows.

At the same time, efforts in the attendance and integration of migrants evolved relatively slowly on the level of the central government. Nonetheless, subsequent reforms of the foreigners' legislation contributed to more profiled policies, and instruments of regularization also opened more secure statuses for many migrants.

In parallel, local social responses in Barcelona and Madrid have been developing since the early 1990s, not least due to the role of local authorities in social service delivery which had expanded through decentralization over the past decades. For many years, local authorities have responded to growing numbers of international migration by their own means, within existing and newly developing programmes. Since 2005 specific funding from the central government has supported this work.

On all levels of government the understanding of integration is now summarized by the concept of interculturality. This approach shares the recognition of migrants' equality in rights, opportunities and obligation, and of cultural and ethnic diversity. This diversity is to be brought into dialogue with mainstream views and institutions in order to contribute to conviviality and social cohesion. It is not meant to serve to separate group formation and segregation, whether voluntary or forced. Interculturality in this sense is generally expressed as a middle way between coercive assimilation and multiculturalism. In this vein, normalization expresses the final goal as well as the process to arrive at an integrated, cohesive society. Normalization refers to the access of migrants to mainstream services, together with all other citizens and social groups, acknowledging that the existing programmes and perspectives have to be adapted to new and changing needs. It further recognizes that in some instances migrants have particular needs, concerning legal advisory or language proficiency, for example. Mutual interaction and changes on both sides – migrants on one side and local society and institutions on the other – is supposed to accompany this process.

In line with a more general emphasis on the role of the local in migrants' reception and integration, participation is advanced specifically on the local level of government. At the moment, the role of political participation is becoming more prominent and local voting rights now exist for some groups. According to the Spanish constitution (Article 13.2) foreigners may exercise local franchise in Spain when reciprocity allows for the same rights of Spaniards in the respective country. Nine nationality groups will have this right in the municipal elections of 2011. Still, this excludes important groups such as the Chinese and Moroccans which are among the top 10 major groups in both Barcelona and Madrid. Struggles for political participation and voting rights have been on the agendas of migrant organizations for many years and this is also reflected in the official policies of the city of Barcelona.

The role of migrant organizations is prominently recognized on all levels of government, too. Their formal participation exists through consultative councils on both national and local levels. The first dialogue between the central government and migrant organizations took place in the early 1990s. In 1995, migrant organizations' representation was formally institutionalized with the Forum for the Social Integration of Immigrants. While the forum seems to have worked relatively well during its first mandate, the second conservative legislature (2000–2004) was accompanied by less support inside and greater protest and contentious action outside the integration forum. In recent years the Socialist government started to resume intensive efforts for dialogue and negotiation with social actors and migrant organizations. Notwithstanding remaining critiques, government efforts have received more positive assessment by migrant and other non-state actors than in previous phases. Since its installation the national-level integration forum has mainly included Madrid-based organizations, with one exception of a Moroccan organization from Barcelona. Hence, this is one of the elements that contribute to notable differences among migrant organizations in Barcelona and Madrid. Further, the models of local governance in each city lead to different approaches to the role of migrant organizations, participatory channels and resources, despite a similar understanding of integration. The city of Barcelona introduced a municipal immigration council in 1997. It is meant to provide a platform for exchange and dialogue between the municipality and the migrant organizations, substituting and complementing the limited political rights of migrants. It is one of the local councils dedicated to relevant urban issues which the city has used as a participatory element since the 1980s. Membership in Barcelona's immigration council is in principle open to any migrant organization and their number has grown from 16 to 32 in the course of the council's existence. Political representatives of the local parliament and from the municipality also participate in this council as well as a few other non-state actors.

The Foro Madrid came into existence almost ten years later in 2006. Its composition is of a more mixed character where ten migrant organizations are represented, a sixth of all members. The election procedure includes credits attributed by a commission composed of municipal officials. This reflects Madrid's characteristic feature of a relatively weak and a more hierarchical relationship with non-state actors. Its focus is more strongly on intercultural dialogue and exchange.

As regards the national-level forum as well as the Foro Madrid, the delivery of services to the migrant community is a criterion for membership, in addition to the representation of 'the most relevant ethnic groups' in the country or city. This puts emphasis on migrant organizations' role in policy implementation and service delivery, whereas the Barcelona council more strongly resembles a channel of participation for certain social groups. As a consequence, only very established organizations form part of these first two mentioned councils. These, in turn, partly overlap as a consequence of the predominance of Madrid-based organizations at the integration forum.

Economic support specifically addressing migrant organizations is not systematic. Migrant organizations are generally not granted support on an ethnic, cultural nor a nationality basis. Still, migrant organizations are eligible within existing funding lines, in equal conditions to other non-state actors, in line with an approach to interculturality and normalization. As a consequence, their funding for social projects has been most important, and here specifically those designed and expanding to address reception and integration of migrants. Again, in this field, important local differences emerge, and not only due to local approaches.

On the central government level, the existing involvement of non-state actors in the delivery of social services toward different social sectors, and increasingly to international migrants, has also meant economic support to projects by migrant organizations. The criteria to receive this funding require certain experience and thus tend to strengthen those already strong. One of the consequences is that migrant organizations have found it difficult to compete with established social service providers. In fact, very few have been granted funding. Some, however, have managed to become more established. These again, so far have been located mainly in Madrid. Further, there is a strong overlap between the recipients of subsidies for service delivery and formal representation in the national-level integration forum. This is also promoted by the established criteria for membership in the forum which require experience in service delivery.

On the local level, in Barcelona migrant organizations have been provided with some sporadic resources only. With the introduction of new lines of subsidies and the *xarxas d'acollida*, non-state actors and migrant organizations are incorporated more strongly into local social service delivery, for this is accompanied by exchange and working group participation. On the Madrid city-level some migrant organizations benefited from the subsidies for projects for migrant reception since 1991 which have grown over the years. The sums provided in these schemes are relatively high when compared to the situation in Barcelona. In the latter city organizations have received a few thousand euros. In Madrid most projects received between 10,000 and 50,000 euros. Whether a stronger focus on service provision in the state/non-state relationships in Madrid than in Barcelona is a more general characteristic of the respective governance models is difficult to say from this research, but it seems rather likely. Further research is required to more deeply investigate the particularities of governance models as regards the relationship between participation in politics and services in the two cities. For the field of migration on which this study concentrates, strong differences in the ways both cities address collective migrant actors and the linkages these establish between services and politics emerge.

These policies which address migrant integration and their organizations are accompanied by the recognition of migrants' transnationalism. Specifically in terms of development cooperation, migrant communities and their organizations are recognized as transnational agents, in line with the current global debate on the linkages between migration and development. This has led to new initiatives that aim at connecting migrant communities with development cooperation in their places of origin, now summarized by the concept of co-development. Notwithstanding certain vagueness and differences in the formulation of specific instruments, this is articulated on the basis of a positive relationship with local integration and the mutual reinforcement between local and transnational cooperation. One of the consequences is that transnational development cooperation exists on the agendas of migrant organizations. Supported by different local approaches, this is more prominent in Madrid than in Barcelona as will become clear in the next chapter.

These multiple institutional features, thus, play out in the city contexts of Barcelona and Madrid. They importantly shape the formation and action of migrant organizations. The next chapter offers an analysis of the accommodation processes of migrant organizations. It first looks at their formation and change. Second, the next chapter analyses the activities of migrant organizations in particular fields crucial to accommodation. These refer to social and political participation in the place of reception, looking at protest and struggle around irregularity and voting rights, and the engagement with places of origin through development cooperation.

Chapter 4

Migrant Organizations in Barcelona and Madrid

The purpose of this chapter is to analyse the processes of migrant organizations' accommodation in Barcelona and Madrid. It will show how migrant organizations form, what their particularities are and how they act out their concerns and claims. Thereby, the chapter demonstrates how the institutional contexts presented in the previous chapter shape these processes of formation and action. Accordingly, the following analysis draws on qualitative, in-depth research on ten selected migrant organizations which are briefly described in the first section of this chapter. Further, the analysis uses information on other organizations and networks as well as secondary literature on the migrant organizing processes in Spain, particularly in Barcelona and Madrid, although this is relatively scarce (see also Chapter 1 and Appendix 1 on methodology).

In general, collective organizing of international migrants is a recent process in Spanish cities, paralleling increasing inflows. Nonetheless, a number of historical associations exist also, as does, for instance, the 'oldest active foreign immigrants' association in the city [founded in] 1927: the Club Escandinavo de Barcelona' (Morén-Alegret 2002b: 112). The more recent waves of migration from different parts of the world and predominantly from outside Europe have led to many new formations and to the transformation of existing ones. In the year 1985 there were 15 organizations related to 'migratory movements' registered at the Ministry of Interior. Their number grew to 201 in the year 2000 and by 2003 their number had risen to 315 (Morell Blanch 2005: 115). Currently there are 685 associations registered at the National Registry of Associations in this domain (Registro Nacional de Asociaciones 2008). Unfortunately, on the city level data on the quantitative growth is not available, but many new formations, specifically since the early 1990s are documented for Barcelona and Madrid (Veredas Muñoz 1998, Morén-Alegret 2002b, Morales, González, Sánchez 2004).

Often, in the study of migrant organizations within particular political–institutional contexts, numbers of organizations are taken to gauge more or less favourable conditions in the environment. However, some limitations exist as regards the explanatory power of numbers. First of all, in the cases in focus here, data is difficult to obtain due to the administrative particularities of formal registration. Registries termed 'migratory movements' or 'immigration' generally include organizations working in the realm of immigrant support, regardless of whether these are of migrant or non-migrant membership. Distinctions can often only be made on the basis of further investigation. In this research for instance, an organization which appeared to be a Romanian migrants' self-organization from the information available on different websites turned out to be a network of employers predominantly working with and supporting the reception of Romanians. Moreover, registries in Spain generally do not control for the nationality of members or founders of an organization, and no special registration is required for associations founded by non-Spanish, as is the case in some other countries such as Germany. Moreover, social organizations may be registered at the different levels of public administration, for example at the municipal, regional and national levels and in different domains. This implies that organizations of foreign migrant membership may be encountered in the domain 'immigration' but also in domains such as 'culture' or 'sports'. Few surveys have been undertaken so far which could reveal the total number of migrant organizations, that is, of organizations of migrant membership. There exists one, though, which covers Barcelona and Madrid. Both the local registries for 'immigration' in Barcelona and Madrid and the survey reveal an interesting difference. There are more organizations registered in the 'immigration' domain in Barcelona than in Madrid, 69 compared to 41. According to the cited survey data this discrepancy also applies for the category of migrant organizations more strictly. Two hundred and thirty-three organizations were identified in Barcelona and 199 in Madrid.

Table 4.1   Migrant organizations in Barcelona and Madrid

	Foreign Population (2008)[1]	Registered Civic Associations 'Immigration' (2008)[2]	Migrant Organizations (Survey Data)[3]
Barcelona	280,817	69	223
Madrid	566,392	41	199

Source: [1]Ajuntament d'Barcelona, Departament d'Estadística, and Ayuntamiento de Madrid, Dirección General de Estadística, see Chapter 4.1; [2]Ajuntament de Barcelona and Ayuntamiento de Madrid, municipal registries on associations; [3]Morales, Jorba 2010.

Compared to the size of the immigrant population, Barcelona not only displays more organizations in absolute numbers than Madrid, the relative difference is even more striking since Madrid has almost twice as many foreign residents than Barcelona. It is thus plausible to assume that Barcelona's city context is more favourable to the formation of migrant organizations than the situation in Madrid. These contexts have, however, further implications. In general, migrant organizations in Barcelona are smaller whereas at least some organizations in Madrid have a large membership of several thousands as is the case for ATIME (over 15,000 members) and a few others (Morales, González, Sánchez 2004: 10). Since no data exists on size in terms of members of all migrant organizations, the density of organizing in relation to the size of the immigrant population in each of the cities remains an open question. In addition, the meaning of membership and the involvement of members vary and this is also shaped by contextual features. A broad membership often reflects professional service provision on the side of the organization, while in smaller organizations members are likely to participate more actively in the diverse activities. This relates to another crucial question in the study of migrant organizations: whom do they represent? What is the relationship of the organization with those it seeks to serve and represent? In-depth analysis is required in order to better understand the question of membership as part of the process of accommodation.

Hence, one main part of this chapter is dedicated to the analysis of the formation and the particularities encountered among the investigated migrant organizations. Here important local differences emerge, not only in terms of the size or scope of the organization. Specifically, the role politics and services play on the agendas of migrant organizations is influenced by the resources and channels offered by public authorities. This has further implications for the understanding of membership (*vis-à-vis* clients and staff) and the related distinction between 'roots and services' as will be shown. The other main part is dedicated to three fields of action and contention which seem particularly important in relation to the process of accommodation, and cover both local and transnational engagement. Here, the first field concerns social rights and the issue of irregularity; the second field refers to political rights and local voting; the third field is constituted by the transnational action of migrant organizations for development in origin countries. As stated above, before entering into a detailed analysis of the formation, particularities and the diverse activities of migrant organizations in Barcelona and Madrid, those organizations selected for in-depth analysis shall be briefly introduced. Data gathered from these organizations constitute the core material for the empirical analysis presented thereafter.

The histories and characteristics of selected migrant organizations

For the purpose of in-depth study, five migrant organizations were selected in both Barcelona and Madrid. The sample includes organizations related to various nationalities, as the intention was to understand how migrant organizations as such are shaped by the political institutional contexts on the receiving site (Green 1991; see Chapter 1 and Appendix 1 on methodology). Thus, selection concentrated on variation in nationality and in (peak) time of inflows from particular countries in order to cover organizations that relate to potentially more and less established migrant communities facing different conditions and needs.

The five organizations of the Barcelona sample are very heterogeneous in terms of how they emerged. The Centro Peruano de Barcelona (CPB) was founded in 1963 by a group of Peruvians as a students' association, the Asociación de Universitarios Peruanos. With the increasing inflows from Peru throughout the 1990s the organization started to attend to and support those newly arriving and changed its name. Today, the CPB offers legal assistance and other advisory services as well as job exchange programmes. It also organizes political debates on Peru and Latin America and is member of the local immigration council. It has no employed staff.

The Associació Catalana de Residents Sengalesos (ACRS) emerged in 1988 as an association to organize collective financing for short-term return for funerals and other family emergencies. It also assisted newcomers in legal matters and housing. Activities became more diverse over time and 2001 is portrayed as a year of greater openness, including the membership of non-Senegalese. ACRS organizes judicial advisory as well as cultural events such as film screenings and mother language teaching in Wolof and Pular to the second generation, family members, and other interested persons. ACRS is member of the Senegalese umbrella organization in Catalonia, the migrant organizations' network FCIC and the neighbourhood network PICA, which also provides them office space. It is also member of two municipal councils on immigration and on associationism, as well as of the regional-level integration forum. For a few years ACRS has received funding for integration as well as for development projects. So far, all of those active in the organization are volunteers.

The Asociación de Trabajadores e Inmigrantes Marroquís de Cataluña (ATIMCA) was founded in 1995 as a branch of the Madrid-based organization ATIME (see below). ATIMCA offers judicial assistance, social support, job exchange, women and youth projects, projects for awareness-raising on health issues, etc. It is definitely one of the more well-established organizations existing in the city. It counts on employed staff, volunteers and interns (through agreement with a European university network), and receives funding from different levels of government, including the city of Barcelona. ATIMCA is a member of the municipal as well as the regional-level immigration councils.

Ecuador Llactacarú – Asociación de Inmigrantes Ecuatorianos en Catalunya para la Solidaridad y la Cooperación – was constituted in 2001 in the context of the regularization programme of those years. Using a kichwa word (Ecuador distant territory), it makes particular reference to the indigenous and mestizo Ecuadorian identity. Whereas at the beginning the weekly legal service and advisory was most important, at the moment Ecuador Llactacarú is re-organizing itself toward stronger engagement with the country of origin. It is related to social movements in Latin America as well as in Barcelona, where it is located in the Casa de Soldaritat, together with other migrant and social movements. The organization is not a member of the municipal council and also has no employed staff.

Casal Argentí de Barcelona was formally registered in 2002 to provide a network for Argentineans in Catalonia and to develop activities as regards Argentina. During the first four years, the organization served as a platform for meetings and exchange among newly arriving Argentineans, mainly providing social support and basic orientation. Today, Casal Argentí offers judicial service, Catalan language teaching as well as cultural events and gatherings. The organization is member of the municipal immigration council. It has no employed staff.

In contrast to the investigated Barcelona-based organizations, the Madrid sample displays a number of differences and the paths of formation are equally diverse. The Asociación de Trabajadores e Inmigrantes Marroquíes en España, ATIME, was founded in 1989. Different versions concerning the formation of the organization exist. One version holds that it emerged in a context of both a concern with the political situation in Morocco and growing immigration to Madrid with the first issue occupying the agenda until the beginning of the 1990s. The other version sustains that ATIME's exclusive concern from the beginning was with the growing migration among a group of Moroccans (these two versions have been distinguished by Sonia Veredas see 1998: 82, 2001: 18). From early on, ATIME Madrid also had a close relationship with the trade union UGT and at first used their facilities to meet. Thus, there is also the version that 'ATIME Madrid was created from UGT' (Morén-Alegret 2001: 79). ATIME offers a wide range of services in relation to such things as legal, labour-market and social issues, job exchange, housing, education, and culture. Since 1994, it annually organizes the 'Encuentro entre dos Culturas', a high-level event with the participation of state officials and intellectuals from Morocco and Spain. In the meantime, ATIME has spread across the country, with branches like ATIMCA in Barcelona and in many other Spanish cities. It also founded two independent issue-oriented organizations. In 1992 the youth organization Asociación de Jovenes Inmigrantes, AJI, came into existence and in 1997 the Euro-Mediterranean Network for Development Cooperation, REMCODE. ATIME was among the first members of the national-level forum on integration and has received funding from national, regional and local governments.

Voluntariado de Madres Dominicanas (VOMADE, today VOMADE-VINCIT) was formally founded in 1992 in Madrid. It emerged at the end of the 1980s from a group of Dominicans who became concerned with the general disorientation and irregularity of newly arriving co-nationals. This group started to provide legal advice to the female Dominican domestic workers in Madrid, most of whom had irregular status, and started to mediate in some conflicts around the use of public space. Over time it extended its activities and became engaged with trade unions and politicians (Veredas Muñoz 2001: 20). It receives funding from diverse public sources and offers a broad range of activities, including legal assistance, labour market insertion and vocational training, as well as cooperation projects in the Dominican Republic. VOMADE was among the first members of the national-level forum of integration and is a member of the local Foro Madrid. It was also member of the regional-level forum of the Autonomous Community of Madrid.

Aesco was founded in 1992 when the acronym stood for Asociación Española por la Solidaridad y Cooperación con Colombia signalling the solidarity with this particular country and a concern for the developing world more generally. Today, it has been renamed the Asociación América España Solidaridad y Cooperación in response to its attendance to the increasing inflows from Colombia and later from other Latin American countries since the mid-1990s. Aesco relies on a number of offices in the Community of Madrid that offer legal advice and other support for reception and integration. Since 1995, Aesco has also engaged in development cooperation in Colombia, and today also in Ecuador. Among its activities are round table discussions on migration and migrants' integration as well as on Latin American politics. In 2006, the presidential elections in Colombia, Ecuador and Peru were an important issue on the agenda, and Aesco collaborated with the embassies and consulates to make people register in order to exercise their electoral right to vote from abroad. Aesco has received subsidies from national and local authorities from early on. It holds membership at the national-level forum for integration and the municipal Foro Madrid and was also a member of the regional forum.

Aculco was also founded in 1992 in Madrid under the name Asociación Cultural por Colombia e Iberoamérica. It provides information and services predominantly to Latin American migrants and has projects for social and labour-market integration as well as psychological assistance. It organizes a number of annual cultural events and carries out development cooperation projects in various localities in Colombia. This led to renaming the organization Asociación Socio-Cultural y de Cooperación al Desarrollo Por Colombia e Ibero-América in 2000. Today, Aculco holds offices in various Spanish cities such as Alicante, Barcelona, Valencia and Zaragoza, as well as in London and Bogotá and other localities in Colombia. Aculco was a member of the national forum, but has now moved to the reserve list due to its re-structuring in 2006. It is member of the Foro Madrid and also was a member of the regional forum. Acuclo works with paid staff, volunteers and interns, and has received subsidies from many different sources.

The Asociación Ecuatoriana de Inmigrantes Radicados en España, Aecautorie, was founded in the year 2000 'from Ecuadorian women with the aim to support Ecuadorians living in Spain' as written on their flyer. It offers legal advice, support for reception and integration, job exchange and labour market insertion, and organizes cultural events and dance classes. It supported the creation of the Youth Association for Integration in Madrid, AJXIM, in 2005. AECUATORIE is also increasingly oriented towards the youth and newly arriving children on the basis of family reunification. It relies on a volunteer staff and has received little funding so far.

Formation and Particularities

Different trajectories and a common turning point: Papers, papers, papers

Although the origins and trajectories of the investigated organizations differ considerably, they all share a common turning point. This turn consists of the realization of increasing and unattended inflows from the origin country of members and founders of these organizations. The specific moment this occurred varies in between the late 1980s and early 2000s depending on the country in question. From this moment on, the founders and early members of these organizations became concerned with migration, the assistance and reception of newcomers and started to provide support to one another and/or to other newly arriving co-nationals.

'Papers', that is, the question of irregularity and access to residency and work permission were the primary concerns addressed by these organizations at the point of their formation (or transformation in case of previously existing organizations), and the issue has remained high on their agendas. Independent of the organization's size, the nationality or cultural and socio-economic backgrounds of the members, the degree of professionalization the organization achieved in the meantime, the year of foundation, or in which city it is located, there is a strong and repeated reference to the issue of 'papers' in the narrations. The following two excerpts illustrate this; the first from the website of a migrant organization in Barcelona, the second one from an interview conducted in the framework of this study:

> In the first years of the life of the association, the primary concerns concentrated on organizing a solidarity network in order to get papers and a place to sleep, and thereby to facilitate the process of reception of newly arriving immigrants. (ACRS website)

> Since we started in '89 it has not been the same as today, the projects have changed. The only tasks [the organization] fulfilled were to present claims and the issue of papers for immigrants. Because in '89 there was a terrible problem with papers. Not like today. And the only thing [the organization] did was this. Later on, step by step [the organization] started to create new departments, new projects. (Interview transcript, no. 27)

Whereas some of the organizations emerged out of what were, at first, informal networks among migrants who supported one another, in other cases already existing organizations transformed in this context. This is sometimes reflected in the change of names, as can be seen with the Asociación de Universitarios Peruanos which became the Peruvian Centre of Barcelona, CPB.

The rise in inflows and especially the great degree to which these are characterized by irregular statuses have shaped these organizations. Furthermore, the specific features of the immigration regime which complicate the entrance and maintenance of regular statuses has made that this is an enduring issue on their agendas. The general absence of state intervention and support, not withstanding first responses by local authorities, has further contributed to the fact that migrant organizations together with other social actors started to address this situation. Subsequent and selective state funding has further impacted migrant organizations' engagement, an issue to which the analysis returns in the next sections. Their activities have included early protest campaigns and other political action, mediation between migrants and public institutions, as well as the passing of information to migrants on their rights and making them aware that even in an irregular status they are not without rights; this later on often became more formalized in legal assistance. Their work often also covers information on the labour market and mediation in conflicts with employers. The mechanisms of regularization together with the legal improvements for the situation of irregulars described in Chapter 3 also constitute relevant issues on their agendas. Irregularity and social rights for irregular migrants is, thus, the crucial issue in the formation of these migrant organizations and one of the most important aspects of their activities. Further down the protest actions around irregularity will be analysed in greater detail. In this section, the perspective is limited to the importance and role attributed to it by those actively involved in the organizations. For example, Pedro Alvarez, founding member of VOMADE, describes the role of the organization as a mediator and protector for migrants in the early phase in a speech delivered in Madrid in 2002 the following way:

> We gave a *carné del Voluntariado* [of VOMADE] to the associated persons which for many of them was the only documentation they had, but it gave them a certain status and guarantee before the police. (VOMADE 2003: 38)

Over time, new legal measures improved the situation of irregulars and thus awareness for existing social rights also became a topic for migrant organizations. For instance, the Programma GRECO of 2001 introduced the 'sanitary card' as a means of access to medical assistance open to irregular migrants (Agrela, Dietz 2006: 221). Speaking about the important topics on their agenda, one interlocutor thus stressed:

> The issue is, if you don't have any documentation you can get the sanitary card, which gives you the right that a doctor attends to you. The fact is that a person recognizes first that she has this right. (Interview transcript, no. 21)

Legal measures also frequently change and the information on the changes is crucial since the maintenance of a legal status often depends on the fulfilment of the respective requirements. The reform of the foreigners' law 14/2003 introduced mandatory renewal of the municipal registration every two years for any person without permanent residency. In this respect, one interlocutor highlighted:

> It is very important to renovate the *empadronamiento*. To the people who come here, this is one of the most important things I recommend to them. You do have papers, but watch the *empadronamiento*. If you do not have permanent residence permission you can end entirely as if you were just arriving, with the same problems as a recently arrived person. (Interview transcript, no. 25)

While at the beginning activities were often carried out outside regular, formal and established guidelines, over time many organizations acquired considerable consolidation and professionalism. In a retrospect on the history of the Dominican organization VOMADE, a report sustains that 'we do not detail the years before [1992] because [the activities] were carried out in informal ways and were not registered' (VOMADE 2003: 49). For the period between 1992 and 2003 the report gives the following details: more than 42,600 people were attended to by the judicial advisory department; 126,000 received information on the telephone; 6,000 were advised in matters of regularization; and the job exchange services offered support to 15,000 people and involved over 1,000 in vocational training courses (VOMADE 2003: 49). Similarly, ATIME's activity report 1998–2002 presents assistance in the following realms of the organization's judicial service: application for work and residence permissions (via the General Regime [770 people] and through contingents and regularization [1,908]), application for the renewal of work and residence permissions (1,117), application for non-labour related residence permissions (8,193), information on family reunification (8,193), information on student's permission (8,193), exemption from visa (393), and revocation of expulsion order (675), among others (ATIME 2002: 195). Other organizations display similar activities, though many not in such professional terms.

Nonetheless, the role attributed to this type of activity is relatively independent of the intensity and degree of professionalism which characterizes the work of individual organizations. Some of the organizations work with lawyers specializing in foreigners' law. In some instances, these are part of the employed staff, especially among those organizations that became service providers based on public subsidies (see below). Others rely on volunteers donating a few hours a week to support legal assistance and other activities and projects. And even non-professional members and organizations which do not work with qualified lawyers see their role and contribution in this context:

> And we started to prepare ourselves in foreigner's legislation, we studied the law. Eight people. We can say that we are prepared. (Interview transcript, no. 22)

These (partly retrospective) accounts from interviews, self-presentations in written documents, or migrant organizations' websites illustrate how the early trajectory of each of the organizations marks the perception and functioning of the migrant organizations. Independently from their 'real' backgrounds, the strong reference to 'papers' and to the concern for the needs of growing migrant communities show how this situation led to a (re)direction of attention and activities to these inflows and to the difficulties migrants encountered in this situation.

The urgent needs of first arrivals and in particular the central role of 'papers' have ceased to be exclusive priorities for many migrant organizations. In general, the situation of migration is perceived to be more settled than at the beginning, in particular compared to the situation at end of the 1980s and in the early 1990s. This can be related to legal changes that have slowly contributed to the improvement of the situation.

> When a foreign person arrives in Spain, s/he has to solve basic issues. To have ones' documents in order. Now a little less. Now the rights of the person without documentation are recognized. (Interview transcript, no. 21)

This is not to say that irregularity has ceased to characterize the situation of many migrants, or that it disappeared from the agendas of migrant organizations as an issue to be tackled. But due to legal changes over the years the situation changed and this is reflected in the experiences of the organizations. The introduction of a permanent residence status and the right to family reunification in 1996, the strengthening of administrative resources regarding migration, and the signing of bilateral agreements on labour migration and other measures have improved the legal situation for many migrants. The possibilities to access residence and work permission after some years of stay in Spain or through other legal instruments such as regularization programmes have moreover contributed to regularizing more people. And the expansion of social rights for irregulars has often improved the situation of these. Accordingly, a more settled situation means that more people in some national groups have achieved a more secure status over time and settlement has already started to take place.

> Before, everything was foreigners' law, it is how do I get my papers, and now that I have papers, it is how do I get citizenship, how can I bring my children. It is how can I get married, how do I get divorced, how can I get my titles recognized, how do I study, how do I get my drivers licence recognized, how do I buy a house. (Interview transcript, no. 21)

The question of papers or in other words irregularity was thus crucial at the time of the migrant organizations' formation and it is still today the single most important issue on the agendas of most of them. But over the years agendas generally expanded toward new topics such as vocational training, cultural events, the youth, women and (transnational) development cooperation. For some of the organizations changes imply that these have extended their support and services to increasingly diverse nationalities. The following citation refers to the changing inflows of immigration to Spain. At the same time, it reflects the changes in the communities which direct themselves to and receive support from this organization:

> Many people from Colombia came because they were about to introduce the visa. When they introduced the visa it stopped a lot. And the Ecuadorians came. Until they introduced the visa. Now there are Bolivians arriving. (Interview transcript, no. 21)

The fact that migrant organizations start to serve people from diverse national and cultural backgrounds poses crucial questions concerning self-understanding and representation which is generally based on ethnicity, both from the perspective of the migrant organizations as well as from the side of public authorities. Therefore, this issue of ethnicity will be analysed in more detail in the next section. This section concentrates on the observation of changes. Not all organizations broaden-up their public, though. Some remain concentrated on one nationality group and re-orient toward new topics. For instance, Ecuador Llactacarú began providing support and assistance when their group of reference grew very rapidly over a few years at the beginning of the twenty-first century. After the introduction of entry visa requirements, the number of inflows from Ecuador dropped and the conditions for new arrivals are now also different. From the experience of this organization, those who still arrive in Spain do so within established frameworks, some based upon an existing bilateral agreement for labour migration and others predominantly within the frameworks of family reunification and other established networks. In this new situation, Ecuador Llactacarú now re-orients its work toward engagement in the country of origin. These topics stood on the agenda since the creation of the organization in 2001, but moved or remained on a second stage in the face of the urgent needs of new arrivals.

Divergent relationships between politics and services

So far this chapter has shown how the Spanish immigration regime and the limited political responses to new immigration has influenced the formation of migrant organizations. This was soon accompanied by formal state recognition of the role of migrant organizations. This has led to the installation of consultative councils as well as to inclusion into the system of welfare provision, although this has been very selective. Studies on migrant organizations in Spain generally observe a transformation 'from protest associations to service providers', supported by public subsidies and in parallel with other social actors (Veredas Muñoz 1998, 2003, Morén-Alegret 2002b: 154–6, Martín Pérez 2004a, 2004b). Nonetheless, several studies show that migrant organizations are also engaged in protest articulation and use different channels to voice their claims (Morén-Alegret 2002b, Morell Blanch 2005: 117–18, Laubenthal 2007: Chapter 6). In addition, the involvement in and the relationship to street protest, participation in formal politics and incorporation in social service provision greatly differs across the organizations. This difference is particularly stark between the two cities investigated and thus represents partly different processes of accommodation in this respect. Therefore the situation in each of the cities shall be presented separately in the following.

Barcelona

In Barcelona '[i]n general, the foreign immigrant associations are small organizations modestly funded or not funded at all' (Morén-Alegret 1997: 7). This observation from the mid-1990s still applies to the situation more than a decade later. Municipal funding has not been a major source of financial support for most migrant organizations. Of the investigated organizations, only two had received support from the municipality, and one of them only a small amount for the past three years. When taking into account the diverse funding lines of the city, concentration on a limited number of organizations can be observed with the same names appearing in different categories such as 'reception and integration', 'social welfare' or 'women'. The separate funding on the level of districts also benefits these organizations. The majority of the beneficiaries of municipal funding are members of the municipal council for immigration. However, the inverse relationship does not exist. Not all members of the council receive funding by local authorities. With the funding to the local reception and integration of migrants introduced by the central government in 2005, local subsidies for non-state actors have very recently grown in Barcelona (see Chapter 3, Table 3.3).

Four of the investigated five organizations (CPB, ACRS, ATIMCA, and Casal Argentí) are members of the local immigration council; some are also represented in the regional-level council, while none of them forms part of the national-level integration forum. There, only one Barcelona-based migrant organization holds membership. In addition, ACRS is not only a member of the immigration council but also of the municipal council on associations. Ecuador Llactacarú, in contrast, is not a member of the municipal consultative council, nor has it made any attempts to become a member. There are also no other accounts of a migrant organization which saw its attempts to apply for membership in the council frustrated. The regulation of the council itself defines membership in principle as open to any migrant organization, provided some basic requirements such as official registration and a two-year operation history.

In this situation, the local government is an important addressee of interests and claims, both through formal channels and in street protest (see also further down, fields of action and contention). National level institutions, in turn, are hardly accessible for the Barcelona-based organizations and the central government in Madrid is far away. Members of the local immigration council critique the comparably little influence migrant organizations may exercise on the municipality's policy. Often, those interviewed in this research were concerned that the council would meet very seldom; that this form of participation was very limited to only a few meetings in the course of a year. Based on an ethnographic study, it has also been argued that the immigration council in Barcelona was only an instrument for legitimizing local authorities' policies and that conformity predominated in the council (Però 2007). In spite of such critiques, participating migrant organizations see the council also as a forum for access to information, exchange and influence and positively evaluate its existence.

> [If we are not there] maybe we don't get the information. If you are there, you can give your opinion, give your ideas, work together, know more people and at the same time participate together with other associations. (Interview transcript, no. 27)

Thus organizations also actively try to enter the permanent commission, which is the core organ of the council, meets more frequently and is in closer interchange with the authorities. The council is valued as a platform of information on municipal policies, procedures and legal changes. It is seen as a platform for voicing interests, opinions and claims. This applies to daily problems encountered in the city, such as the extension of city school yard hours to provide younger (immigrant) children an afternoon play area. Other topics concern, for example, opening hours of public institutions during ongoing regularization programmes or local voting rights. This evaluation is voiced in spite of the limited influences on local policies felt by the actors.

In addition, participation in the municipal council also engages migrant actors in exchange among each other, although here as well disagreement on certain issues exists. In various interviews, council members articulated a 'need to work together' with other migrant organizations and other non-state actors. Indications of existing relationships further include cross-references to other migrant organizations positions' in conversations, the fact that they exchange mobile phone numbers, as well as a the existence of a number of networks and collaborative events and protest campaigns in which a greater part of migrant organizations has collaborated.

In addition to local policies which constitute rather favourable conditions here, although financial resources hardly exist, other third actors in the local setting also play a role for the support of migrant organizations as argued in Chapter 2. Social actors, non-governmental organizations and trade unions among others have generally been supportive of the formation and interlocking of migrant organizations in Barcelona. They have encouraged their formation, supported their claims and sometimes existing organizations provide migrant organizations with a place to meet or an office space. At the same time, these are also competitors for attention and resources from public authorities. Collaboration and conflict has characterized the relationship between non-state actors and migrant organizations as well as among each of these two types of actors.

An important role in Barcelona is played by the trade union Comisiones Obreras (CCOO) where anti-Franco movements in the late 1960s and early 1970s and the parallel arrival of the first immigrants, students and refugees from authoritarian regimes came together. From these circles a number of migrant organizations also emerged. In addition, in 1988 CCOO initiated the foundation of SOS Racism to address discrimination and xenophobia against migrants, following the model of its French predecessor. Around a third of the founding members were foreign immigrants (Morén-Alegret 2002b: 128–30).

In 1990, in the context of the regularization programme, the Federació de Col.lectius d'Immigrants a Catalunya (FCIC) emerged as a multi-ethnic immigrant network supported by many other social actors, especially CCOO and SOS Racism. FCIC has gone through different phases of more and less engaged activism, and recently re-organized with the participation of Casal Argentí and ACRS. Upon its foundation and again in its re-organization FCIC's aim is to coordinate migrants' claims and protest from within the migrant communities. In the course of time, the relationship between FCIC on the one side and CCOO and SOS Racism on the other side worsened. Many migrant organizations increasingly felt that SOS Racism was taking over leadership from non-state actors in the field of migration, placing the migrants on a second stage.

The criticism also included that the majority of funds as well as recognition by public authorities was directed to SOS Racism while migrant organizations hardly received any support. The resolution of the first FCIC congress in 1994 stressed that 'it is necessary that immigrants talk with our own voice and that this voice (...) should be representative and independent' (cited by Morén-Alegret 2002b: 142). Today again, the re-organized FCIC puts strong emphasis on the independence of migrant organizations from political parties and non-state actors in its statements. Many of its earlier members remain wary of the reorganization, however. This is probably a sign of further diversification and disagreement among migrant organizations in the city.

Throughout the 1990s the FCIC together with other local actors had an important role in the struggle for migrants' rights. In 1996, FCIC and the Federation of Neighbourhood Associations of Barcelona (FAVB) initiated the Assemblea Papers per a Tothom (assembly 'papers of all'), supported by both trade unions CCOO and UGT. In the course of its existence, the assembly has addressed migrants' rights, reform (and abolition) of the foreigners' legislation, regularization as well as political and voting rights (see further down for more detail).

Over the years some migrant organizations have held a more critical and distant relationship towards the trade unions while others collaborate intensively with them. For instance, ATIMCA is member of the Coordinadora de Entidades de Inmigrantes en Cataluña, a network composed of 14 organizations of different nationalities and CCOO. The Coordinadora holds regular meetings once or twice a month where information on diverse issues is exchanged. Further, some migrant organizations also hold 'agreements of collaboration' with CCOO, like ATIMCA and ACRS. On the basis of these agreements migrants are channelled to the trade union's services offered through CITE, particularly on labour-related and legal matters. It is rather likely that the active involvement of the trade unions and other social actors in Barcelona, partly supported by the municipality in the case of local immigrant reception service SAIER for example, is a reason why migrant organizations in Barcelona have received little funding for the provision of legal assistance and other social services to migrants. They have also not been engaged in vocational training courses and other more specific labour market issues, as opposed to Madrid. This division of tasks is specifically promoted by trade union representatives who see the role of migrant organizations as more cultural and their political role as only transitory in the absence of full political rights, while social services and support, they believe, should not be provided by ethnic actors (Interview transcript, no. 6; see also Morén-Alegret 2002a: 59). In sum, the particular city context in Barcelona contributes to a relatively large number of small organizations. These are not so strongly engaged in services as other non-state actors in the city. Only recently are subsidies expanding toward more organizations in Barcelona. At the same time, participation in formal politics exists and is not related to service provision, a situation which differs from the one in Madrid. Local authorities are the relevant addressees, in spite of criticism. Furthermore, networks with other social actors and street protest also exist.

Madrid

In Madrid, the majority of the migrant organizations in this sample had already received recognition and public resources at a relatively early point in time. Most other organizations in the city remain outside public attention, however. Whereas these organizations have received considerable state funding from different governmental levels, on average migrant organizations have received scarce economic support amounting to only 3 per cent of their average budget (Morales, González, Sánchez 2004: 15–16, Table 11). This implies that most organizations have not received any financial state support. Thus, what may be considered a selection bias of the sample reflects the bias in the relationship between migrant organizations and public authorities, in which the study is particularly interested. Against this background, the study reveals that local interaction replicates the relationship on the national level and that on both levels (subsidies for) services and formal politics are closely related.

Two of the investigated organizations, ATIME and VOMADE, have been members of the national-level forum for integration since its constitution in 1995. In 2001, Aesco and Aculco also became members in the course of increasing migration from Colombia; all four organizations have remained in the national forum throughout the years, with Aculco now on the reserve list. From a relatively early point, these four organizations have also received funding from the national government. ATIME and VOMADE since the early 1990s, Aculco together with other organizations has received support since 1998, reflecting an overall increase in public funding for the provision of services to migrants.

As regards the membership in the national-level integration forum, in-depth investigation shows that the first members were not national representations of smaller branches across the country by the time they entered the forum. These organizations emerged among migrant communities in Madrid at the end of the 1980s or the beginning of the 1990s (see description above). They were smaller organizations of territorially-limited scope, often operating in only one of Madrid's districts. Relatively quickly, they spread throughout the city and sometimes across the greater metropolitan area. In the meantime, some Madrid-based migrant organizations have spread across the country and often also beyond, toward other European immigration destinations and more frequently toward their countries of origin. VOMADE, for example, has remained predominantly in Madrid, although plans exist to open an office in Barcelona as well. Aesco has offices in a number of municipalities in the metropolitan area of Madrid, such as Alcobendas or Getafe. Aculco has branches in Valencia, Alicante and other localities all over Spain. ATIME is the most widely spread organization in Spain in this respect and holds offices all over the country.

At the local level, the election procedure to the newly created Foro Madrid in 2006 brought VOMADE, Aculco and Aesco among the ten migrant organizations on the council. Similarly, the municipality has also subsidised member organizations of the national-level forum, including ATIME, its youth organization ATIME-AJI, Aesco, Aculco and VOMADE. Apart from these organizations, very few others, between two and four annually, have received funding from the municipality.

Local and national funding not only reinforce one another. Membership in both consultative councils is also linked to public subsidies and experience in the delivery of services which are criteria for membership. In this situation there are a number of mutually reinforcing processes at work. First, conditions for the granting of subsidies that support the delivery of services are related to previous successful handling of subsidies and their efficient management. This leads to the fact that those organizations which previously received funding are most likely to receive further funding. Second, conditions for membership in the national forum also include criteria of successful provision of services, and related to this the handling of public resources. Accordingly, those organizations which have received public funding at a very early point are also the ones represented in the national forum. Third, local funding in Madrid predominantly benefits the same organizations, based on the same principles of professionalism and experience. Fourth, the Foro Madrid de Diálogo y Convivencia also uses the same criteria linking membership to successful service delivery. Therefore it is not surprising that Aculco, Aesco and VOMADE are among the ten migrant organizations in the local forum.

Since the Foro Madrid is a relatively new body, at the time of this research no experience with formal local participation could be observed. Beyond this, access to municipal authorities, in particular for smaller organizations, is very difficult. Bigger and more established organizations nonetheless hold informal or un-institutionalized contacts with the local authorities. Even for these, access is rather limited, though. In some instances, a number of migrant organizations have been invited to exchange information on certain topics like regularization programmes or within broader frameworks such as the First International Congress on Local Policies for the Integration of New Neighbours, where the central ideas of the Plan Madrid were elaborated. However, in the interviews interlocutors repeatedly sustained that access to the authorities was difficult in the city of Madrid. Some also pointed out that relationships with the smaller municipalities were more intense and that the authorities there were also more open to exchange and collaborative events. In addition, since the investigated organizations are either members of the national-level forum for integration or excluded from any contact with the municipality, the local administration is sometimes also less important as an addressee for their claims and concerns.

As in Barcelona, migrant organizations and non-state actors in Madrid also make references to the support and interactions between each other. Among those actors supporting migrant organizations, the trade union UGT is most frequently mentioned. ATIME is reported to have had early relations with this trade union as explained above (see above, Description of selected migrant organizations in this chapter). Various documents and conversations of VOMADE also refer to early relationships with UGT and the support encountered among the trade unions in general. This is also the venue that brought migrant organizations into contact with the public authorities from the central government at an early stage. In the early 1990s there were no organizations of territory-wide migrant representation, and hardly any organization of migrant representation would have fulfilled the criteria of successful management of public resources (which also seems to have only been a criterion introduced in the forum's regulation later on). In this situation, the political closeness and relationships to UGT and through it to the then party in government, the socialist PSOE, are most likely the grounds upon which these migrant organizations entered the system of public subsidies and the national-level forum for integration (Veredas Muñoz 2003: 214). Aesco until recently had its office in Madrid in a building where PSOE and UGT district sections also had their address. In 2007, Aesco's president became a delegate in the regional parliament of the Community of Madrid for PSOE. VOMADE's ex-president has in the meantime become the socialist party's spokesperson for immigration and integration.

Relationships to the trade unions and specifically to UGT and to the Socialist Party PSOE have seemingly been crucial for the access to national-level institutions. The support from the local level to the same organizations, however, cannot be traced to these party relationships and also the fact that the same migrant organizations remained members of the integration forum after the 1996 change in government cannot be explained by this either. The party in government in the city of Madrid since the 1990s has been the conservative Popular Party (PP). This party also governed nationally from 1996 to 2004. Some organizations had entered the integration forum before, under Socialist rule in the mid-1990s, but others entered at the end of the decade. Once these organizations achieved certain recognition and were connected to a certain level of public resources, the criteria rather worked in their favour.

Hence, the generally favourable environment for migrant organizations in Spain has meant selective advantages for some Madrid-based organizations. These have become established service providers and political interlocutors with relatively good access to the national government. Exchange with the local government in Madrid, in turn, has been rather informal, and few established relations exist here. This situation replicates the hierarchical relations observed in Madrid's model of local governance (see Chapter 3, Local governance in Barcelona and Madrid). Many other organizations are basically excluded. This city context has thus promoted a few well-established migrant organizations while relegating others to a more marginal position. It contributed to an overall smaller number of migrant organizations, especially when compared to Barcelona, where only half as many migrants live. In the second main part of this chapter on fields of action and contention it will be shown that this affects the nature of mobilization and protest. Some organizations in Madrid are by now too established and others too weak for more radical protest action. Here differences compared to Barcelona become visible. Before moving to this part, the next section focuses on the effects of this situation for the meaning of membership and the question of representation, because this is crucial for the understanding of the process of accommodation. Here some further differences between organizations and cities can be observed.

The meaning of membership, ethnicity and representation

The particular context has implications not only for the formation and activities of the organizations, it also influences membership relations and, related to this, is relevant to the question of representation. Most of these organizations and specifically their highest representatives at the forefront claim to represent large memberships and whole ethnic groups. This is reinforced by the political–institutional contexts, discourse, participatory regulations and funding criteria. At the same time, the great importance these organizations give to the support of migrants and to the delivery of services, assistance and legal advisory, paralleled in some instances by access to public funding, has made it so that the communities they address and the scope of these migrant organizations reaches well beyond actively engaged members, and these sometimes are also from many different national backgrounds. This has contributed to a situation where there is a marked distinction between the categories of members, clients and staff, and where 'roots' and 'services' refer to different functions of the organizations. These distinctions are most clear-cut among the Madrid-based organizations of this sample of which a majority is highly established and subsidized as deliverers of social services. Some similar features can be found among less-funded and Barcelona-based organizations as well, though.

Members, clients and staff

The diverging relationship between these organization and those they seek to support and represent can best be described by the categories of members, clients and staff. Generally, the organizations count on a core group of (active) members, but mediation, protest action, and in particular assistance and social services are meant to support a broader circle of people which can rather be described by the category of clients. Whether these are formally considered members is related to the ways in which services are provided. Some of the organizations ask for a contribution for each particular service, others do not charge for any kind of service or consultation, while still others charge only for certain services. Sometimes, organizations make their clients members to allow for access to their services and others ask for fees from their clients and offer reduced fees to their members who pay an annual quota. In this situation, the number of members or clients and their contributions are likely to be higher when an organization offers a needed service. This, in turn, is more likely when an organization already receives public subsidies which allows to offer a broader range of services.

In the same vein, migrant organizations give an account of their size not necessarily by the number of their members, but often what matters is the number of 'people attended'. For instances, in its annual account for 2001 VOMADE lists 42,657 persons attended with their judicial services, 15,000 in their job exchange, 1,050 in vocational training courses (Álvarez 2003: 49). Following the same logic, ATIME refers to over 15,000 members in Madrid (Morales, González, Sánchez 2004: 11). ACRS reports to have 400 members, but it is unclear what this membership implies since it reflects two thirds of all Senegalese living in Barcelona. For those migrant organizations which receive public funding this logic derives from the requirement to report on their scope and successful management of the services for the purposes of evaluation and future applications. What is more, the logic of referring to 'people attended' is more widespread, even when not related to subsidies and service provision. It is generally a way of stressing the importance and representativeness of an organization. Speaking about the first years when the organization offered regular meetings as a '*reunión de acogida*' (first reception meeting) one afternoon a week, one interlocutor stressed:

> This circle allowed us to attend to thousands of people, in the first year 7,000 people passed through the association. (Interview transcript, no. 17)

Besides the two categories of members and clients, the third category of person enrolled in migrant organizations which can be distinguished is that of the staff, be it volunteers or paid personnel. Those working and actively engaging themselves in the organizations are still predominantly engaged migrant members of the organizations. However, the category of staff is becoming more varied, pluri-ethnic and also non-migrant. On the one hand, migrant organizations find solidarity and support among people from diverging ethnic backgrounds – mostly native Spanish but not only – who donate their time and support to these organizations. On the other hand, and more importantly, this trend toward more varied categories of people involved is a consequence of professionalization. Many services require professionals, lawyers, social workers, psychologists and others with comparable qualifications. Hence, staff, volunteer or paid, is frequently recruited on the basis of qualification. This further includes internships, often by students and young professionals, as an increasingly widespread practice. As a consequence, the socio-cultural closeness and ethnic representation supposedly reflected by migrant organizations is partly put into question by this increasing internal heterogeneity:

> Surprisingly, the only Arabic speaker in the locale of this Moroccan migrant organization is my interlocutor; the two young women – one being an intern from Italy, the other one probably Spanish – attending a female client who spoke

no Spanish could not communicate with her; we interrupted the interview so that
my interview partner could help them out. (Field note made 2006)

Before further discussing the role of ethnicity for the internal dynamics of
these organizations and the question of representation, the distribution of tasks
which accompanies the differentiation along these categories and even among
those actively involved should be pointed out. Visible indications of task
distribution encountered in this field research are the limitations expressed by
many interlocutors regarding their insight into certain processes and positions of
their organization as a whole. Although actively involved in the organization's
activities, some interlocutors recommended talking to another person (most
often the president) on certain subjects due to this person's involvement
in formal participation and other external relations. Frequently, those not
personally present in a consultative council preferred not to give their opinion on
its workings or the position the organization holds on particular political topics.
Where different members of the organization represented the organization in
different councils, the particular person interviewed preferred to talk about the
council she participated in, and not others, pointing to the limited knowledge
of the topics discussed there. This division of tasks is relatively independent
of whether the organization received subsidies or not. A few available studies
have also pointed to the low affiliation rate within migrant organizations (Nadal,
Oliveres, Àngel Alegre 2002: 78) and a low degree of activism of members or
even founders after the first years among migrant organizations in Spain (Veredas
Muñoz 1998: 622). As a consequence, numbers of organizations and the size
of membership give only limited insight into ongoing dynamics. Institutional
contexts here also shape what numbers and membership express.

Roots and services

In addition to membership and the degree of involvement, ethnicity is another
crucial aspect in relation to migrant organizations and to the question of
representativeness. The investigated migrant organizations, as well as many
others, were founded by and are composed of a majority of migrants who share
one particular national background. This is reflected in the names the founders
of the organizations have chosen, expressing a relationship with one particular
nationality or country. In the course of their existence, this situation has become
more complex, though.

Some organizations have opened up to clients of nationalities other than their
own national origin. Moroccan organizations, for instance, claim to serve migrants
from many other places, primarily from Arabic and Sub-Saharan African countries,
but also from Eastern Europe, although they estimate that their clientele is still 80
to 90 per cent Moroccan in background. According to VOMADE's annual report
2005, the organization provided services to people from 47 nationalities (VOMADE
2005: 16). This situation also led to their re-naming of the formally exclusively

Dominican organization into VOMADE-VINCIT to signal openness to other migrants (VOMADE 2003: 48). This heterogeneity applies more intensively to those migrant organizations which have received funding for their services, but not only those. In this context in which intercultural dialogue and exchange is promoted from national and local level institutions, general openness toward all ethnic groups is also expressed by migrant organizations.

'Roots' and services are, however, looked at very differently, notwithstanding a certain ambiguity.

> People look for their roots, their associations to affiliate, and go there. But when they are in need of legal assistance, they continue to come here. (Interview transcript, no. 9)

> If you have a legal problem, it doesn't matter whether you are Chinese, Colombian, Moroccan or Bulgarian. The judicial assistance is the same to everybody. (Interview transcript, no. 21)

At the same time, this person as well as many other interviewees and documents emphasize cultural closeness and mutual understanding when reasoning about the needs of migrants for directing themselves to a particular migrant organization and to be represented by it:

> Listen, where do I have to go, where am I feeling close, where would they talk to me in my dialect, in my language, where do they understand me. (Interview transcript, no. 21)

'Roots' strongly refer to the claim of legitimation and representation of migrant organizations as mediators for a certain ethnic community. This is also expressed in terms of electoral participation by a few interviewees. They claim to represent and therefore attract votes from the broader ethnic group once (local) voting rights exist. Services, in turn, are often provided to a broader range of nationalities. It is this number of members as clients or 'persons attended' in services that generally indicates the size of an organization here. In this respect, size is a criterion for subsidies for service provision as well as for participation in consultative councils, most explicitly in the national-level forum and in the Foro Madrid. Somewhat contradictorily, representation is also related to ethnicity. Members of consultative councils are to represent the 'plurality of migration' and include all relevant nationality groups. Given the fact that the most established and funded organizations are also the ones which attend to persons of many different nationalities, this indicator seems contradictory on the level of political institutions as it remains ambiguous on the side of the organizations.

These findings put into perspective what the numbers and size of migrant organizations can signify beyond the consideration of organizational density of a certain ethnic group and a more or less favourable environment for the formation and existence of migrant organizations. The multiple institutional levels which constitute each city's context and the often selective nature of the opportunities these offer have shaped migrant organizations, their formation, and also the internal dynamics and the meaning of membership. These organizations have emerged in the struggle around legality and 'papers'. To different degrees and in partly different ways they are today involved in service provision and politics. This is influenced by the forms of recognition and resources, and the conditions specifically connected to these. Rather than downplaying the role of migrant organizations, the findings show that migrant organizations play a social and political role and are addressed as such by diverse actors albeit their relationship with the migrant communities as a whole or even with many of their members can sometimes be considered weak. It is the aim of the following second main part of this chapter to show how migrant organizations engage in activities to improve the rights and situations for the populations of their concern in three selected fields of action and contention.

Fields of action and contention

After having presented the analysis of migrant organizations' formation and their particularities, the question addressed in the following is how this situation and the factors that contributed to it play out in the activities and mobilization of migrant organizations in particular fields of action and contention. Thus, the following sections present an analysis of protest action and campaigns in the realms of social and political rights and of transnational (development) cooperation encountered among migrant organizations.

Protest on (ir)regularization

Protest action for the improvement of migrants' rights, their legal situation and specifically their regularization has always been a topic on the agendas of migrant organizations in Barcelona and Madrid. The claim for regularization has been the object of many campaigns and protest actions, including the occupation of public buildings and churches, throughout the years. In addition, dealing with these issues is not limited to these more publicly visible actions and mobilizations. Formal channels of participation and less contentious protests by migrant organizations' networks are also platforms for the articulation of claims for migrants' rights. Changes in institutional contexts such as the installation of the national-level integration forum and the degree to which it has been open for dialogue, have influenced the nature of protest. Specifically, when dialogue is restricted, contentious action is more likely to occur and find support. The chosen forms of action further stand in relation to the individual actors' position in the consultation, formulation and implementation of policies as will be shown.

Already the first foreigners' law of 1985 was accompanied by a regularization programme (1985/86) in order to confront a critical situation for many migrants. However, the programme is broadly considered as poorly planned and badly communicated to the public and those potentially affected (Cornelius 1994: 353). Many persons residing and working in Spain were left without authorization. Of the 40,000 application 23,000 were finally approved (see Chapter 3, Table 3.3). In this situation, many social actors, trade unions, non-governmental organizations and the still few existing migrant organizations voiced their discontent in different campaigns in the major cities and other localities across the country on the shortcomings of the legislation and the programme.

Protest action continued in the following years. At the turn to the 1990s pro-regularization campaigns had gained tremendous visibility, most strongly in Madrid. Protest action also occurred in Barcelona, though, and there new migrant networks emerged too. In response to the protests and in order to rectify the 'administrative errors' of the previous programme, the government opened a new regularization programme in 1991 (Cornelius 1994). The programme specifically addressed Moroccans, as this group had been particularly disfavoured previously. Again the whole process was badly prepared, had little credibility concerning its intentions, and disseminated information poorly. This contributed to a relative failure of the programme and only 3,000 Moroccans were legalized. In the face of continued protest by non-governmental organizations, trade unions and migrant organizations, a broader regularization programme was opened in the second half of the year which finally allowed 100,000 migrants to legalize (Cornelius 1994: 353–4). The pro-regularization movement in Madrid brought together a large number of church-based groups, non-governmental organizations, solidarity associations, trade unions, migrant organizations and the left party Izquierda Unida, and received the support and signatures of over 100 organizations. Among other events, two major demonstrations took place in Madrid (Laubenthal 2007: 133). The occupation of churches in Madrid by the Moroccan organization ATIME in 1991 and 1992 were crucial events which found broad support from the above mentioned social and political actors (Danese 2001: 81). In Barcelona the migrant organizations' network FCIC came into existence in this phase, meant to provide a broader platform for migrants' political mobilization and claims. In these years FCIC stayed in intense contact with another network Catalunya Solidariá amb la Immigració, which brought together various non-governmental organizations like SOS Racism, Caritas and trade unions, particularly the CCOO. During this early phase, both networks held nearly weekly meetings (Morén-Alegret 2002b: 137–8). These initiatives are crucial not only because they voice migrants' claims, but also because they contribute to the dissemination of information on the requirements once the regularization programme is set-up. The Madrid-based groups in particular also officially collaborated in the dissemination of information and application materials (Cornelius 1994, Danese 2001: 77). Most likely Barcelona-based groups were similarly active, but obviously not officially recognized to the same degree or at least not at the central government level.

Throughout the second half of the 1990s new networks emerged both in Barcelona and Madrid working for migrants' rights, regularization, and to different degrees the improvement or abolition of migration regulations. Contentious protest actions comparable to those of the first years are not documented for this phase. This has to do with the government's relatively open attitude on dialogue with non-state actors, including intensive meetings and consultation processes on the most important regulations issued in these years. Even before the formal implementation of the integration forum, the government recognized migrant organizations as interlocutors and invited three Madrid-based migrant organizations, ATIME, VOMADE, and ARI Peru, together with other non-state actors for consultation at the presidential palace (Veredas Muñoz 2003: 218). After the installation of the national-level integration forum in 1995, the most important changes such as the introduction of the quota system for labour migration, the 1996 implementation rules to the foreigner's legislation, and the 1996 regularization programme were subject to dialogue in the forum, and this dialogue received altogether positive evaluation by those involved (Veredas Muñoz 2003, Martín Pérez 2004b, López Sala 2005). It has obviously also deactivated more contentious actions, such as those in the early 1990s. Nonetheless, 'papers for all'-campaigns continued in parallel and these used different means and channels. In Madrid for instance, 48 migrant and non-migrant groups together signed a manifest in 1998 that demanded an end to the criminalization of migration and the exploitation of migrants as cheap workers as well as regularization of all undocumented migrants and their full access to rights equal to nationals. In this phase, division among the actors becomes visible, with some opting for a more moderate and pragmatic course. Accordingly, some major organizations – those which were already very established by then and often represented in the national-level forum for integration as, for example, ATIME – stayed at the margins of more conflictive initiatives (Veredas Muñoz 2001: 19). Protest action also continued in Barcelona, specifically through the Assemblea Papers per a Tothom, a network initiated by the FCIC with support from the Federation of Neighbourhood Associations of Barcelona (FAVB) and the trade unions (Morén-Alegret 2002a). In these years, the assembly, the FCIC and other migrant organizations organized various meetings, debates, and demonstrations to voice their standpoint and to articulate their claims for the improvement of migrants' rights. Already in 1995 Assemblea Papers per a Tothom also engaged in a campaign for voting rights, as will be explained below.

The end of the year 1999 brought a new foreigners' law (LO 4/2000) which was also accompanied by a regularization programme. However, only around 60 per cent of the applications found a positive response and over 100,000 applications were rejected. In the face of the high numbers of those remaining in irregular status, protest by social and political actors grew stronger. In the meantime, national elections had brought the conservative PP into a majority government. As announced during the electoral campaign, the government immediately started to work on a reform of the recently approved law. Their reform (LO 8/2000) focused on a stronger separation between regular and irregular migrants and is generally considered more restrictive (Gortázar 2002, Fauser 2007).

Throughout the year 2000, this change in migration policy as well as the unfulfilled expectations on the regularization programme gave way to strong protest. At the end of the year 2000, a greater demonstration took place in Madrid with around 2,000 participants protesting against the newly elaborated restrictive reform and in favour of a revision of rejected applications for the regularization of the 2000 programme. More radical activities in Madrid did not find greater support by migrant organizations. Although the occupation of churches and other public buildings took place there, this was supported by only two migrant organizations, the then newly founded Ecuadorian organization Rumiñahui and the Asociación de Emigrantes Marroquíes en España, AEME. Throughout the protests increasing dispute on the forms of protest led to a separation within Rumiñahui[1] and the withdrawal of the organization from some of the initiatives. The main activists in the Madrid protests were people and groups related to anti-globalization movements and other more informal and fragmented networks of mainly Spanish people, with the involvement of some individual migrants (Laubenthal 2007: 136–7).

In Barcelona the most important actor in the protests was the Assemblea Papers per a Tothom. Activities there took a more contentious form and included the occupation of ten churches throughout the years 2000 and 2001. On 20 January 2001 about 600 irregular migrants of mainly Pakistani, Bangladeshi, and Sub-Saharan African backgrounds occupied the Santa Maria del Pi church and participated in a hunger strike (Morén-Alegret 2002b: 143, Laubenthal 2007: Chapter 6). The protesters demanded the regularization of all migrants, no sanctions or repression against participants and supporters, papers for all, and a meeting with the Delegado del Gobierno, the representative of the central government. Organizations like SOS Racism and CCOO-CITE and some migrant organizations distanced themselves from the movement when the situation became more conflictive (Laubenthal 2007: 138). Yet, others continued their support, especially those associated with the Assemblea Papers per a Tothom and FCIC. In addition, actors like the Federation of Neighbourhood Associations of Barcelona (FAVB) supported the occupation and publicly expressed their solidarity. The president of FAVB went to visit the protesters (FAVB 2001). Moreover, the demonstration in Barcelona produced 5,000 participants (Laubenthal 2007: 119). Even the mayor Joan Clos visited the enclosed hunger strikers. After a few days, the Delegado del Gobierno offered to revise 15,000 of the previously disapproved applications of the 2000 programme. The occupants rejected this offer and protest continued in Barcelona as well as in some other Spanish cities and localities. Finally, the government saw itself forced to open a new programme in 2001 (Pumares 2003: 57). Whereas in the first stage over 160,000 migrants were regularized, the second stage included more than 220,000 (see Chapter 3, Table 3.3)

---

1   Since then Rumiñahui has also become a member of the national-level integration forum.

Local differences between Barcelona and Madrid in the contentious nature of protest reflect the fact that migrant organizations in the Spanish capital are today either too established or too weak to engage in highly conflictive activities. The more established ones opted not to engage in the heavily contentious actions. At the same time these have also always continued to work for the regularization of irregulars as can be seen in many of their declarations, documents and from their website, and they were able to make use of other channels of influence on public authorities.

In the years following this strongly conflictive phase, the situation became calmer again. Nonetheless, migrant organizations and other social actors have continued to issue public declarations, participate in protest demonstrations, and make use of their own publications. They have organized many events to claim migrants' rights and new networks emerged in both cities. In 2002 some of the largest Madrid-based organizations, including Aesco, VOMADE, and ATIME, the trade unions UGT, CCOO, USO, the regional federation of neighbourhood associations and other non-state actors as well as the political party Izquierda Unida Madrid founded Red Ciudadana por la Igualdad (Citizens' network for equality) (Red Ciudadana 2002). The founding manifesto of Red Ciudadana, signed by 25 organizations, demands a change in the conservative governments' migration policy, the recognition of the rights of migrants and the regularization of those in irregular status and their social integration. Among other aspects it claims to decouple citizenship from nationality. One of the events which Red Ciudadana organized was the '48 hours of protest against the foreigner's legislation and its reform', a cultural event with lectures, film screenings and talks by legal experts in Madrid in November 2003. Throughout the year 2004 Red Ciudadana joined a country-wide campaign claiming migrants' rights and immediate regularization as well as the recognition of the right of citizenship based on residency under the title 'Pro regularization, pro human rights and pro the right to citizenship'. Signatures collected in the framework of this campaign were handed over to the parliament on the day of the elections to the European Parliament, 13 June 2004. Related to other campaigns in Europe which also claimed citizenship of residence and political rights for non-communitarian migrants, the Madrid-campaign pointed out that there was also

> another question which is even more urgent: to make accessible the condition of residency to hundreds of thousands of people which today do not even have this opportunity. (Red Ciudadana, Press Release)

Since the change in government after parliamentary elections in 2004, most non-state actors, including migrant organizations, have all reacted favourably to the direction of matters of migration of the newly elected socialist government. From the beginning, the new government started to actively involve social actors, set up the Mesa de Diálogo Social with the participation of the administration, trade unions and employers, as well as migrant organizations in some instances, depending on the topic discussed. Moreover, the new government also strengthened the competences of the integration forum, and important initiatives such as the implementation rules to the foreigners' legislation, the Strategic Plan for Citizenship and Integration, and a new regularization programme were discussed and generally positively approved by the forum.

As regards the latest regularization programme from 2005, the situation in Madrid is again somewhat different from that in Barcelona. In this case, not only the general climate on dialogue and less conflictive opposition *vis-à-vis* the government played a role, but also the direct incorporation of some of the Madrid-based actors into the consultation around regularization and its implementation contributed to their approval. In the interviews conducted for the purpose of this research, these actors highlight the fact that they were actively involved in the preparation of the process, and even though not all their considerations are reflected in the procedure, they show their consent with the process as a whole and the achievements made in relation to some technical aspects 'trying to regularize as many persons as possible'. In this respect, exchange is valued not only on the national level, but also regarding local authorities.

VOMADE, Aesco, Aculco and ATIME were among the information points contracted by the Ministry of Labour and Social Affairs for the dissemination and preparation of the programme. According to a survey undertaken by the Migration Observatory in Madrid (2005), Aesco attended to 3,000 people at its five information points in and around Madrid. VOMADE attended to 921 at its Madrid headquarters, ATIME had two info points, and Aculco had one. The major part of this work consisted of face-to-face and telephone consultation provided by their judicial departments. In this respect, interlocutors also point out the strong involvement and expertise of their respective departments. Throughout the implementation, the administration and the non-state actors worked closely together in formal and informal exchange, as the cited survey as well as the interviews conducted in this study show. This is not to say that there were no critiques or that the organizations did not encounter obstacles concerning the administrative procedures. These commonly consisted of confusing information on the valid documents to be presented, difficulties due to the overload of the administration and social security offices, unwillingness of employers to sign the needed contract for the regularization, dismissal of employees, and the failure of employers to pay social security once the application had received favourable response (thus making the authorization invalid) (Observatorio Madrid 2005: 33–4). As a consequence of remaining problems, protest also continues. Red Ciudadana, for instance, publicly criticized that in many cases, employers which had signed a work contract with migrants within the regularization programme failed to pay social security, rendering the regularization invalid (Red Ciudadana, Press Release).

In Barcelona, Assemblea per la Regularització Sense Condicions (assembly for regularization without conditions, previously 'papers for all') made some attempts at more radical action, but did not receive the same support as some years before. In June 2004 the assembly organized occupations of various churches, among them the Cathedral of Barcelona as well as the Iglesia Santa Maria del Pi to support their claim for broad regularization. Around 500 irregular migrants from India, Bangladesh, Pakistan, Ecuador and Colombia enclosed themselves in the cathedral on 5 June 2004. After interventions by a number of public officials for voluntary and calm withdrawal, the police dissolved the occupation in the early morning hours of the following day (*El Mundo*, 6 June 2004). Some smaller protests, demonstrations and occupations, as for instance in the Casa de la Solidaritat, continued. On this occasion, the delegate of the central government, the authorities of the city of Barcelona, the regional government of the Generalitat, the trade unions CCOO and UGT and the migrant organizations' network Coordinadora de Entidades de Inmigrantes de Catalunya published a document together which demanded an end to the occupations (Coordinadora 2004). Altogether, the more radical protest forms hardly found support among the broader migrant and pro-migrant communities, nor from the public authorities or the media. Nevertheless, different actors in Barcelona collaboratively voice their critique concerning the regularization programme and other legal changes. In a collaborative statement, Assemblea per la Regularització Sense Condicions, SOS Racism and the Coordinadora de Entidades de Inmigrantes de Catalunya voiced their criticisms of the conditions of the regularization programme since relevant groups would hardly be eligible, specifically those currently not working and mainly women with children. In addition, the fact that the specific conditions of the programme were negotiated between the government and the Mesa de Diálogo without migrant representatives was another aspect that was criticized (*Europa Press*, 27 October 2004). This, in turn, demonstrates that Barcelona actors closely follow the involvement of migrant organizations on the national-level, even though formal channels are open mainly to Madrid-based organizations. In cases when even these are excluded protest is likely to grow and become more contentious in Barcelona as well.

When asked whether they were engaged in contentious action or about other ways the regularization programme of 2005 had affected their work, those migrant organization representatives in Barcelona that have regular contact with the authorities referred to the channels successfully used in this respect.

> Yes we talked about it. In the sense of informing and instructing the people. What is the regularization about? What are the conditions? Giving information how to inform the people. (…). They gave information to the organizations which represent the migrants, which present the documents of the migrants. (Interview transcript, no. 45)

They point to their role as mediators concerning the exchange of information and the improvement of procedures, for instance concerning opening hours of the offices receiving the applications. This exchange occurred within and around the municipal council, in direct interchange with the administration and with the national government representative, the Delegado del Gobierno.

Throughout different phases migrant organizations have engaged in political mobilization for regularization and the rights of (irregular) migrants. Protest action becomes more conflictive (in the case of church and public building occupation) and more broadly supported when the political situation at the level of the central government is perceived as restrictive and lacking dialogue. In other instances, as was the case during the 2005 campaign, when national and local contexts are perceived to be relatively favourable, contentious action lacks broader support. Less radical forms of protest articulation include press releases, demonstrations, campaigns, as well as the use of available channels of participation and exchange with authorities, and legal means used in the daily work of these organizations.

Local struggles for voting rights

In parallel to regularization and the recognition of migrants' social rights, many of the above described campaigns also sought increased political participation and sometimes explicitly called for migrants' voting rights. The need for protection and social rights of irregulars and their regularization were more urgent issues, though. Explicit claims for voting rights have remained on a second stage for many years (see also Méndez 2005). For example, the 2004 campaign of Red Ciudadana demanded 'regularization, human rights and citizenship of residence', but did not make explicit reference to voting rights. On many other occasions the claims for the regularization and (social) rights of irregulars and those for political rights and integration of (regular) migrants are interwoven. More focused voting rights campaigns have become more intensive in the last few years and these, in turn, also frequently refer to the need to solve the problem of irregularity. Although this is a shared perspective across many places in Spain, some differences between Barcelona and Madrid exist here as well.

What emerges from this research is a more favourable environment for political mobilization and claims for political participation in Barcelona, specifically earlier in the 1990s. This is also expressed in local policies that officially demand local voting rights in the Carta Municipal of 1998 (Ajuntament de Barcelona 1998). Local authorities are in turn considered a venue to present the claim. In Madrid, voting rights have not been a visibly local issue, but access to the national-level forum among the majority of the migrant organizations of the sample has in recent years offered channels to voice this claim, in parallel to its explicit recognition and advancement from the national-level government in the few last years (see Chapter 4).

In Barcelona, prominently and for the first time publicly visible, a broad campaign for local voting rights for non-EU citizens accompanied the municipal election in 1995. The FCIC, Assemblea Papels per Tothom and other migrant and non-governmental organizations initiated a campaign around these elections when, for the first time, foreign EU-citizens residing in Spain were allowed to vote. The slogan of that campaign was 'Igualtat de Drets, Democràcia per a Tothom' (Equality of rights, democracy for everybody) (Morén-Alegret 1997: 13). In fact, when asked for how long voting rights had been on the agenda, migrant organizations' representatives in Barcelona referred to a time frame of at least ten years or more (in interviews conducted in 2006 and partly 2007). This holds true even for those organizations which had not existed by that time. With different degrees of intensity, voting rights remained a topic on the agenda of every campaign for the rights of migrants, although frequently more urgent social rights and access to regular statuses covered the top of the agendas.

Among the more recent initiatives in Barcelona is the '1=1. Tothom Ciutadà' (One equals one, everyone a citizen), led by SOS-Racism. It advocates a concept of citizenship decoupled from nationality and based on residency. It claims voting rights for migrants beyond the constitutional conditions, seeking to abolish the requirement of reciprocity agreements which would give Spaniards the same rights in the respective signatory state; it further claims political rights on all levels of government. This campaign receives great support from trade unions, pro-migrant and migrant organizations, as well as university and research institutions and a number of municipalities in Catalonia. The activities around the campaign include public debates with political parties and migrant organization representatives, concerts, the collection of signatures, the encouragement of municipalities to approve a resolution, and other public and media campaigns.

In some of these statements, the concept of residency is related to municipal registry and is therefore open to irregulars. More often though, reference is made to 'any person living (and working) in Spain', leaving more room for interpretation on how exactly 'living' was defined. This vagueness in defining 'citizenship of residency' is relatively typical. This is a consequence of the fact that residency constitutes the basis of legitimacy for claiming both social rights and regularization for irregular migrants as well as political rights and electoral participation for which regular residency is a generally accepted precondition.

In the Barcelona context, migrant organizations make use of formal participatory channels in direct and indirect ways, for instance through contact to politicians in formal and informal meetings, by individual organizations and through existing networks.

> Even to the [regional] parliament we presented a report on the issue. (…) There were two co-fellows of the Coordinadora [de Entidades de Inmigrantes en Cataluña] who presented a document on the issue. (Interview transcript, no. 45)

This also includes the immigration council, and even though the municipality does not have the competence to grant local voting rights, it was nevertheless used as one venue to articulate the claim.

> I had meetings apart from the [municipal immigration] council and also within the council in order to make it an issue to be considered and to put pressure on it, that the immigrant, at least in municipal elections, can vote. Of course, this is also a proposal we presented. We are making a common proposition.

> The city hall cannot decide it, but it is taking strength to communicate it to the
> government. What we want is to use all channels which could be official in any
> way in order to make our voice heard. (Interview transcript, no. 25)

In fact, the city and its representatives make reference to the position of the immigration council when presenting their own claim on that matter:

> These days, there is a clear line, which is the right to vote. Of course, this is a line
> of demands for them [the migrant organizations], it is a basic right. (Interview
> transcript, no. 23)

However, interlocutors also frequently highlight that although there was hardly any opposition to their claims, nothing had happened either. As for the immigration council, disagreement within the council finally meant that no common statement was issued. While some were in its favour, others were more distant, and not all considered the issue as important to the same degree. A third group presents itself as moving beyond limited claims and aims at a new migration policy, which leaves behind any separation between migrants and Spanish nationals and gives immediate access to nationality for all migrants. These voices are represented by FCIC and its members, among these Casal Argentí and ACRS.

The situation in Madrid differs from the one in Barcelona. On the one hand, stronger claims for voting rights are altogether more recent. The interviewed migrant organizations' representatives dated the emergence of the issue in 2002. On the other hand, references to national-level institutions are stronger given the access some of these organizations have through their participation in the integration forum. At the same time, the Madrid-based organizations hardly make reference to the local government in this question or even point out that the granting of voting rights was not within its competences. This resembles the municipality's general attitude where voting rights for non-communitarian migrants before the recent generalized debate was not an issue, and retrospectively public officials maintain that at the end of the 1990s, when intensive work for migrants' participation began, the right to vote was still 'utopian' (Interview transcript, no. 52).

It appears that the stronger claims for local voting rights in Madrid started around the 2003 municipal election. In this period, Red Ciudadana with its members joined the campaign 'Aquí vivo, aquí voto. Por una Ciudadanía Plena' (I live here, I vote here. For full citizenship) which originated in Andalusia. The campaign was initiated by the Plataforma Tod@s Iguales, Tod@s Ciudadan@s, (platform all equal, all citizens), a network of 18 migrant and solidarity organizations from Southern Spain. The campaign advocates voting rights for migrants based on the condition of residency, and pushes for viewing migrants not as workers, but as citizens. This claim is focused on political rights at the local level as a first step and considers citizenship something 'gradual' from municipal, to regional, national and European levels. As in Barcelona, this campaign also claims to go beyond limited constitutional conditions. In addition, it makes reference to the regularization of migrants.

In the context of the 2003 municipal elections, the Green Party candidate to the Madrid mayor's office, José María Mendiluce, in particular, promoted migrants' voting rights – both in local and regional elections – and organized a number of public meetings and press conferences together with various migrant organizations and networks, among which Aculco's president participated. This initiative included symbolic voting for migrants on the day of elections, 25 May 2003, for which an additional ballot box was put in the polling stations (*Europa Press*, 20 March 2003).

The Madrid-based organizations of this sample also highlight the importance the issue has gained in the integration forum where it has been discussed for a few years.

> This issue was fundamental in the national forum for the integration of immigrants. (…) There I myself brought in the issue. That was two years ago. (Interview transcript, no. 36)

Migrant organizations and campaigns welcome the initiatives from the parliament and central government to extend local voting rights. This is also reflected in the official statement of the integration forum. Still, this statement remains critical of the condition of reciprocity and demands a change of the constitution. In addition, the integration forum mentions here the 'transnational character of the participation of migrants' (Foro 2007: 14). Thereby the Foro expresses its view on the compatibility of local and transnational participation, in line with its recognition by the Strategic Plan for Citizenship and Integration, and the same applies to local governments' approaches. This recognition of transnational orientations is most strongly reflected in the concept of co-development, to which migrant organizations and policy documents make increasing reference.

Transnational development cooperation

The two previous sections have analysed the relevant fields of action and contention of migrant organizations in Barcelona and Madrid where these seek to improve migrants' situation and social and political rights in the receiving cities. In parallel to these engagements migrant organizations are increasingly becoming involved in transnational action, development cooperation and co-development more specifically. In different ways this action, too, is shaped by multiple institutional contexts and these also result in some local differences. This is the topic of the analysis presented in the following.

The investigated organizations in Barcelona and Madrid, as with many others, include transnational activities on their agendas. According to the survey on migrant organizations in Barcelona and Madrid cited at the beginning of this chapter, between 70 and 80 per cent of these are involved in some kind of transnational activity directed at the country of origin (Morales, Jorba 2010). In this respect, the primary research presented here found that organizations actively promote transnational participation in presidential elections where citizens are allowed to vote from abroad, such as Colombia, Ecuador and Peru. From these and other countries, migrant organizations convene round table discussions on the political and socio-economic situation in the origin country. Depending on their leverage, organizations aim to put pressure on the respective governments in order to improve their situation as emigrants and citizens abroad, or at least seek to do so, for instance concerning consular procedures, the sending of remittances, or social security agreements. Some also aim to put pressure on the government of their origin country to act in their favour before the Spanish institutions. Migrant organizations in Barcelona and Madrid, thus, cover many issues of transnational political mobilization and action identified among organizations in other European localities as well (Østergaard-Nielsen 2003). Furthermore, these migrant organizations also engage in development cooperation and co-development projects. This latter type of projects is more strictly related to migration in various ways. Projects may involve greater migrant communities, take place in migrant source regions and/or refer to issues related to the migratory process, namely irregularity, return, and emigration (see Chapter 3).

Various interviewees in this research expressed the need to participate 'here' and 'there'. Not seldom is the wish to work for the improvement of living conditions of migrants on the side of reception and of their families on the side of origin already expressed in the founding statutes of organizations. Further, the investigated organizations not only retain contact to other social and political actors in origin countries, most of them also have formalized partnerships or co-organizations there. For instance, Ecuador Llactacarú, which was founded in 2001 in Barcelona, initiated the Association of Families of Migrants Ecuador Llactacarú in Ecuador at the end of the same year. The Ecuador-based co-organization brings together the families left behind and seeks to provide them with support and facilitates cross-border dialogue. On its homepage Ecuador LLactacarú highlights that in the near future it will also engage in development cooperation which it had not done so far:

> In the future, when the work of the *asociación* has become more established, we will initiate the promotion and implementation of different projects in development and cooperation, with the aim to improve the living conditions and family, social and productive networks in Ecuador. (Llactacarú website)

This is one indication that the cross-border activity is not yet intense in Barcelona, whereas in Madrid transnational cooperation is stronger among migrant organizations according to this and other research. The above cited survey found that 13 per cent of the organizations in Barcelona and 20 per cent of those based in Madrid are actively engaged in cross-border activities in the country of origin. Among the latter, engagements are also more varied and cover a plurality of aspects whereas transnational topics encountered among those in Barcelona are more limited (Morales, Jorba 2010).

From the Barcelona sample only one organization had been enrolled in transnational development cooperation at the point of this research. ACRS had joined an existing project in Senegal in 2005 where it supported micro-credit systems among women and for which it received funding by the Fons Català.

A number of further indications exist that suggest that transnational cooperation for development is only recently coming on the agendas of migrant organizations in Barcelona. A preparatory study of Fons Català (2006) for co-development projects among Sub-Saharan African migrants in Catalonia highlights that almost any organization encountered was pre-occupied with the situation in Catalonia, the exchange of information concerning application for residence permits, the reception of and support to newcomers as well as their regularization, the need for a place to meet in a familiar environment, and awareness-raising in Catalan society of migrants' cultural and migratory experiences. Since these organizations have not received much funding, cannot rent an office, and cannot rely on professional staff, the report concludes that this hampers their engagement in development as well. Nonetheless, their study found organizations willing to engage within its frameworks. Another study (Ruiz 2003) carried out among Moroccan migrant organizations in and around Barcelona which originally planned to organize co-development and capacity building workshops had to redirect its focus in the face of the so far limited interest or capacity among the migrant communities. Conversations held in this present study with representatives from Catalan development agencies confirm this impression. Representatives of migrant organizations related to Latin American countries also highlight that among Latin American organizations development cooperation was hardly an issue. However, this seems to be changing in the context of growing attention on the matter. One indication is that the Barcelona-based Latin American federation Fedelatina, a group of almost ninety organizations from in and around Barcelona, joined the REDCO-network (Network of Migrant Organizations and for Co-development). This network was initiated by ATIME's development organization REMCODE in early 2008 and brings together organizations from Madrid, Barcelona and some southern Spanish cities.

So far, Barcelona's city context has been less favourable to transnational engagements than the one in Madrid (see Chapter 3). Migrants' transnationalism and the promotion of co-development was not yet part of the agenda of the municipality when this research was carried out, although this is now changing with the recent integration plan. The consortium Fons Català has focused its co-development initiatives on Africa exclusively and furthermore works together intensively with the smaller municipalities across Catalonia rather than with authorities from Barcelona city. In addition, other needs still cover the top of the agendas of migrant organizations and since the vast majority of the organizations in Barcelona have hardly received funding for their support of migrants and migrant communities, resources to expand action are scarce.

Among Madrid-based organizations, involvement in transnational development cooperation seems generally stronger and this specifically applies to the organizations of the sample. These are well established and were able to access local and national funds for their work in Madrid. Given their privileged location in the capital, some also successfully accessed national funds for development cooperation. And crucially, the city of Madrid started to work on co-development by the end of the 1990s and prior to this, had already funded migrant organizations' transnational development cooperation. In this context, ATIME founded an organization exclusively dedicated to development cooperation, the Red Euromediterránea de Cooperación al Desarrollo, REMCODE, as early as 1997. For its development projects REMCODE has received support from the national-level development agency AECID and from some municipalities in different Spanish regions as well as from private foundations. Aesco had emerged as an organization concerned with the development in Latin American and already carried out projects in Colombia in the mid-1990s when it started to work for migrants in Madrid. For both types of projects the organization has received funding from the city of Madrid. Aesco first worked with Colombian counterparts and later on opened offices in Bogotá, Pereira, Cali and in the meantime also in Ecuador's capital Quito. VOMADE opened an office in Santo Domingo in 1995, three years after the formal registration in Madrid. This was at first meant to maintain relationships across borders with returning members of the organization. At present, this counterpart and other collaborations with local committees all over the Dominican Republic deal with many different topics around migration and development. Aculco is also engaged in transnational cooperation and opened an office in Bogotá in 2003. In the meantime the organization holds offices in at least three other Colombian localities and also received support from the municipality in Madrid and other sources for projects in Colombia. And even though the less-established organization AECUATORIE is not active in matters of development cooperation, there are plans to apply for the newly available co-development funds from Madrid. Moreover, in its flyer, AECUATORIE voices its goal to contribute to awareness on 'co-development' among the immigrant youth.

In their explanations of the active or planned engagement into development, interlocutors in this research in both cities frequently expressed a concern about the consequences and root causes of migration.

> We feel that the immigrants, we, have to be involved in these projects and we have to cooperate, even if it is with few resources. (…). And this, somehow, first, can help to stop this immigration, sometimes uncontrolled, and then, also makes sure the immigrant does not to forget his origins and the reality. (Interview transcript, no. 37)

Another example are the explanations given by VOMADE in many documents, public articulations and its website concerning its work in the Dominican Republic and the places where it holds offices. The rationale is explicitly based on the high intensities of migratory out-flows which characterize these places. Similar motives are expressed by representatives from other organizations as the following interview excerpt shows:

> Definitely one of the important factors of immigration is the situation in the country of origin. It is not that I think [migration] was something totally negative, but in legal ways. Therefore, one of the first projects we made in development cooperation was related to the region, from which, according to statistics, as we realized, most of the immigrant population in Madrid is coming. (Interview transcript, no. 20)

In line with this perspective, there are projects which deal with classical development cooperation such as healthcare, the malnutrition of children, rural development or potable water. Furthermore, some transnational projects also cover migration-related issues. These projects focus on the prevention of (irregular) migration, labour market insertion of returnees, as well as information for potential emigrants. Some of these initiatives have received public support, in particular from the city of Madrid within its concept of co-development. To illustrate the diverse kinds of projects on the agendas of migrant organizations, Table 4.2 displays a few examples of projects from Madrid-based organizations which were financed by the city of Madrid.

For example, Aculco describes the objective of one of these projects in its brochure as preventing young women from migrating by offering them possibilities and capacity building for the production and commercialization of art crafts in a Madrid-based fair trade shop. VOMADE is currently conducting an information campaign called 'Inform yourself, and then decide'. Starting from the perspective of their work in the receiving cities some of the transnational projects connect these experiences across borders to places in the origin countries:

> [In the place of origin] inform them a bit, bring them closer the reality in Spain, the policy in Spain, which they will confront, that they know a little before they arrive here. That they know at least how to buy a metro ticket, to get the sanitary card, things which are the most basic, but necessary to know. And once they are here, it is all the work of social services, support them in the process of adaptation, psychological assistance, and everything. (Interview transcript, no. 20)

As one step further, interlocutors also refer to the official recruiting process in the frameworks of existing bilateral agreements on labour migration between Spain and several countries. In this respect, they seek recognition as mediators

Table 4.2   Development and co-development projects of migrant organizations in Madrid

Year	Title/Subject	Organization
1995	Health care	AESCO
	Vocational training/micro-entreprises	VOMADE
1996	Socio-educational	AESCO
1999	Vocational training/micro-enterprises	AESCO
2001	Socio-educational	AESCO
2002	Centre for Information, orientation and advisory of potential migrants from Colombia to Spain	AESCO
2003	Socio-educational	AESCO
	Socio-educational	ACULCO
	Prevention of immigration of the feminine population with high risk in the Eje Cafetero and in Bogotá, Colombia	ACULCO
	Orientation and formation of Dominican female migrants in case of migration to Spain, Dominican Republic	VOMADE
2005	Integrated programme for voluntary return and prevention of unorganized migration to Spain in the metropolitan area of Pereira	AESCO
	Nuestras manos en Madrid – Agro-industrial project working with women, including the commerzialization through Fair Trade Shops in Madrid	ACULCO
2006	Junto es possible – Fase 2	ACULCO

Source: Ayuntamiento de Madrid. Programma de Cooperación al Desarollo (various years).

and experienced partners in the provision of assistance. In the same way some of their projects in Madrid which offer vocational training follow the objective to contribute to migrants' labour market insertion in the place of settlement and in the place of origin in the event of return.

In many of these projects and initiatives irregularity and the support to regularization plays an important role. In the context of the 2005 regularization programme in Spain, Llacacatarú Ecuador participated in an information campaign in 12 Ecuadorian provinces. The goal of this initiative was to advise and support the families of migrants living in Barcelona and other Spanish cities associated with the organization about the requirements and procedures of the programme. Similarly, during the pro-regularization campaign of 2001 Rumiñahui had organized family members in Ecuador to support their claims in Madrid (Laubenthal 2007: 140). Other organizations also report that they gave advice and information to requests from abroad, via email predominantly, on the possibilities and conditions of immigration to Spain or on certain legal questions. But only among Madrid-based organizations more formalized transnational migration information services were encountered, in line with the cities approach on co-development.

Summary of the Spanish city cases

The accommodation of migrant organizations in Barcelona and Madrid is shaped by partly different city contexts. This is also to say that some elements of the national framework and some similarities of the cities lead to common elements among migrant organizations. Migrant organizations in both cities formed or transformed along with increasing inflows from the respective country of origin of the founders and early members of the organizations. This took place between the late 1980s and early 2000s in the cases investigated here. The situation newcomers have encountered is characterized by the existence of a relatively large informal economy, inappropriate legal and administrative measures and a complicated bureaucracy, all of which contribute to precarious statuses and irregularity of migrants. This makes leaving and falling back into irregular status a permanent concern, and little direct state intervention has accompanied this situation. In this context, 'papers', or in other words access to and maintenance of regular status, and other aspects related to the urgent needs of newcomers in many senses (for example, a place to sleep, the need to find a job, insecurity and lack of protection) are the first concerns of these organizations. Over time, changes in the immigration regime contributed to a more secure status for more people and access to more (social) rights for irregulars. These subsequently also became part of the work of migrant organizations as intermediaries towards the migrant communities. Relatively soon new topics came on the agendas of the organizations, such as youth and culture, and diverse aspects of integration covered more space. While some smaller organizations re-orient toward new topics, others broaden their agenda and also reach out beyond the scope of their original national reference group. This pertains mainly to those organizations that receive public funding for the services they offer. Others also engage in newer and more diverse activities, but to a lesser extent and with more limited resources.

Hence, whom do the organizations represent? Generally, migrant organizations in both cities are connected to one nationality and country. This is reflected in the names the organizations carry. Since part of the work of the most established migrant organizations addresses wider migrant publics in their services, beyond one national group, this has also led to a change in the names of organizations by adding broader categories (for example, Latin American or foreign workers). This applies predominantly to those which receive subsidies in both cities. Smaller organizations outside public funding rather re-orient when inflows decline and continue to concentrate more strongly on their own ethnic group, although seldom exclusively. At the same time, the rationale given for the existence of migrant organizations and their mediation between migrants and authorities is based on shared roots, culture, and common knowledge. Accordingly, migrant organizations attending to a broader public beyond the scope of their original reference group show certain ambiguity in their perspectives on (ethnic/national) 'roots' and (client) services. This is in turn promoted by conditions for formal participation and funding. Criteria for formal participation refer to representation of relevant ethnic communities in the city – or country, in case of the national-level integration forum. At the same time the scope of service delivery is relevant for representation in the local Madrid and the national-level forum which support the need of a broad clientele. In addition, the approach on migrants' integration expressed by interculturality as it is articulated on all levels of government further contributes to this openness. Interculturality acknowledges ethnic and cultural diversity but advocates dialogue and the non-separate, 'normalized' treatment of different ethnic groups. This also applies to the work of migrant organizations and the publics they address.

Some relevant differences concerning the type of involvement into support, assistance and protest action for migrants' rights can be identified between the organizations in the two cities. In general the recognition of migrant organizations as relevant actors on all governmental levels in Spain is not accompanied by specific funding for ethnic actors. Nevertheless, migrant organizations have benefited from public subsidies, specifically for the delivery of services. Until recently migrant organizations in Barcelona have received very little funding for assisting newcomers and the delivery of services to them, though. With the introduction of central government funds for local measures of migrants' reception, regular funding for these activities by non-state actors now exists. From these funds, a number of migrant organizations have benefited. Still, there are also organizations outside public funding that are members of the immigration council in Barcelona. The possibility of exchange with public authorities is valued there, in spite of criticism as to the limited influence migrant organizations can exercise. In Madrid, a concentration and mutual reinforcement of national and local funding can be observed which tends to support a small number of organizations. Further, the successful management of service delivery is a criterion for membership in the national-level integration forum as well as in the local Foro Madrid. Following from this, there is not only an overlap of those nationally and locally funded but also of those represented in consultative councils on both levels. This bias in state-migrant actors' relationship is reflected in the sample of this study. The majority of the investigated migrant organizations in Madrid are well established, participate in consultative councils on various governmental levels and receive economic support from a wide array of administrative departments. When they emerged they were small, local organizations in Madrid, which benefited from mutually reinforcing recognition and support over time. The vast majority of Madrid-based organizations are excluded both from economic support and access to the authorities.

In both cities, migrant organizations engage in manifold activities outside the formal channels of participation in the struggle for migrants' rights, regularization and political participation. This includes a wide array of forms and venues – from round table discussions, press releases, usage of own radio programmes and members' journals, to public events, and demonstrations. Migrant organizations have also engaged in protest actions for migrants' rights and specifically for regularization. Contentious forms such as occupations of public buildings and hunger strikes have found greater support when formal access channels were closed. This concerns on the one hand the access of individual actors and on the other hand the general dialogue between the government and migrant organizations. The more established an organization has become the less it is willing to participate in radical protest. Moreover, being established generally means also the possibility to use other channels of influence. Further, there is a direct relationship between access to public authorities being closed and greater support for more radical action. In the very conflictive situation in 2000 and 2001, the occupation of churches and hunger strikes found greater support among migrant organizations and other non-state actors as well as local politicians in Barcelona. In Madrid similar actions were seen with greater reservation by the migrant organizations as well as by most other actors. While some migrant organizations in Madrid had been involved in similarly contentious action in the early 1990s, they have become rather established in the meantime and do not participate in more radical actions any longer. The broader field of migrant organizations in Madrid, which are numerically fewer than in Barcelona, also seem less well-connected among each other and with other social actors. In 2004 and 2005, the more open approach of the newly elected central government towards more comprehensive migration policies and dialogue with social actors and migrant organizations has deactivated support for more contentious action in both places. Nonetheless, critiques and campaigns continue to call for the improvement of the situation of irregulars, their regularization and other aspects related to migrants' rights, including political participation.

Further, advice for migrants and more formalized services often address the same concerns as the more explicit political activities, through formal political channels and in contentious action. In both Barcelona and Madrid, the informal dissemination of information and formally institutionalized advisory services accompany political struggles for migrants' rights and regularization. Both forms aim to mediate between the authorities and migrant populations. Participation in consultative councils serves as an information channel in both directions, i.e. for migrant organizations and for the public authorities. This has also been recognized by state institutions distributing information through the organizations. During the 2005 regularization programme, this took the form of contracted information points among some of the Madrid-based organizations of this sample. Whereas daily services and less institutionalized forms of advice support the access to existing rights, formal and non-institutionalized political action in the form of campaigns, manifestos and demonstrations articulate struggles for the extension of rights to (irregular) migrants.

Voting rights have become a more prominent issue in the last years. Until recently, the rights of irregulars and their regularization, critiques concerning migration regulations and claims for political rights, specifically the right to participate in elections, have been articulated together. For many years, more explicit claims for political rights had remained on a second stage and are only now more independently articulated. At least in Barcelona, however, in the mid-1990s the first municipal elections allowing for the participation of EU-citizens were accompanied by a campaign claiming these rights for non-EU foreigners as well. In Madrid, the issue came later onto the agenda of migrant organizations. Current initiatives make use of formal and non-institutionalized venues and again reflect local conditions. In Barcelona, the municipality and its representatives have recognized local voting rights for migrants since 1998 in their official declarations. Even though the granting of voting rights is not a local competence, the immigration council serves as a platform allowing for a mutual reinforcement of migrant organizations' and local authorities' call for voting rights. In Madrid, where the local authorities have not been proactive in this matter and where organizations were not provided with a formal participatory channel before 2006, little importance is attached to the influence on the local level on the matter. In addition, given the national-level representation of some of the organizations and the recent advancement of the central government and parliament, the national-level integration forum is a more relevant platform.

Both the claims for regularization and for voting rights are based on the concept of citizenship residency. Most frequently, articulations do not express a clear-cut distinction between regular and irregular residency. This is an expression of the rather gradual understanding, from the *de facto* residency of irregulars to regular residence and from there to citizenship rights equal to those of Spanish nationals. The same applies to many documents by local authorities referring to any citizen living in the city, leaving open how exactly a citizen is defined. This resembles the dynamics of an immigration regime in which persons often achieve regularization after some time in an irregular status and even as irregulars they still have access to certain social rights through municipal registration. This situation renders clear-cut distinctions relatively difficult.

In parallel with the strong focus on reception and an advocacy for citizenship based on local residency, transnational engagements with places of origin exist. Some migrant organizations formulated a focus on the improvement of living conditions and socio-economic development in the country of origin in their statutes, often from the beginning. Active engagement in origin countries, however, often lagged behind when the first needs of newly arriving migrants were seen as more urgent. Transnational activities are now taking more shape. For some organizations, this goes along with the availability of funding from national and decentralized development cooperation. Current discourses and newer institutional arrangements around migration and development linkages and co-development bring additional attention to migrants' involvement in development cooperation. Here, migrant organizations from Barcelona and Madrid display different degrees of intensity as well as differences in the types of projects they engage in. In Barcelona, the municipality itself has no particular focus on migration–development linkages so far. The municipal development consortium Fons Català, however, has a clear programme in this respect and addresses African communities specifically. This is reflected in the fact that only one organization of the Barcelona sample of Senegalese migrants is involved in development cooperation. In contrast, some Madrid-based organizations have received early funding for projects in (developing) countries of origin in parallel to the support of the reception and integration from local and/or national levels since the second half of the 1990s. Four out of the five organizations of the Madrid sample are involved in transnational development projects. These projects cover classical development cooperation as well as issues related to migration, namely the prevention of irregular migration, the return of migrants, and support for regular migration. This latter aspect can be found in more institutionalized forms among Madrid-based actors, although some organizations in Barcelona make reference to similar topics – for instance, through responding to emails from abroad – but they do not address these topics in formalized cross-border projects and they have not received funding for such projects. The treatment of aspects related to migration within cross-border projects is favoured within the subsidy schemes of the city of Madrid and reflects its definition of co-development. Hence, in both cities migrant organizations are engaged in the struggles for rights and the improvement of living conditions for the local migrant communities as well as for the places of their origin. The intensity and forms of these engagements vary according to the particular city context and the often selective support migrant organizations have encountered there.

Chapter 5
Migrant Organizations in Established Immigration Contexts

The previous two chapters have presented the processes of accommodation of migrant organizations in cities of recent immigration. It has become clear how multiple institutional levels which constitute particular city contexts have influenced this accommodation. This chapter now focuses on more established places of immigration in Europe where international migration has already had a longer trajectory for several decades. It covers three established immigration countries and selected localities there in order to show, first, the differences in the processes of accommodation of migrant organizations as they are shaped by divergent contexts. Second, the analysis presented in this chapter reveals some commonalities among migrant organizations in established places of immigration that have often been absent in or at least did not receive systematic attention from available scholarship. These appear when contrasted to new immigration places as will become shown in the next chapter.

The chapter draws on literature concentrating on Germany, putting the city of Berlin at its centre, the Netherlands with Amsterdam as the city example as well as the UK where the role of localities for migrant organizations has generally been emphasized (Soysal 1994). The analysis of the situation in the British localities here concentrates on the more proactive cities, particularly Birmingham and some other places which developed multicultural approaches on migrants' integration in the 1980s. To different degrees the northern European immigration cities all have been affected by 'guest worker' and/or post-colonial immigration since World War II. The immigration of guest workers, later joined by their families, was most important in Germany and this type of immigration is also responsible for relevant inflows to the Netherlands. Immigration to the latter country includes post-colonial migrants too, while this type of migration has been central in the UK. These characteristics of their immigration regimes make these destinations distinct from the recent immigration places where irregular migration is a characteristic feature (Baldwin-Edwards, Arango, 1999, King et al., 2000). These types of inflows are also best reflected in the available research on migrant organizations in established immigration cities on which the following analysis draws. There were other types of inflows, most importantly ethnic German re-settlers in the case of Germany for example or Irish migrants in the UK. In addition, in all three countries refugees and asylum seekers contributed to important inflows, especially in the 1990s. Today, migration and settlement patterns are more diverse all over Europe. There exists specifically high-skilled migration, different forms of low skilled migration, often organized around temporary stay, as well as asylum seekers and refugees, and irregular migration has become more important since the 1990s all over Europe (Layton-Henry 2004, Martin 2004, Muus 2004). The conditions of entry, stay and work regulated by the immigration regime but also the policies of reception and integration are different for these different categories of immigrants and this should also contribute to at least partly different processes in the accommodation of migrant organizations emerging in these contexts. Little research has specifically accounted for the impact of these differences on the formation and activities of migrant organizations in the established immigration localities. Therefore the chapter concentrates on the more historical and the more well-researched types which allow for contrasting with the accommodation processes in recent immigration localities.

While the role of the immigration regime for the processes of migrant organizations' accommodation has generally been neglected, most insights exist on the shaping forces stemming form the institutions of integration. Existing comparative migration scholarship has specifically pointed to the differences across established immigration places in the policies addressing the reception and integration of migrants (Brubaker 1994, Soysal 1994, Castles 1995). Germany is known for a relatively exclusionary and assimilationist context which makes it more difficult for migrants to organize, although the city of Berlin is acknowledged for its more open environment (Vertovec 1996a, Koopmans 2004). The Netherlands and Amsterdam stand as the paradigmatic case of a liberal, multicultural and encouraging context for migrant organizations both on the national and local levels (Vermeulen 2006: 69–76). Localities in the UK, in turn, are perhaps more important to migrant organizations than in many other countries because formal venues for migrant organizations to participate on the national level have been absent, while more opportunities exist on the local levels (Soysal 1994). Multicultural policy approaches in some British localities have further strengthened their role, at least in those places. In addition, the different policy approaches have also had varying implications for the recognition or rejection of migrants' transnational orientations and activities as regards the origin country. In general, where authorities recognized transnational ties this was premised upon temporary stay and eventual return of migrants. Where settlement and migrants' integration into the receiving society was more actively promoted, migrants' transnationalism received little attention or was negatively perceived. More than yet in recent immigration cities, responses to migration and to migrant organizations in established immigration countries and localities have changed over the decades. It will therefore be important to account for these changes and the ways these are reflected in the processes of migrant organizations' accommodation. The argument put forward in this chapter, as was the case for the analysis of the recent immigration cases from Spain (Chapters 3 and 4), is that migrant organizations are shaped by political–institutional contexts from multiple levels. As discussed in Chapter 2, the political institutions relevant for the accommodation of migrant organizations concern the approach on migrants' integration together with the existing state/non-state actors' relationships, both on national and local levels, as well as the immigration regime. It is the intention to show how these play out on migrant organizations' formation and in their local and transnational activities.

Some differences in the material and presentation as compared to the previous chapters have to be mentioned. The latter were based on primary research conducted by the author and presented an in-depth investigation of issues revealed predominantly through qualitative research. In contrast, this chapter now makes use of existing secondary literature and data available from it, supplemented by some primary data collection. Rather than following individual organizations' trajectories as has been done for the Spanish cases, the following presentation is interested in the more general paths of the processes of accommodation in these established places, their contrasts with each other and with the places of recent immigration. As regards the political–institutional contexts, each country and city-section presents an overview of the major phases, events and turning points that have shaped migrant organizations' formation, their activities and claims. This is also to say that the most recent developments will only briefly be mentioned since their effects cannot yet be observed. They may, however, provide an outlook on potential future changes in the accommodation of migrant organizations.

National restrictions, delayed integration and some local recognition: The case of migrant organizations in Berlin

Immigration and the immigration regime in Germany

Post-war immigration to (West) Germany[1] has been composed of guest workers, later joined by their families, most of whom came from the Mediterranean. They constituted the most important type of inflows for many decades in Germany, both in terms of numbers and in the public and political debate. Asylum seekers are another relevant category with numerically high inflows, mainly in the 1990s. In addition, ethnic Germans who first came as displaced persons and refugees from the eastern parts of Europe and the Soviet Occupation Zone immediately after the war and later as re-settlers form a relevant migrant category in post-war

---

1   This sub-chapter concentrates on immigration to the German Federal Republic, or in other words, until 1990 it concerns only West Germany. There was immigration to the German Democratic Republic as well, including foreigner workers from Vietnam or Cuba, for instance. The city of Berlin, in turn, has been in a special situation as a divided city for several decades. In the following, for the period until 1990 the focus is mainly on West Berlin. With German reunification, Berlin became the capital of the German Federal Republic. In 1991, the parliament decided to also move the seats of government and parliament from Bonn to the new capital and both officially started to work there in 1999. In addition, Berlin is one of Germany's city-states and thus has more competences than other major German cities.

Germany.[2] The following concentrates on the changing conditions of entry, stay and work for those who originally came as foreigners or (guest) workers. These are also the groups which have received the most attention in the research on migrant organizations, on which this sub-chapter draws.

German labour recruitment started in 1955 in order to confront labour market shortages of the expanding post-war economy and it ended in 1973 with the oil crisis. During this period, the German government signed bilateral agreements with several Mediterranean states, of which most are members of the European Union today. Since the Turks were the last group to arrive in large numbers and have outnumbered all other groups since 1972, and because they are considered culturally 'more different' from German mainstream society, mostly because they were Muslims, the Turks came to be associated with immigration in Germany in general (Martin 2004: 231). Turkish migrants are at the centre of the discourse, and the majority of empirical studies available on migrant groups in Germany concentrates on them.

The guest worker policy was originally focused on the temporary stay of migrants, on their rotation in exchange with other workers, and their expected return (Schönwälder 2001: 245–57). Relatively soon the practice of rotation had to be dropped since the industry protested to keep the workforce they had already trained and which had become familiar with the working procedures. Still, longer stay and settlement had not been envisioned. Family reunification or family

---

2   At the end of the World War II a high number of displaced ethnic Germans and refugees came to Germany from the former German eastern territories (today Poland) and other parts of eastern and south-eastern Europe where their ancestors had settled several centuries ago. Around 12.5 million came to Germany, West and East. Another 3.8 million moved from East to West Germany before the building of the Berlin wall in 1961, and around 600,000 left the German Democratic Republic afterwards. Between 1950 and 1988 1.6 million ethnic Germans came, mainly from eastern Europe, and in the four-year period until 1992 another 1.4 million (Mahnig 1998: 46–9). In the last years, only a few thousand re-settlers come to Germany annually. The immigration of ethnic Germans is regulated by very different regulations as those affecting guest worker immigration. The German constitution of 1949 allowed ethnic German re-settlers to come, premised upon the persecution they faced due to their German ancestry. They are automatically eligible for German citizenship and have therefore full access to social welfare and the labour market. In addition, a broad range of social measures has existed to support their integration into society and the labour market, although this has been cut back significantly since the early 1990s (Seifert 2000: 134–6). While the numbers had been very small during the cold war, the arrival of ethnic Germans dramatically increased around 1989. As a consequence, several legal reforms restricted the circle of persons eligible for application, premised on the perspective that these persons were now following economic considerations rather than repression in the newly democratizing countries. Today, the general assumption of persecution persists only for residents of former Soviet Union, while all others have to prove this individually. In addition, language requirements in particular have been elevated as a sign of German heritage (Bundesamt für Migration und Flüchtlinge 2009: 49–57).

formation was not in the mind-set. Guest worker recruitment was a state enterprise, highly regulated, and organized by state agencies which had offices in various cities of the countries with which agreements had been signed. Guest workers enjoyed equal treatment in the labour market, including payment and rights of participation in Germany's well-established frameworks of codetermination in the workplace as well as in the trade unions. The social rights of foreign workers were basically equal to nationals and state-funded welfare agencies catered to their specific needs (see next section). The number of foreign workers reached 1 million in 1964, and after slightly declining in the recession of 1966–67, grew again. In 1973 there were 2.6 million foreign workers in Germany (Thränhardt 1999: 24).

In 1973 the recruitment ban put an end to this policy. What followed was a 'policy of consolidation of immigrant employment' which aimed to reduce the number of foreign workers (Seifert 2000: 136, Schönwälder 2001: 496–584). The major part of guest workers had returned to their origin countries, but others settled more permanently (Thränhardt 1999: 31). Already some years before the ban, family reunification had started, partly related to the recruitment practices of big firms which were inclined to recruit family members and, in some sectors such as in Berlin's textile and metalworking industries, specifically women were recruited (Schwarz 1992: 123). One of the consequences of family reunification and family formation was that the share of non-working migrants living in Germany grew. In 1970 the employment rate of foreigners in Germany was 70 per cent. By 1982 it had dropped to 50.8 per cent (Jahn, Sen 1984: 135). This, however, was not only an effect of arriving spouses and children. It was also a result of growing unemployment which specifically affected foreigners, and the fact that subsequent legal changes after 1974 prohibited newly arriving family members from working, at least for the first years of their stay. These regulations were meant to discourage family reunification. Policies and debates around stronger restrictions had, however, the opposite effects from those expected, and contributed to longer stays of migrants who feared that in the future even temporary work in Germany would be impossible for them (Mahnig 1998: 48). Thus, after some decline in the years immediately following the ban, the foreign resident population in Germany grew again at the end of the 1970s and reached 4.67 million in 1982 (Thränhardt 1995: 24). This number has grown steadily. In 2009 there were 6.7 million foreigners living in Germany, 8.7 per cent of the population. A quarter of these hold Turkish citizenship. In addition, there is another 8.5 million first generation migrants who are German citizens, either naturalized foreigners or ethnic Germans (Bundesamt für Migration und Flüchtlinge 2009).

In the 1980s, migration policies officially pursued three main goals: to promote the integration of legally residing foreigners and their families, to restrict further immigration and to encourage return (Martin 2004: 230). Still, the official narrative maintained that Germany was not an immigration country. Integration was at the centre of political attention for only a few years and included mainly social policies supporting education and labour market incorporation. Most policies of the 1980s focused on the other two aspects, return and restriction. In addition to stricter border controls, restriction generally targeted family reunification. This led to the lowering of the age barrier for the arrival of migrants' children to 16 years by sub-national authorities following the recommendation of the federal government. This policy was first implemented in Berlin in 1981 (Mahnig 2004). In 1983 the government introduced a new law for the promotion and support of voluntary return and reinsertion. Other attempts to deport migrants in cases of unemployment or reliance on welfare benefits could not be implemented, however.

During the 1980s legal and financial initiatives were set-up or continued in order to support return and reintegration in origin countries. For example, between 1973 and 1983 the German Ministry for Development directed 80 million Deutschmark (DM) into a special credit fund to support the investment of Turks in Turkey, matched by funds from the Ankara government (*Der Spiegel* 1983). Today return still constitutes an important element of migration (and development) policies. In the second half of the 1990s, for instance, a debate began on the return of refugees who had fled the war in Yugoslavia. Accompanied by a mixture of coercion and incentives, the majority of Bosnian refugees ultimately returned. This was achieved not least through the conditioning of financial assistance to Bosnia on its open doors to returnees (Thränhardt 1999: 41–2). A broader range of programmes and economic support still exist today for return and reinsertion, and in recent years development agencies in Germany have also initiated a small number of pilot projects for migrant organizations' development activities in origin countries. To date, a more specific approach in this respect, comparable to the one observed in the Spanish cases, does not exist.

Further measures during the 1980s targeted irregular migration. Forms of irregularity had existed before, but it generally meant that migrants entered the country without authorization or as tourists but often received work and residence permission because of the good chances of becoming employed relatively soon (Vogel 2003: 168–9). When irregular entry and work became more contested, the government approved a law to combat irregular employment in 1982 (Mahnig 1998: 48). Since that time irregular entry and work has remained an important topic in Germany's immigration policies. According to recent estimations there are between 196,000 and 475,000 irregular migrants residing in Germany (Bundesamt für Migration und Flüchtlinge 2009: 183).

Especially since the 1990s immigration to Germany has greatly diversified concerning legal statuses and origin countries. Numbers of asylum applications had been very small prior to 1980, but displayed significant increases at the end of the decade due to the political changes in eastern Europe and the war in Yugoslavia. This rise gave way to a heated debate which finally led to a change in the previously relatively liberal asylum regulations, including the amendment of the German Constitution. This and subsequent European regulations led to a significant drop in the number of applications. In 1998, for the first time in ten years there were less than 100,000 applications; another ten years later there were less then 20,000 (Bundesamt für Migration und Flüchtlinge 2007). Furthermore, over the last two decades, Germany has selectively opened new venues for migration into the country, both high and low skilled, most of which are focussed on temporary stay. In parallel, the newer policy also shows commitment to the promotion of migrants' integration through a whole range of respective programmes. As in other countries, this goes along with rising requirements – concerning language proficiency to name but the most prominent example – for the access to citizenship and permanent stay and residency, as well as in relation to entry (in the case of marriage migration, predominantly).

Hence, for many decades the majority of migrants in Germany have encountered relative stability in terms of work and stay as well as regarding social rights and state attention. This was originally meant to be of only transitory nature and return programmes have supported this idea. This was also accompanied by exclusion from political rights, especially electoral participation and citizenship as will be discussed in greater detail in the next section.

The national German policy context for migrants and their organizations

The evolution of policies on migrants at the central government level in Germany can broadly be distinguished into three phases. Until the late 1970s, the approach was rather characterized by non-policies with few specific programmes for migrants in the face of the expected transitory nature of migration and the return of the guest workers. In the following decades, more emphasis was put on migrants' integration following an approach based on assimilation. State and state-funded welfare and social policies did, however, exist for the guest workers in the first phase, while they expanded in the second phase during the 1980s and 1990s to include workers' families and especially their children. Exclusion of foreigners predominated in relation to political rights and access to citizenship, though. Around the year 2000 a new phase started. Access to German nationality now recognizes a *ius soli* right to the second generation of migrants. Further, migrant organizations are now also officially recognized and invited to dialogue, whereas they had received very little attention from the central government before.

Until late into the 1970s no particular policy at either the national or local level existed which would have targeted the potential stay, settlement and integration of foreign migrants living in Germany, since the transitory nature of guest worker immigration predominated. Migrants were expected to return and neither their further integration in the diverse social realms of German society nor their cultural adaptation to it were issues of concern. (Schönwälder 2001: 314–23). On the contrary, ties to the country of origin and the language skills of migrants and their children were welcomed since they were seen to facilitate reintegration after return. Still, some provisions to accompany longer term stay existed. For example, in 1964 all federal states introduced preparatory classes for newly arriving children. In some German states, all courses were taught in German, in others in the mother language, while some opted for a mixed model (Mahnig 1998: 55). Guest worker policies stressed the equal treatment and pay in the labour market as well as social rights. This was mainly a success of the trade unions which wanted to avoid a 'race to the bottom' for the native work force (Seifert 2000: 102). In addition, the established German state-funded welfare agencies took over the delivery of social services and support to migrants. Although no formal agreements exited, a distribution emerged with the Catholic Caritas taking care for the Italians, Spaniards and Portuguese; the Protestant welfare organization serving the Greek, and the Workers' Welfare Association (AWO) addressing the Yugoslavs, the Turks and all other migrants from outside Europe (Puskeppeleit, Thränhardt 1990: 47–50). These services soon employed or trained staff of migrant background in order to offer bilingual assistance in German and mother languages to the respective groups. As they still do today, they provided social advisory information as well as assistance to migrants. Moreover they served as mediators and channelled migrants toward mainstream public services such as social welfare. In addition, they also organized cultural activities and provided meeting places for migrant groups. These mainstream organizations also acquired a political role, representing interests and acting as the (often self-declared) voice of the migrant groups. Some of them also included migrant organizations on their boards. This substantially shaped the formation of migrant organizations. On the one side, self-help was less important since most issues were covered, and on the other hand there was a certain interrelatedness and also dependency among emerging migrant organizations and the welfare agencies (Hunger 2002, see below).

By the end of the 1970s it had become clear that the halt of recruitment had not stopped migration and fewer migrants than expected had returned, and that instead the migrant population was growing, mainly on the basis of family reunification and births, paralleled over time by increasing numbers of asylum seekers. Social problems and growing unemployment, problems on the housing market and residential segregation grew in parallel. In that period integration became an important issue for the central government. Among other efforts, this led to the creation of a foreigner's commissioner in 1978. The commissioner's memorandum of the following year recommended substantial changes and demanded the recognition of Germany as a country of immigration, an idea which was officially rejected until the 2000s. In the 1980s Germany's policies on migrants were characterized by the double orientation of 'integration or return' (Meier-Braun 1988), including greater ambivalences. Policies, and more so the discourse, emphasized the integration of those in the country, including the need to adapt to the German language and habits. Still today, this includes the impossibility of dual citizenship. At the same time, while rejecting dual orientations of those who wish to stay and become German citizens, transnational ties are recognized as part of the lives of those who have their home abroad. This is expressed in the report of the commission on the foreigners' policy from 1983. It defines integration as:

> (..) a social process of incorporation [Ein- und Zuordnung] of different societal groups. Integration is neither static nor unilateral, but requires contributions for adaptation from all. This means that foreigners have to make their own contributions to integration in that they have to adapt to the way of life and the

conditions in the workplace which exist in the German Federal Republic. This requires, in other words, the learning of the German language, the renunciation of extreme national–religious behaviour that would disturb peacefully living together in our society and the adaptation to the existing norms and patterns of behaviour. It is not the aim of this process to separate the foreigner from his ties to his home [Heimat]. This would not be integration but assimilation. (cited in Meier Braun 1988: 30)

In the 1980s and 1990s little advancement occurred in relation to political rights and citizenship. There is still today no local voting right for non-European citizens, although this has remained a contested issue, in particular since access to nationality has been difficult. For many decades no birth right was granted on a *ius solis* basis. This meant that access to German citizenship for second generation children of foreign migrants was as difficult as it was for their first generation parents. However, in 1991 a reform of the nationality law facilitated the access to nationality for children born in Germany (Thränhardt 1999).

Broader reforms occurred in relation to social policies. In 1980 the government deployed a broad programme for labour market and social integration. It was mainly focused on the youth, who were often coming to Germany after several years of schooling in the country of origin with no knowledge of German. Other programmes were set up that supported adult migrants' vocational qualification as well as access to and information on existing social programmes. The budget for the programmes for language and vocational education as well as that for other social services rose from 3.1 million DM in 1968 to 88.4 million DM in 1985. In 1990, integration programmes were financed with 90 million DM (Soysal 1994: see Chapter 4, Seifert 2000: 134–40, Mahnig 1998: 52–5). Language, education, vocational training and labour market insertion have remained the most important part of integration programmes in Germany, especially when it comes to youth.

More comprehensive policies and broader legal reforms started around 2000 when a new nationality law went into force. Since that time, children born in Germany to non-Germans are automatically German citizens. However, they have to decide whether they wish to keep their parent's nationality or remain Germans upon reaching the age of 18 and before they turn 23. As stated above, dual citizenship still does not exist in official policies, but there are many exceptions today (Gerdes, Rieple, Faist 2007). Further, the period of residence required for naturalization has been lowered from 15 to eight years (Seifert 2000: 138–40). The immigration law of 2005 also stresses the need and support for migrants' integration, while the general course on immigration restriction is upheld. Since 2006 the German chancellor invites representatives from politics, the media, trade unions, churches, welfare agencies and migrant organizations to the annual integration summits. In its first meeting the participants of the summit agreed on the elaboration of an integration plan, which the government published in 2007.

When it comes to the role of migrant organizations it is important to note that the right to association has existed for foreigners, but ethnic and minority groups have not been provided with specific recognition, and a specific state budget for their support has not existed (Soysal 1994: see Chapter 6, Koopmans, Statham 2000, Østergaard-Nielsen 2003: 261). At the local level, however, participatory channels and consultative councils have existed in a number of cities and smaller villages in Germany since the 1970s (Andersen 1990). Some local governments have also granted funding to migrant organizations, but Berlin is an exception here for its greater focus in this respect as will show in the next section. Today, migrant organizations also participate in the national-level dialogue on integration, while Muslim religious organizations participate in the German–Islam dialogue. The integration plan from 2007, in turn, states that the incorporation of migrant organizations into the formulation and implementation of integration measures was one of the basic pillars for successful integration policies. The installation of the Federal Council for Integration in 2011 is the latest expression of this course. Around a third of all members are representatives from migrant organizations (Bundesbeauftragte für Integration 2011). In addition, for some years migrant organizations have received funding from different ministries and national agencies for their projects. They are officially considered a 'pillar of voluntary engagement' and a few migrant organizations are already registered as entities allowed to accept young men and women to undertake their 'voluntary social year' there (Deutscher Bundestag 2010). Migrant organizations are, thus, now forming part of changing state/non-state actors' relationships and more diverse non-state actor involvement in the realm of social policies. This resembles a greater shift from previous decades when migrant organizations were still seen with greater reservation.

Local policies on migrants' integration and their organizations in Berlin

At the beginning of the 1970s, earlier than other cities and levels of government, the local government of Berlin officially declared its support for the integration of migrants, given that the migrants were also willing to integrate. At the same time the city's approach opted for a general restriction on further immigration and supported return. The local government set up integration measures, especially in the realm of education and training for the second and third generation, in order to support their adaptation in the face of more permanent stay. Other measures addressed social problems and urban conflicts that were associated with residential segregation and the fear of ghetto formation. One important element of these policies was settlement bans (for districts with over 12 per cent foreign immigrant population) that Berlin introduced a week after their approval by the Federal Ministry of Labour and Social Affairs in 1975. The bans prohibited any non-European Community citizen from settling in the districts of Kreuzberg, Tiergarten or Wedding. Officially this policy remained in force until 1990 although it had been declared unconstitutional already in 1979 (Schwarz 1992: 124–30, Mahnig 2004: 24–5).

In 1981 the Christian Democrats won the local elections, after a campaign with a clear restrictive approach on immigration and a literally xenophobic dictum (Hunger, Thränhardt 2001: 109). In the years to follow, the city's policies pursued the two-sided strategy of control and immigration restriction on the one hand and the promotion and support to migrants' integration into the local and German society on the other. In his first government declaration, the city's new mayor Richard von Weizsäcker stated (cited by Schwarz 2001: 131):

> In the opinion of the Senate, our foreign co-citizens in the long run have to choose between two options: Either return to their old homes, or stay in Berlin; this implies the decision to become a German citizen permanently.

Successive Senators of the Interior have stood for the more restrictive parts of Berlin's migration policies (Gesemann 2001: 16). Already in 1982 one major step was taken in that direction with the restriction of family reunification for children by lowering the age barrier to 16 years, which caused great protest and mobilization by migrants (Gitmez, Wilpert 1987: 107, Blaschke 1996). Most other German states followed this example during the 1980s. Furthermore, Berlin also supplemented the federal governments' financial incentives for voluntary return with additional funds (Mahnig 2004: 26). On the side of the more proactive integration policies, an important initiative was the installation of a foreigners' commissioner for the first time at any local or regional level in Germany. This position was meant to serve as a communication channel and mediator between migrant organizations and the authorities. Over the years the commissioner's position came to express the more liberal part of Berlin's integration policies and shifted partly toward a multicultural orientation in the 1990s (Vertovec 1996a, Blaschke 1996, Schwarz 2001). Berlin, however, never pursued a multicultural agenda comparable to Amsterdam or Birmingham and its approach can rather be characterized as intercultural, based on the recognition of cultural diversity and an emphasis on dialogue and non-separation.

Three elements are characteristic of Berlin's policies on migrants' integration: (a) a proactive course on naturalization, (b) information and awareness campaigns as well as multicultural events, and (c) the establishment of linkages with migrant organizations. One of the first initiatives of the office of the foreigner's commissioner was a naturalization campaign which particularly aimed to motivate the children of migrants to acquire German citizenship and thus to become full members of German society (Hunger, Thränhardt 2001: 120). In spite of the relatively restrictive national legislation of the time, Berlin used its discretionary competences to a broad extent. As a consequence, especially in the 1990s, Berlin, together with Hamburg, had the highest rates of naturalization of all regional states. Since the year 2000, though, this process has slowed down and other regions display higher naturalization rates today (Thränhardt 2008: 15–18). In 2006, Berlin started a new campaign advocating that 'the German passport has many faces' (Berlin 2006). Secondly, Berlin's policies put great emphasis on public relations and media campaigns in order to promote mutual understanding and especially the tolerance of local society *vis-à-vis* migrants' cultures. This included publications in the series on 'Berlin's minorities', poster-billboard campaigns, round table discussions, public lectures and information campaigns for migrants' on available services. In addition, the city initiated and supported cultural venues and events such as the Werkstatt der Kulturen in 1993 and the carnival of cultures which it has organized annually since 1996 (Vertovec 1996a: 391, Schwarz 2001: 137). Thirdly, during the 1980s Berlin's authorities started to establish linkages with migrant organizations. Whereas on the national level migrant organizations were still seen as a potential way out of German society, inhibiting integration and promoting ghetto-formation, Berlin had developed a more positive approach (Schwarz 2001: 133). This has taken place in the broader framework of changes in state/non-state actors' relationships. Here, a general shift occurred away from the exclusive classical welfare policies toward support for self-help initiatives, neighbourhood associations and generally smaller, less-established agencies (Schwarz 1992: 143–8). This generally meant the incorporation of new non-state actors into social initiatives and the provision of welfare services. Together with a changing approach to integration of a more intercultural character, this has opened venues for migrant organizations, too. Since 1985 migrant organizations have received financial support from the city of Berlin through many different local programmes and from different departments, some of which support services and assistance to different social groups. In addition, the commissioner's fund for social affairs has also supported them, and there is a specific funding scheme for social initiatives (in the 1990s the so-called '*Fink-Topf*'), of which a greater part went to migrant organizations. At the beginning, the budget of the *Fink-Topf* was 10, later on 20 million DM of which 40 per cent went to organizations of Turkish, Russian, Polish, Tamil, Arabic and other migrants. Through these funds 70 to 80 organizations were financed (Blaschke 1996: 14–15). Due to the many different sources, a full overview of subsidies for migrant organizations was and still is impossible (Ohliger, Raiser 2005: 7). Severe financial constraints in the 1990s led to a reduction of subsidies (Blaschke 1996, Schwarz 2001). The budget of the commissioner was around 8.5 million DM in the 1980s, and 7.5 in the 1990s. Yet, it is unclear to what degree this has also affected migrant organizations. It is estimated that Turkish organizations received 350,000 DM annually throughout the 1980s and 850,000 DM annually in the 1990s, which testifies a considerable rise in subsidies (Uiterwaal 2004: 20, cited by Vermeulen 2006: 79). With these subsidies, the city supports assistance, vocational training, education, as well as information, meeting points and cultural projects (Hunger, Thränhardt 2001: 122). This has led to a considerable reconfiguration of the pattern of migrant organizations, as will be shown in the next section (Schwarz 2001).

Recognition and support to migrant organizations from Berlin's authorities is generally premised upon the idea that there is a critical limitation to migrant organizations 'where the emphasis on cultural distinctiveness is accompanied by a conscious retreat into an 'ideological' (*weltanschauliches*) ghetto which displays hostility to the outside, and aggressive pressure for solidarity on the inside' as stated in the foreigner's commissioners report from 1985 (cited by Schwarz 2001: 135, translation MF). Since then, public officials have emphasized that funding is not primarily given on an ethnic basis, but is intended to promote projects for integration and social problems among migrant groups. Those considered most likely to successfully approach the respective target groups are granted funding (Interview with public officials from the integration department in Berlin, 2010). Thus, the recently articulated understanding on promoting diversity and cohesion can be seen as a continuation of a long-held perspective expressing an intercultural approach (see below). Compared to a city such as Amsterdam (especially during the 1980s), which has a stronger ethnically-based multicultural understanding, this funding is project related, while structural subsidies are generally very rare and with support going to more established organizations rather than to the very small ones (Vermeulen 2006: 80).

Interaction with migrant organizations has not been limited to subsidies, though. The foreigner's commissioner held close formal and informal relationships with a great variety of migrant organizations (Schwarz 2001). Consultative councils have existed in some of the city's districts (*Berliner Zeitung* 1997). On the city level, a consultative council in the realm of migrants' integration did not exist before 2003, but other forms of exchange, consultation and dialogue did. An important instrument is the Procedure for the Hearing of Migrant Organizations proposed by the commissioner in 1982 (Schwarz 2001: 134). This instrument was used in the 1990s to discuss the draft report on the situation of the integration of foreigners presented by the authorities (Fijalkowski, Gillmeister 1997: 256) or more recently in the elaboration of the first integration plan in 2005 (Berlin 2009).

Berlin's more recent policies on migrants are summarized by the first official integration plan, approved in 2005, which carries the title 'Encouraging Diversity – Strengthening Cohesion'. Many aspects resemble a continuation of the previous approach, although the restrictive overtones of the early 1980s are absent in Berlin's official declarations today. The newer documents consider diversity as a more adequate approach acknowledging the heterogeneity of migrants, which is not exclusively related to culture or ethnicity.

> [Migrants] do not represent a homogenous group. They speak different mother tongues, belong to different religions, have very different socio-economic backgrounds and maintain different lifestyles. (Berlin 2009: 5)

This is similar to initiatives in other European cities such as Amsterdam or Birmingham as will be shown in the following sections of this chapter, but seems less related to other aspects of diversity and other (potentially marginalized) sectors of society. However, Berlin's multicultural experiences also never were so strongly focused on group-based multiculturalism and ethnicity as those other examples. In line with this, the members of the Consultative Council for Integration and Migration, created in 2003, are representatives from public authorities, employers and trade unions, social actors as well as six migrant organizations, reflecting particular world regions.

Migrant organizations in Berlin

Shortly after their arrival, guest workers in Berlin as in other German cities started to form so-called worker associations (Gitmez, Wilpert 1987, Thränhardt, Dieregsweiler 1999, Østergaard-Nielsen 2003: see Chapter 4). These served as spaces to come together in familiar environments, organize cultural events and provide social and psychological support to their members. These newly emerging organizations not infrequently were related to welfare organizations that catered to specific migrant groups. Thus, typically Turkish worker's associations organized under the auspices of the Workers' Welfare Association (AWO) (Schwarz 1992: 139). In Berlin, as well as in other university cities, foreign students also started to organize and some joined those worker's groups. A major part of the early organizations had or established linkages with political forces, parties or oppositional movements in the country of origin. Often they also became politicized through political changes in the origin country as for instance in the takeover of the military regime in Greece, 1967–1974 (Jahn, Sen 1984). Some of the Turkish association were affiliated with Turkish political parties, others had linkages with religious groups of Turkish and international Islam; in some organizations (as in some political parties) these came together (Özcan 1989, Østergaard-Nielsen 2003). In the context of relatively stable legal and social situations for the guest workers generally, cultural, religious and leisure activities were most important. There were already two Islamic organizations in Berlin in the 1960s (Schwarz 1992: 139). Since it was relatively easy for migrants to incorporate with the German welfare state, and the German welfare organizations played an important role in the state-funded provision of specific services to migrants, this lowered the need and the legitimacy for migrant organizations to take over this role (Diehl 2002: 217, Hunger 2002). Mainstream organizations also hired migrant staff according to the clientele they dealt with which strengthened this situation. Some social services were among the activities of the early workers' associations, but these were dealt with in rather informal ways. Often other informal networks related to kinship and hometowns also supported the reception of new arrivals in finding a job and an apartment (Gitmez, Wilpert 1987: 94–5).

The recruitment stop brought fundamental changes to the immigration regime. New inflows now mainly stemmed from family reunification, more permanent settlement occurred and for many migrants the idea of return was at least postponed. This has also contributed to a growth in the number of migrant organizations in Berlin according to many observers (Gitmez, Wilpert 1987, Schwarz 1992), although a systematic survey on the total number of migrant organizations has never been undertaken. One study reveals that there were 58 Turkish organizations in the 1970s. Their number grew to 140 in 1980s and reached 204 in 1990s (Vermeulen 2006: 88, Table 4.1). According to an interview with the foreigner's commissioner, the authorities had knowledge of about 500 migrant organizations in the mid-1990s (Vertovec 1996a: 390).

The growth in numbers also reflects a more varied picture of the types and activities of organizations. Turkish migrant organizations in Berlin, for instance, include leisure, youth and sport clubs, parents' organizations, cultural and theatre associations, religious congregations, self-help and assistance groups, as well as professional, business and trade associations (Gitmez, Wilpert 1987, Özcan 1989, Soysal 1994: see Chapter 6). In general, although most migrant organizations have more narrowly defined goals, their activities cover a broad range of issues (Fijalkowski, Gillmeister 1997: see Chapter 5). Available data for the Turkish migrant organizations shows that since the 1970s the four main activities are interest representation, religion, as well as cultural and socio-cultural activities (Vermeulen 2006: 88, Table 4.1).

Thus, many new initiatives emerged and institutionalized in parallel to the changing environment of Berlin's integration policies. Moreover, the specific focus of the city on the civil society sector and self-help associations has brought new issues and projects onto the agendas of existing organizations. Some started to engage in youth projects or neighbourhood meeting centres for which funding was available. Sports associations developed socio-cultural and youth projects and political groups now offered advice and educational activities for youth or women (Schwarz 1992: 184–6).

During the 1980s, interest articulation and claims for migrants' rights also started to gain more importance. In 1981 a large demonstration took place in Berlin as a response to the local government's policy to lower the age barrier for reunification of children with their parents living in the city. This event has been considered a turning point, specifically for the many Turkish organizations in Berlin which previously were oriented toward Turkey and which were rather characterized by political frictions concerning the situation in Turkey than by cooperation on behalf of migrants' rights in Berlin (Gitmez, Wilpert 1987: 107). A number of migrant organizations set up umbrella organizations in order to count on a broader platform for interest articulation. One example is the Islamic Federation founded in 1980 by 19 Islamic associations and mosques as a representation of Turkish Muslims. One of its main goals at its point of formation was official state recognition of Islam, alongside the Christian Churches and Jewish Community. Another example is the Turkish Community of Berlin which was founded in 1983. In 1990 it had 13 member organizations (Soysal 1994: 108). Today, it represents 55 organizations which cover a wide range of sports, culture and parents' associations, mosques and religious groups, youth and women organizations, socio-cultural clubs and social assistance projects (TGB 2011). The Turkish Community of Berlin was recognized at an early stage by the city officials and invited to meetings and hearings. The same applies to the Turkish Federation in Berlin (today of the broader region Berlin-Brandenburg) which also came into existence in 1983 (Gitmez, Wilpert 1987: 108, Özcan 1989, Schwarz 1992: 140, Soysal 1994: 108, TBB 2011). The majority of umbrella organizations that formed throughout the 1980s were of local or regional scope while nation-wide networks were rare, although some local branches claimed national representation. This has changed since the mid-1990s when national umbrella organizations emerged. Before, though, differences were particularly striking when compared to the situation in other countries such as the Netherlands where national umbrellas were strong and nationally recognized and represented (Soysal 1994: see Chapter 6).

In Germany, country-wide campaigns or protest marches for migrants' rights have been relatively rare and the same applies to local mobilizations in many instances. Yet migrants' claims, as measured by newspaper coverage, are more intense in Berlin's local public discourse on immigration and migrant's situations than in other German cities (Koopmans 2004). Political claims concern the improvement of legal statuses and conditions of residency as well as active and passive voting rights. Facilitation of naturalization through the acceptance of dual citizenship is a crucial issue, particularly for Turkish organizations in Berlin, while for other migrants from the European Union this is less important (Fijalkowski, Gillmeister 1997: 251). In addition, in a study on migrant organizations in Berlin from the mid-1990s, migrants' representatives reported that intense contacts to local authorities were more important for the advancement of their concerns than demonstrations and public protest action (Fijalkowski, Gillmeister 1997: 256). Interest articulation is also one of the four main activities since the 1970s, as already stated.

Berlin's authorities with their somewhat ambiguous approach between assimilation and multiculturalism, welcomed the overall growth of migrant organizations and the emergence of umbrella networks as a means for interest articulation. At the same time, they demanded that ethnic organizations should not serve as a retreat from German society (Schwarz 1992: 135). In line with this, cooperation in multi-ethnic (or multi-national) networks and especially with mainstream actors has been an important expectation. Although not without conflicts, cooperation and collaborative events and campaigns between trade unions, welfare agencies, political parties and other non-governmental organizations have existed. In general, as has been encountered in other places, migrant organizations criticize the fact that native German organizations receive more recognition and generally dominate discussions (Schwarz 1992: 185–6, Fijalkowski, Gillmeister 1997: 257, Yurdakul 2006).

The decade of the 1980s is also generally portrayed as a phase when a shift from 'homeland to host-land'-oriented engagements occurred (for instance Özcan 1989). Statistical data on transnational activities (related to the country of origin) among migrant organizations in Berlin also suggests a decline over time (Vermeulen 2006: 88, Table 4.1). Here, a number of features seem to interplay. Return constituted a relevant orientation of national and local policies in Berlin still in the 1980s. This was increasingly considered as opposed to integration, though. The relatively sceptical attitude toward persistence of 'home' country relations among settling migrants is likely to have contributed to relegating migrant organizations' transnational activities to a generally less important position. The particular stand point taken by individual migrant organizations also seems to influence their trajectory. In spite of the fact that the foreigner's commissioner held an equal approach on all migrant organizations, independent of their political-ideological standpoint and has sometimes been criticized for being too inclusive, the aforementioned organizations have taken different paths in this context. A recent comparison shows that while the Turkish Federation Berlin-Brandenburg receives around 1 million euros annually from local and national ministries for a great variety of projects, the Turkish Community has a comparatively small budget of only 27,000 euros (Yurdakul 2006: 443). It is rather likely that this is influenced by their diverging positions with the former advocating in favour of total immersion into German society, while the latter opts for integration with cultural difference and close contact with Turkey. Nonetheless, case studies also show that orientations and engagements with the country of origin have remained relevant among many organizations, and that these different activities have often existed in parallel for many decades among migrant organizations in Berlin (Gitmez, Wilpert 1987, Çağlar 2006, Yurdakul 2006) as in other German cities and localities (Jahn, Sen 1984, Østergaard-Nielsen 2003: see Chapter 4, Sezgin 2010). Their co-existence has often been neglected by scholarship on migrant organizations in Germany, although this is now changing. Of course, there are also many other organizations which do not share this characteristic. Compared to other European cities, references to the 'homeland' in the public discourse are, however, stronger in Berlin. But they are less intense when compared across Germany (Koopmans 2004). This may be explained by the fact that the Berlin's authorities encouraged migrant organizations to engage in local politics, services and exchange more strongly than has been the case in many other German localities. Today, new (Turkish, but probably not only) hometown associations emerge in Berlin, but these as well address integration, education and the second generation (Çağlar 2006). So far these seem to be rather small scale, though, and no indication exists that these are currently evolving toward professional developmental actors as in some of the cases encountered in Spanish cities.

The emergence and decline of Dutch minority policies: Changing contexts for migrant organizations in Amsterdam

Immigration and the immigration regime in the Netherlands

Post-war immigrants to the Netherlands originated in different countries and world regions, but consisted predominantly of inflows from the (former) colonies in Indonesia and the Caribbean and of guest workers from Mediterranean countries. In the early days none of the groups arriving was considered nor called immigrants and most were expected to return after temporary refuge or work. In addition, more than 400,000 Dutch citizens left the Netherlands after World War II and the first positive net immigration occurred in 1961. Similar to Germany, the Netherlands was reluctant to become an immigration country in the first decades of immigration (Entzinger 1994: 195–201, Rath 2009). The Netherlands acknowledged the *de facto* reality of immigration and settlement several decades early than Germany, though. What is more, the Netherlands recognized and supported ethnic groups and cultural diversity from the 1980s onwards, although this recognition has become the object of great controversy over the years, as will be shown.

A greater part of migrants to the Netherlands were Dutch citizens from the (former) colonies who enjoyed full rights. With Indonesian independence in 1949, Dutch citizens started to emigrate to the Netherlands (300,000 people in the 1950s and 1960s). The arrival of these 'repatriates' (most of whom had never been to the Netherlands before) was accompanied by great suspicion by many Dutch officials who worried about their different cultural habits and their sometimes low socio-economic status. A whole range of state programmes was set up to help them adjust to Dutch society. Today, this group is often portrayed as an exemplary case of successful assimilation (Rath 2009: 676). In addition, 12,500 Moluccans came from Indonesia, mostly soldiers who had served in the Dutch army, along with their families. Their stay was meant to be a temporary solution until they would be able to return to a free Moluccan republic, which however only survived for a short time (Muus 2004: 267). The Moluccans were hosted in camps, later on in separate residential areas and fully cared for by the state. This ambivalent government policy contributed to their separation and marginalization and finally was abandoned in response to riots and occupations by Moluccan youth at the end of the 1970s (De Graaf, Penninx, Stoové 1988: 205).

Immigrants from the Caribbean have often also been Dutch citizens. From Surinam immigration slowly grew in the 1960s, and peaked before independence in 1975 and again before 1980 – prior to the expiry of the bilateral agreement on settlement and residence of mutual subjects which allowed Surinamese to settle and work in the Netherlands. Around 150,000 people, mainly from the Afro-Surinamese working class and the descendants of Indian indentured workers, settled in the Netherlands (Rath 2009: 676). Dutch citizens also arrived from other Caribbean islands but in smaller numbers.

Due to these inflows, labour shortages did not become critical until the late 1950s. During the 1960s the government signed bilateral agreements with Southern European countries as well as with Turkey and Morocco. Subsequent to more spontaneous recruitment by private companies, the state introduced a monopoly on labour recruitment in 1968. As a consequence, controls become stricter and established clearer rules for recruitment, admission and employment (Van Amersfoort 1999: 147). Two years later a governmental report defined the official guidelines of the policy on foreign workers based on temporariness according to labour market needs, support for return and the delegation of social assistance to private organizations (Mahnig 1998: 65).

With the economic recession in the early 1970s recruitment came to a standstill and a number of further control measures were introduced (Van Amersfoort 1999: 146–50, Muus 2004: 268–71). Among the measures taken at first were financial incentives for return through the transfer of acquired welfare benefits, for example, as well as through development aid and support for migrants' investment in origin countries organized by the Dutch Ministry for Development Cooperation. These were, however, stopped by the mid-1980s. These programmes issued limited results at high costs and were increasingly seen as opposed to the spirit of integration into Dutch society (De Haas 2006: 34). Immigration controls and regulations became stricter, for example, with the introduction of entry visa requirements which were imposed on Surinam, Morocco and Turkey in 1980 (Penninx, Schoorl, van Praag 1993). Restriction also targeted family reunification, but not to the same degree as in Germany, and restrictions also did not target asylum seekers or the immigration of persons with certain qualifications. A law from 1983 which restricted marriages between second generation migrants and those from origin countries had to be rescinded due to immense public pressure (Mahnig 1998: 66). In relation to access to the labour market, Dutch regulations seem to have worked flexibly. In spite of the standstill of recruitment, regulations left open a number of back doors, especially for those already in the country as well as arriving family members and some other categories (Muus 2004: 268–71).

Irregular migration has also existed throughout all phases, and has become a contested issue at different points in time. In the 1950s and 1960s irregular migrants were considered 'spontaneous guest workers', and since they easily found a job they subsequently received permissions for work and stay (Van Amersfoort 1999: 147, Rath 2009: 677). This practice became more difficult with the official state recruitment after 1968. Nevertheless, in the course of time, several regularizations have taken place, the most important ones occurring in 1975 when 18,000 applications were presented and most accepted, a smaller one in 1980 and again in 1992. Smaller regularizations of more local scope have also existed, not least due to migrants' mobilizations (Bousetta 1997: 225). In addition, more informal practices existed for legalizing foreign workers and their families who already had been living in the Netherlands for several years without legal residency and work permissions. In 1995 the parliament discussed a proposal that aimed to formalize these practices, but this attempt was shut down. Instead, a one-off regularization programme was carried out in 1997 open to irregulars who had resided in the Netherlands for the last six years. Today, political and public discourse has become more restrictive on irregular migrants and new provisions ensure that these have no access to social services and welfare benefits (Muus 2004: 277–9).

Other inflows to the Netherlands were composed of so-called 'invited' refugees of which a smaller annual quota were accepted, between 250 and 500. For these fairly extensive reception and assistance programmes exist. These do not apply to individual refugees and asylum seekers, although in practice many of them have received comparable treatment, with one important exception: asylum seekers are not allowed to work (De Graaf, Penninx, Stoové 1988: 206, Entzinger 1994: 199). When numbers of asylum applications started to grow more significantly at the beginning of the 1990s, several legal and administrative measures were subsequently introduced to confront this increase, partly also with the aim to lower the number of applications. At the same time, the government introduced new temporary protection schemes which granted a three-year residence permit, important social rights as well as, at least in the third year, the right to work. If return is not feasible after this period, the conditional stay transforms into a permanent residence authorization (Muus 2004: 272–7). In addition, there are several provisions which allow for highly skilled migration, professionals, students and academics. Over the last decade or two, Dutch authorities have generally increased immigration controls and restrictions, comparable to other European countries. Newcomer Policies specifically target potential migrants who now have to participate in integration and language courses before arriving in the Netherlands (Van Amersfoort 1999, Muus 2004: 280–81, Rath 2009).

The Dutch national policy context for migrants' integration

Similar to Germany, the Netherlands consistently declared over several decades that it was not nor was to become a country of immigration (De Graaf, Penninx, Stoové 1988, Entzinger 1994). This marked the first phase of Dutch policies on migrants until 1980. Subsequently official policies followed an approach based on multiculturalism. This included recognition, participation and economic funding to migrant organizations. Only ten years later, though, critiques slowly drew policy away from this approach and today put more emphasis on cultural adaptation while the political role of migrant organizations is less prominent. State and state-funded assistance to migrants' arrival and subsequent settlement and integration has existed from early on, while only in the past one to two decades have migrant organizations played a role in the implementation of social policies.

   Throughout the first decades of international migration to the Netherlands, the newcomers were generally considered temporary residents and this includes not only the guest workers, but also the (post)colonial groups of Moluccans, Surinamese and Caribbean migrants who arrived in search of temporary work or refuge. State attendance for each of these groups differed due to their different historical relation with the Netherlands and the resulting legal statuses, as well as due to the point in time and the specific political context of arrival. This implied that some groups received more comprehensive assistance while others received less support. Migrants from the (former) colonies held Dutch citizenship, spoke Dutch and were approached more openly by the state and society (De Graaf, Penninx, Stoové 1988, Koopmans, Statham 2000: 28–9). Soon private initiatives emerged that started to offer social services to the different groups like the Foundation to the Assistance of Foreign Workers or the welfare foundations for Surinamese and Antillean immigrants. With the expansion of the welfare state in the 1960s and 1970s (Entzinger 1994: 202) these initiatives started to receive state funding and were brought under the direction of the Ministry of Welfare in the framework of community development policies. In general, programmes for migrants were based on the maintenance of their cultural habits and ethnic identity, since they were expected to return and reintegrate in their 'home' country, rather than to adjust to the Dutch society (De Graaf, Penninx, Stoové 1988: 208, Penninx, Schoorl, van Praag 1993, Mahnig 1998). The Dutch repatriates who came to stay from the beginning encountered special governmental programmes. Social workers and home visitors supported and instructed them in the best way to adapt (Rath 2009: 676).

In the 1970s it became increasingly clear that return rates had sharply declined, that settlement took place, and that, as a result of family reunification and some new inflows of refugees and also growing immigration from Surinam, the number of migrants was increasing. At the same time, social problems became more evident and economic recession had worsened the conditions for migrants specifically. This gave way to an official shift in Dutch policies on migrants following the Ethnic Minorities report presented by the Scientific Council for Governmental Policy of 1979 and the Minorities Bill of 1983 (Entzinger 1994: 205, Duyvené de Wit, Koopmans 2001, Muus 2004). Both documents affirmed that settlement was a reality and that Dutch society had become multicultural in character. The bill had three objectives: (a) to reduce economic and social deprivation for members of ethnic minorities; (b) to prevent and counteract discrimination and improve the legal position of foreigners in general and target minority groups in particular; and (c) to create the conditions for targeted ethnic minorities to increase their participation in Dutch society and to contribute to their 'emancipation'. An important element in these policies is that integration was to take place without the loss of cultural identity.[3] Multiculturalism in the sense of group-based identities was, thus, continued. It was, however, no longer meant as an element of return, but as an integral part of Dutch society (Penninx, Schoorl, van Praag 1993: 161, Entzinger 2003: 62–9). Further, the new approach was accompanied by restrictions on further immigration, but this did not include barriers for family reunification (nor for asylum seekers) as in Germany (Mahnig 1998: 72).

The character of this new policy can be understood as the combined effects of the existing institutional set along two lines. On the one side the Dutch welfare state ideology is generally opposed to the formation of minorities and is characterized by a strong presence of the state in the social policies that work to avoid it. On the other side the historical institutionalization of state/society relations is organized

---

3   It is important to note that minorities did not refer to all migrants or foreigners, but to those who specifically faced difficulties and deprivation in the Netherlands defined as target groups (and for which the Dutch state felt specifically responsible). The following national, social and legal groups were defined as 'ethnic minorities': migrants from Suriname, the Antilles and Aruba, the Moluccans, Mediterranean guest-workers (Turks, Moroccans, Italians, Spaniards, Portuguese and Greek, ex-Yugoslavians, Tunisians, Cape Verdeans), gypsies, political refugees, and a domestic semi-nomadic group (Entzinger 1994: 204).

along religious and secular 'pillars' (Soysal 1994, Van Amersfoort 1999, Duyvené de Wit, Koopmans 2001, Entzinger 2003). Dutch 'pillarization' includes the idea that determined groups should have their own social, cultural and political institutions and rights. Although this structure had lost prominence in Dutch society by the 1960s, it partly revived in relation to international migration.

The new approach of the 1980s brought a broad range of cultural and religious rights and freedoms to migrant communities, mainly in the realms of education and broadcasting. For example the Dutch state has subsidized Muslim, Hindi and Chinese schools,[4] along with Calvinist and Catholic ones, and it has also supported mother language teaching (Penninx, Schoorl, van Praag 1993: 168–70, Entzinger 1994: 206–7, Duyvené de Wit, Koopmans 2001: 6). Minority policies of the 1980s also improved political rights and the legal position of migrants. The reform of the nationality law in 1985 introduced birth-right access to nationality for the third generation and facilitated access to Dutch nationality for migrant children and non-Dutch spouses. In 1992 the government introduced dual citizenship which was subsequently taken back a few years later. Local voting rights for foreign migrants were introduced in 1985. Social rights and social security provisions for migrants are basically the same as for nationals, and in the 1980s the government initiated a range of programmes in order to improve the labour market participation of migrants and to combat discrimination. Employers have been required to report on the ethnic composition of their workforce, although positive, affirmative actions were rejected (Penninx, Schoorl, van Praag 1993: 162–5). The organization of social services for migrants also changed with minority policies in the 1980s in three main respects. First, decentralization brought the major part of social programmes to municipal authorities for which they receive funding from the national level. Second, services to migrants were now incorporated into local public mainstream services. This changed the role of the older foundations and other initiatives from the direct support of migrants toward advice and assistance to both the authorities and migrant organizations. Thus, third, migrant organization were to advise the formulation of welfare policies and programmes in order to help existing programmes and services to adapt (De Graaf, Penninx, Stoové 1988: 231).

Migrant organizations acquired an important role in this new setting. They were meant to contribute to group emancipation through cultural activities and contact with mainstream society as well as advise policy formulation. Economic support to migrant organizations from the national government gave priority to local activities and subsidized these through the municipal authorities. State funding also supports national-level umbrella organizations. The functions

---

4   The first Islamic school was founded in 1989, and by 2002, there were already 35 Islamic primary schools. This shows that the Muslim community in the Netherlands took advantage of the opportunity structures opened by minority policies (Vermeulen 2006: 72). It further illustrates that once implemented, many rights and institutions continued to exist, even though some changes in the orientations and the public discourse indicate a greater shift away from minority policies of the 1990s.

supported by the state are those which a) promote migrants' interests; b) provide informational, cultural and 'emancipation' activities; and c) offer training to volunteers as professional organizational leaders. Therefore migrant organizations often received structural funding and in addition benefited from a broad range of further measures including advisory services, capacity building and leadership training (De Graaf, Penninx, Stoové 1988, Soysal 1994: see Chapter 6). A nation-wide study from the early 1980s revealed that 70 per cent of the over 2,000 identified organizations already received funding (De Graaf, Penninx, Stoové 1988). Yet, migrant organizations were not meant to have an active role in welfare policy implementation by that time.

In order to achieve equality and adaptation among mainstream institutions, consultative councils on the national and local levels have been introduced. At the national level the National Consultative Council for Ethnic Minorities was established which had eight sub-councils for the different minority groups. The council is to be heard on relevant minority policy changes and can act on its own initiative. In addition, municipalities are required to set up their own local councils for migrant organizations' representation (Penninx, Schoorl, van Praag 1993: see Chapter 6, Soysal 1994: see Chapter 5).

Ten years after the initial minorities' policy, Dutch authorities arrived at the conclusion that these had failed. In particular, economic disparities and social problems persisted. Critiques insisted that the policy had contributed to high levels of state-dependence on the part of migrants. Furthermore, the immigrant population in the Netherlands had grown due to new inflows and these inflows were more diverse in terms of origin countries and more heterogeneous concerning other cultural and socio-economic characteristics (Entzinger 2003: 69–77). Therefore, existing structures and instruments were no longer considered adequate to confront the situation. In 1989, again the Scientific Council's report entitled Foreigners' Policy initiated a partly different course. The report distinguished between measures in three policy fields. In the field of immigration it advocated a restrictive course accompanied by the demand to furnish those accepted with equal rights to those of nationals and to offer comprehensive integration measures. In the field of integration policies it stressed the role of the labour market, school and education for youth and adults, including the learning of the Dutch language. In the third field of cultural policies the report emphasized the recognition of the multicultural character of Dutch society, but advocated for a clear separation of integration and cultural policies. The latter should be open to all migrants (and Dutch) and no longer pursue the goal of collective emancipation of specific groups (Mahnig 1998: 76). From here on what were formerly called minority policies were now renamed integration policies and targeted programmes concentrated on the labour market. In general, these newer policies are also less focused on minorities and more on individuals. A Newcomers Policy started in 1996 to support but also to direct migrants to integrate into Dutch society. Newcomers, for example, have to take Dutch language classes, and integration courses are either recommended or obligatory depending on the legal status (Muus 2004: 283).

While migrants' return, reintegration and other aspects potentially related to development hardly played a role in the 1980s and 1990s, migration and development reemerged as a political topic in the Netherlands in the 2000s. Several measures in the realm of development cooperation now exist generally aiming to improve migration management and to combat irregular migration. There are now also capacity building workshops and conferences on migrants' engagement with development in their hometowns and countries. These activities are, however, considered a private initiative of individual migrants and groups. Systematic economic support to migrant organizations in development cooperation does not exist (De Haas 2006: see Chapter 3).

In sum, group-specific measures in the first decades of post-war immigration to the Netherlands were premised upon return perspectives. A short phase during 1980s put greater emphasis on ethnic minorities' cultural identities as part of Dutch society and aimed to support collective emancipation. Although many things changed, numerous institutional structures and social, political and cultural rights supporting this particular type of group formation remain. Since the turn of the millennium, probably for the first time in Dutch history, group identities are broadly rejected in the social and political debate on the integration of migrants in the Netherlands. More pressure is now placed on adaptation to the language, culture and norms of the majority society. The state has remained the key institution to organize this integration (Rath 2009: 679).

Amsterdam's policies on migrants and their organizations

Amsterdam's policies on migrants have paralleled the course taken at the national level to a great degree. They have undergone similar changes at the respective turning points described above (Vermeulen 2006: 73). In the early phases of migration, Amsterdam's authorities shared the view on migrants' temporary stay just as authorities from other places and governmental levels in the Netherlands. Together they dealt with some social issues and needs that emerged among the different communities, but more comprehensive approaches seemed unnecessary. Specific services were provided by Dutch private organizations and foundations, many of which had been subsidized by national and also local funds. In line with the national level policy shift, Amsterdam revised its course on migrants in the 1980s when the city also moved toward a multicultural policy. This policy also aimed at both the improvement of migrants' socio-economic and political integration and the recognition of cultural identity in its own right and as a means of collective emancipation.

With the decentralization of welfare policies in the 1980s (De Graaf, Penninx, Stoové 1988: 213, Soysal 1994: 69), the municipalities became equipped with greater competences and now controlled greater resources in confronting migration and ethnic diversity. Whereas previously the government had directly funded the institutions and foundations that offered services to the different migrant groups these issues were now integrated in the local mainstream services. In parallel, in 1981 Amsterdam's authorities started to subsidize migrant organizations from the minority target groups. These were to perform the following three main activities: a) to promote and preserve cultural identities, b) to emancipate their constituencies and c) to represent community interests. Originally, political and religious organizations were not meant to receive funding, but the municipality recommended that they establish socio-cultural organizations which allowed for their funding as was the case in relation to the Islamic Center in Amsterdam for instance (Vermeulen 2006: 74).

Similar to the national level, the Amsterdam local authorities set up five consultative councils in 1985 (one for Turks, a second for Moroccans, another for Surinamese, Antilleans and Ghanaians, another for refugees, one for Chinese and Pakistanis and a further one for Southern Europeans). The members of each of these councils were appointed by affiliated migrant organizations. These councils were allocated a secretary and their own budget. Their task was to act upon consultations with the authorities as well as on their own initiative and give advice on local policies in general and on migrants in particular (Kraal 2001: 22). In addition, migrant support organizations are also officially recognized as a form of participation to advance migrants' interests. This course has structured the process of accommodation of migrant organizations to a considerable degree by enhancing their legitimacy, recognition and resources. And it has shaped their organizing around ethnic and national identities which also meant that groups of the same national and ethnic background had to work together in those sub-councils. Often broader ideological differences existed between left- and right-wing groups as well as among more moderate and more radical visions or different religious strands and beliefs. The councils somehow forced them to enter into closer contact with each other and with the authorities, and created for networking and the formation of federations (Vermeulen 2006: 75).

At the end of the 1980s, Amsterdam's authorities arrived to a similar conclusion as that of the central government which deplored the many remaining problems concerning the socio-economic position of migrants. In 1989 the City of Amsterdam published a memorandum entitled Municipal Minorities Policies that outlined the fundamental changes of those policies, but not their abandonment. It followed two main objectives: a) to increase the accessibility of scarce goods and services in the labour market and in fields such as education, health and welfare in order to resolve the disadvantaged position of migrants; and b) to fight discrimination and racism, including by means of positive (affirmative) action. The memorandum also demanded more influence of migrant communities in the projects affecting them, in the consultative councils as well as in neighbourhood projects. It highlighted the key role of migrant organizations for the integration of migrants into the society. In this sense migrant organizations were not only to be part of policy formulation but also more strongly involved in policy implementation, in particular *vis-à-vis* groups difficult to reach by municipal authorities. Greater emphasis was now on their will to cooperate with each other, with Dutch mainstream organizations and the local authorities, while more nationalist discourse were received with reservation (Kraal 2001: 21–2). In the subsequent years authorities became increasingly dissatisfied with the results of minority policies and with the concept of target groups and group-specific instruments, including the role of migrant organizations and councils.

The Power of a Diverse City draft memorandum of 1999 outlined the diversity policies that came to substitute minority policies (Kraal 2001, Uitermark, Rossi, van Houtum 2005). The new policy tried to instil two main views: on the one hand that the social problems of minorities not only concerned migrants (and their second and third generation descendants), but also women, disabled people, gays and lesbians. On the other hand it followed the view that individual migrants need and should not be associated with deprived minorities and that minority groups are not homogenous in the first place. This implies a move away from ethnic criteria and group-based approaches to more problem-oriented policies (Kraal 2001). The focus of newer policies and instruments is more on individuals and the idea that everyone should have equal opportunities. Collectives and specifically minorities play a less important role. Policies now address all inhabitants of the city with the aim to make everyone feel 'at home' and count on equal opportunities in the social and political life of the city (Kraal 2001: 23–4, Antalovsky, Wolffhardt 2002: 109–12).

These changes have important implications for the role of migrant organizations. First, in the 1990s conditions for funding changed, shifting from structural support to project-based finance for specific activities. Thus, rather than financing the workings of ethnic organizations as such, projects which address relevant issues and are of high-quality receive support (Kraal 2001, Uitermark, Rossi, van Houtum 2005: 630). Furthermore the distribution of funds changed in that period. For example, while the total amount of subsidies for Turkish organization had grown in the 1980s and was still high in the 1990s, the average amount that individual organizations received decreased (Vermeulen 2006: 76; Figure 4.4). This is to say that while economic support from local authorities in Amsterdam in the 1980s had grown together with the number of migrant organizations (although not to the same degree), in the 1990s the rising number of organizations were not met by rising financial resources. After 1998 there is a great decrease in the total amount of subsidies. The second implication of changing policies for migrant organizations is that their role in policy formulation has diminished. The group-specific councils lost their role at least since the mid-1990s and since 2004 there exists only one Council for Integration and Diversity. This new council does not represent organizations but rather individual experts with knowledge in the realm of migrants' integration (Uitermark, Rossi, van Houtum 2005: 630). Professional expertise and civil society engagement are the criteria mentioned for the selection of members, and here great emphasis still seems to be given to migrants' own experiences, since current members appear to have some sort of migration background (Amsterdam 2011). The third consequence for migrant organization is that dialogue and interethnic cooperation are now taken even more seriously than already proclaimed since 1990. This also involves a tendency toward new types of organizations which are less focused on collective emancipation, more pragmatic and more open to 'everybody' (Uitermark, Rossi, van Houtum 2005: 632). Organizations of the older type have lost legitimacy and recognition in this process.

Migrant organizations in Amsterdam

Throughout the first decades of post-war immigration migrants in Amsterdam often formed informal networks and emerging formal organizations were often leisure and social clubs serving as shelters for migrants by providing a familiar environment (De Graaf, Penninx, Stoové 1988, Penninx, Schoorl, van Praag 1993, Vermeulen 2006: 89). These were frequently orientated toward the country of origin, to which many would return sooner or later. These first organizations were often politically engaged with the situation in their respective countries and some also supported the improvement of living conditions there. For example, a quarter of the 50 Afro-Surinamese organizations which existed in Amsterdam in the year 1980 supported the development of their home-country by sending money to schools or hospitals (Vermeulen 2005: 956–9).

In the 1980s and 1990s, similarly to Berlin, the overall number of migrant organizations in Amsterdam increased and the pattern also became more diverse (Vermeulen 2005: 958–60, Tables 2 and 3). While there was one Turkish organization registered in 1970, there were twelve in 1980 and 64 in 1990. By the year 2000 their number had grown to 185. Even when taking into account that the number of Turks in Amsterdam also grew in that period, the degree of organizational density still grew stronger (from 0.96 organizations per 1,000 Turks in the 1980s to 3.5 per 1,000 in the 1990s). This is particularly striking when compared to Berlin where the size of the Turkish migrant population is four times larger but where fewer new organizations emerged in the same period (Vermeulen 2006: see Chapter 4). Similarly, Surinamese organizations, including those from Afro-Surinamese migrants, grew in number from 25 in 1970 to over 200 in 2000.

During this period, not only more but also new types of organizations came into existence (Vermeulen 2005, Vermeulen 2006: 88, Table 4.1). These cover a broad range of activities such as sport, youth, women or media. Their main activities are socio-cultural and interest representation, as well as religion – but this is only relevant among some migrant groups, such as Muslims or Hindus. The high incidence of both socio-cultural and interest representation on the agendas of migrant organizations in Amsterdam, but also in other Dutch cities, is in line with the character of minority policies which aimed at group emancipation and collective participation (De Graaf, Penninx, Stoové 1988: 229, Vermeulen 2006: 89). In the same way, service delivery has not been a relevant activity for migrant organizations in Dutch cities (De Graaf, Penninx, Stoové 1988, Soysal 1994: Chapter 4). Social services to migrants were at first provided by private, state-founded foundations and since the 1980s by local mainstream services. For Surinamese organizations in Amsterdam this was different (Vermeulen 2005). Local policies assigned an important role to local (Afro-)Surinamese organizations in order to attend to the arrival of larger numbers of Surinamese in the mid-1970s, while policy-makers and public officials from various government levels as well as Surinamese leaders still expected their return. From 1974 onwards Surinamese organizations started to receive local state funding to serve the deprived segments of newly arriving migrants. Between 1975 and 1984 these received an equivalent of 2 million euros a year. In this positive environment the number of Surinamese organizations grew from 25 to 104 between 1970 and 1980, and numbered 215 in 1990. The reorientation toward mainstream services in Amsterdam in the 1980s subsequently led to a withdrawal of those subsidies. This has contributed to a certain decline in the number of their organizations after 1990.

Scholars have also pointed to the low level of active membership participation within migrant organizations as well as to their little involvement in mobilization and protest action in Amsterdam and other Dutch cities (Penninx, Schoorl, van Praag 1993: 176–80, Soysal 1994: Chapter 6, Bousetta 1997). Scholars on the Dutch situation frequently point to the fact that local voting rights and participatory channels for migrant organizations were given to them 'unsolicited' (Penninx, Schoorl, van Praag 1993: 180). Still, in the positive environment migrants' involvement in the local integration discourse is remarkable. Migrant voices are responsible for 21.4 per cent of all claims (identified in the local newspapers) in relation to immigration and ethnic relations in Amsterdam. Local comparison reveals that this figure is greatly above the share of migrants' own claims in Berlin (as well as in other German cities), and below those from the British city regions around Birmingham and Bradford (Koopmans 2004: 464, Table 3). In addition, interest representation is a goal at least among a relevant number of organizations as stated above.

As explained in the previous sections, the general approach on migrants' integration and particularly on migrant organizations had changed in the 1990s toward more project-based subsidies and a greater emphasis on their involvement in the delivery of services. At the end of the 1990s a clearer shift toward diversity politics occurred in Amsterdam which put an end to the previous multicultural minority approach. Therefore, it is likely that the nature of activities reflected in available data has also changed. Unfortunately, however, it remains unknown to which degree, for example, the above mentioned socio-cultural activities or those in the realm of education which are also reported in the data from the 1980s and 1990s reflect particular services rather than festivals. Further research is required to determine the involvement of migrant organizations in service delivery and the effects this has had for the role of members and also whether there are cross-effects concerning their involvement in politics. It is relatively likely that those engaged in services are also the ones which receive more political recognition. In addition, these should also count on the necessary resources to be more politically engaged in formal politics and claims-making. Other organizations, in turn, may share a more distant relationship with the authorities, whether freely chosen or due to difficult access to either one of these realms. Yet, the newer situation has already led to a certain reconfiguration as regards the legitimacy of 'old-generation' organizations which are now considered too (self-)centred on identity issues. These find themselves now excluded from dialogue. In contrast, 'new-generation' organizations (likely to be led by people from second and third generations, younger and with a greater proportion of women) now have a more specific focus on problem–solution and are also more strongly orientated toward diversity and intercultural openness. Project-based subsidies encourage these organizations to put more emphasis on their character as service providers (Uitermark, Rossi, van Houtum 2005).

Concerning transnational origin-country-related activities, changes have also occurred over the decades. In the 1970s and 1980s many different organizations were oriented toward the 'home' country. Many organizations of Turks, Moroccans or Surinamese, for example, actively supported or opposed the political situation in those countries, which were characterized by political turmoil, colonial independence or military rule (Van Amersfoort, van Heelsum 2007, Penninx, Schoorl, van Praag 1993: 176–80). Since then, transnational activities have generally declined. The above cited data on the development activities of the Afro-Surinamese organizations in Amsterdam reveals a decline from 25 to 10 per cent from 1980 to 2000 (Vermeulen 2006). Nevertheless, this is also to say that it still exists on their agendas. In the case of Turkish organizations, it is well known that many hold contacts to different religious groups and political parties in Turkey (Vermeulen 2005: 90). Interestingly, on their agendas there is even some growth of home-country-related activities (from 2.9 to 4.0 per cent of all activities), although at a very low level. In the Amsterdam public discourse reference to origin countries can also be identified (with a share of 13.8 per cent of all counted public claims by migrants) (Koopmans 2004: 465, Table 4). This is a figure which is higher than in the UK cities but much lower than in Berlin (31.4 per cent), for example, where local policies have been more ambiguous in the encouragement of local involvement as well as in the assessment of transnational activities. Furthermore, hometown associations dedicated to socio-economic development in the places of origin exist in Amsterdam as well, although so far little research exists on these cases. A recent finding of a study on Ghanaian hometown associations in Amsterdam shows that the operating conditions for this kind of organization have worsened in the last decades. According to this study, this is a result of increasingly more exclusionary migration policies which have created more difficult conditions for many migrants and lowered their possibilities to contribute to those associations with their own scarce means (Mazzucato, Kabki 2009: 240). If this finding can be generalized, a decrease in transnational activities should be expected among migrants and their organizations as a result of worsening living conditions for migrants and not because of their progressive integration into Dutch society, as research on migrant organizations has generally expected (see Chapter 2 of this book). At the same time, as the cited study and other findings show, those better established in the receiving place find it easier to actively engage with the situation in their places of origin (Mazzucato, Kabki 2009, Portes, Escobar, Arana 2008). Thus, one should expect a relatively heterogeneous picture in the types of organizations and the types of activities that migrant organizations undertake in origin countries, including many with no transnational activities at all.

Race, multiculturalism, and welfare policies: Migrant organizations in British cities

Immigration and the UK immigration regime

Post-war immigration to the UK and its immigration policies show some differences as compared to other early waves of migration in Europe. At first, the UK also encouraged immigration from Europe in order to meet labour-market shortages and recruited European voluntary workers through a number of government initiatives. These workers were mainly displaced persons from Eastern Europe and there was some immigration from Italy (Layton-Henry 1994: 284). The phase of recruitment was very short, though, and ended in 1950, when more and more people came from the colonies and the Commonwealth as well as from Ireland. Between 1952 and 1962 over 480,000 people came from the new Commonwealth countries of the West Indies and the Indian sub-continent (Layton-Henry 2004: 302, Table 8.1). It is one these migrants that this chapter concentrates as most studies and especially the political instruments have done (Räthzel 1994: 225, Solomos 2003). This immigration was unrestricted until 1962 due to the fact that British citizens and Commonwealth citizens from the former colonies were all considered British subjects with the same right to live and work in the UK. Commonwealth citizens were moreover eligible for British nationality after fives years of residence in the UK. However, in parallel to increasing inflows, discussions started as to limit specifically non-white immigration. This was greatly promoted by a number of racist attacks at the end of the 1950s which gave way to the idea that (non-white) immigration was threatening social peace and cohesion of British society. In order to preserve both, so reformers argued, further immigration needed to be restricted. This is generally considered the basis of the political consensus on immigration restriction among political elites and parties in Britain (Freeman 1994, Layton-Henry 2004).

The Commonwealth Immigrants Act of 1962 ended the previously liberal regime. For the first time, it introduced controls on Commonwealth immigrants based on a distinction between those born in Britain or with British passports and other Commonwealth citizens. The latter group was now required a voucher from the Ministry of Labour along three categories: category A for those who already had a specific job to go to in the UK, category B for those with special skills in short supply, and category C for all others who needed to apply separately, with preferential treatment for those who had served in the British army (Solomos 2003: 58, Layton-Henry 2004: 301). In 1965 the quotas for the voucher scheme were cut back to 8,500 and category C was abolished because enough applications were presented within the other two categories.

Further reforms subsequently defined those to which free access to the UK was granted more and more narrowly (Räthzel 1994). The second Commonwealth Immigrants Act of 1968 extended controls to British passport holders without a close connection to Britain, that is, persons who were neither themselves nor their parents or grandparents born in Britain. This measure was mainly directed at Asians arriving from East Africa when Kenya became independent. The Immigration Bill of 1971 introduced a distinction between 'partials' with the right to settle in the UK and all other Commonwealth citizens and foreigners. The category of 'partials' included all those persons with close connections to the UK through birth or decent and those who had been naturalized in the UK or had been living there for longer than five years. All other persons became subject to full control and were required residence and work permits. These also no longer automatically led to the right to permanent residency or family reunification. Finally, the British Nationality Act 1981 marked a break with Britain's imperial history (Layton-Henry 2004: 305–7). The law distinguished between British citizens, citizens of dependent territories and British overseas citizens. With the law reform, the British nationality legislation now resembled those of other European countries more closely. This policy change was accompanied by measures pursuing irregular migrants and overstayers. It also imposed stricter controls on spouses and dependents, as well as refugees who were legally entitled to enter Britain but whose admissions were refused or being processed over several years (Layton-Henry 2004: 306, 1994: 287–9).

During the 1980s and 1990s legal reforms continued to impose stronger control on immigration and now also on refugees. The absolute right to family reunification (for men who settled in the UK before 1973) was repealed in the 1988 Immigration Bill. It made this right conditional upon the situation of the family member living in the UK, whether man or woman. Asylum applications have been comparably low in the UK compared to other European countries, but started to rise in the 1990s. Whereas in the years 1985–1988 there were only 4,000 applications every year, their number was 38,000 in 1990 and 93,600 in 2000 (Layton-Henry 2004: 326). The government undertook several efforts to limit the number of asylum applications as well as the access of asylum seekers to welfare benefits. Nevertheless, the number of applications continues to rise and asylum seekers form a relevant part of immigration to the UK today. At the same time, asylum seekers can apply for work permission after six months of stay and it is assumed that many rejected asylum seekers have remained in the country illegally. Altogether irregular migration seems to have been relatively low until the late 1990s and has then grown due to a specific demand for cheap labour in certain economic sectors such as cleaning or construction (Layton-Henry 2004: 324–7).

At the end of 1990s a certain re-assessment of immigration can be observed in the UK. The role of migrants in the labour market and their economic contributions now receive greater recognition. A number of reports, white papers and government-commissioned research favour labour migration as needed and good for the country and the economy. Economic changes, shortages in key sectors such as care services, demographic change and an aging population have contributed to this perspective. Consequently, the white paper 'Secure Border, Safe Havens, Integration with Diversity in Modern Britain' from 2002 establishes a linkage between immigration control and the national (economic) interest. It further advocates integration and the need to develop a shared sense of belonging for all those in the country (Solomos 2003: 74). Still, great emphasis is put on tight controls and the idea that 'fair, fast and firm immigration control will help promote race equality' (Home Office 1998, cited by Layton-Henry 2004: 316). The Nationality, Immigration, and Asylum Bill of 2002 introduced further measures in the realms of border control and the deportation of irregular migrants. This, as the previous immigration and asylum law reforms, is seen as a response to popular concerns and specific hostility toward refugees and asylum seekers. In this respect, the newer policies follow the traditional trajectory and legitimization of British immigration controls by pointing to public concerns (Solomos 2003: 75).

Thus, especially during the first post-war decades, migrants in the UK were citizens or had access to citizenship relatively easily. As opposed to Germany and the Netherlands, the stay of migrants was not organized as transitory and access to secure permanent residency and subsequently citizenship existed from early on (Seifert 2000: 107). In a parallel fashion, however, new immigration has become greatly restricted, and family reunification has turned into one of the few remaining forms of immigration. Some authors have argued that the British immigration regime is characterized by a 'colour bar' (Freeman 1994). Reforms have often *de facto* meant restrictions for migrants of darker skin colour and these reforms were also often legitimized with the hostility and rejection against those newcomers in British society. This has led to a broader discussion on the inconsistency, if not incompatibility, of British immigration policies that on the one hand aim at promoting harmonious race relations and the integration of those groups that immigration controls on the other hand aim to prevent from coming (Freeman 1994, Layton-Henry 2004: 317). At the same time, migration is considered 'a private enterprise operation' (Layton-Henry 2004: 328). This is in line with Britain's greater emphasis on the individual and private self-help more generally which is also reflected in the comparatively small direct state attendance that migrants have encountered there as will be shown next (Soysal 1994: see Chapter 4).

The development of race relations policies and the role of the local level

Most immigrants who arrived in the United Kingdom after World War II were citizens or had rights equal to citizens, at least until 1971, some also until 1981. Few special measures were set up to support their arrival and settlement. Changing inflows have not changed this general situation. Since the mid-1960s a broad range of measures have, however, aimed at contributing to 'racial equality'.

Decentralized strategies and local authorities have played an important role in this setting (Soysal 1994: see Chapter 4, Solomos 2003: see Chapters 4 and 5). At different points in time, local conflicts and protest by local politicians on the social problems associated with increasing migration, racist attacks and the political mobilization by racial and ethnic minorities in many urban areas entered the national level and are reflected in parliamentary debates, policy programmes and legislation. The development of race relation policies by the central government, in turn, has also shaped, supported, and constrained responses by local authorities. Each of the different phases of policies on migrants in the UK also involves a somewhat different relationship between national and local levels. The first years of post-war immigration saw little policy responses beyond some ad hoc measures, mainly from local levels. This changed in the mid-1960s when racial equality became a major principle. Race relation policies developed and a growing legislation aimed at anti-discrimination and equal opportunities for members of racial and ethnic minorities. In this phase, urban programmes and local authorities were equipped with resources to confront the needs and problems associated with migration. During the 1980s and until the mid-1990s fewer new efforts on the central government level existed, accompanied by greater control imposed on local authorities. In parallel, local governments developed varying responses ranging from those of resisters rejecting the idea of specific policies on migrants to pioneers with a multicultural agenda (Young, Connelly 1981). While the general national-level approach on integration tended toward assimilationism, cultural rights have expanded since the 1970s and the recognition of ethnic groups and cultures in education and social services especially from local levels contributed to a more multicultural outlook (Castles 1995: 300–301, Koopmans, Statham 1999, Back et al. 2002). In the second half of the 1990s a new phase started in which more emphasis was placed on the diversity of migrant groups and the more general picture of social exclusion. The promotion of 'local autonomy' was one of the strategies to deal with these issues (Back et al. 2002), taking place in the framework of decentralization and the emergence of new forms of local governance which started in that period (MacLeod, Goodwin 1999). Because of the close interrelation between national and local level in the general development of the policies on immigrants, this section describes the respective policies on the multiple levels of government in the UK. The next section then goes into greater detail on how this has involved migrant organizations' participation mainly at the local level. That section will rely on literature from different British cities with a more multicultural agenda, but concentrates somewhat more strongly on the well-documented example of Birmingham.

In the first years of post-war migration in Britain, few particular policies developed to address migrants or their organizations. No specific social policies existed and services for migrants were meant to be no different from those to mainstream society. 'In the 1960s it was argued that there would in any case be little need or demand for services from the young, single men who were the majority of newcomers' (Cheetham 1988: 108). Still in the early 1980s public officials in areas with substantial migrant population were often unaware of this fact or did not see these populations as requiring nor wanting specific services (Young, Connelly 1981: 68). Similar to other countries, settlement of families was not anticipated and cultural difference was not meant to constitute a basis for differential treatment or specific services. Some local governments started to develop ad hoc measures and in some localities special officers were installed to help migrants with their specific problems (Ouseley 1984: 133, Solomos 2003: 97). In parallel, local civil society and non-state organizations became involved in the assistance of migrants. Originally, these initiatives were meant to serve as temporary support to migrants (Messina 1987: 188, Vertovec 1996b). Later many of them became incorporated into the official local structures of race relation policies in the form of so called Voluntary Liaison Committees (VLC) and later Community Relation Councils (CRC) (Messina 1987, Vertovec 1996b).

In the late 1950s racist attacks against black immigrants and the increasing marginalization of migrants moved the issue of race, discrimination and integration of migrants to a prominent place. The instruments which have developed from this observation since the mid-1960s follow two main lines. First, various legal instruments emerged mainly through Race Relation Acts and the related legislative and administrative provisions. Second, new welfare services came into existence in the form of economic support to local governments and agencies and non-state actors through various channels (Soysal 1994: see Chapter 4, Solomos 2003: 80–81). Thus, concerning the first set of instruments, the governments' white paper of 1965 specifically articulated the need to combine the efforts of immigration restriction and the promotion of integration in order to improve race relations and contribute to racial equality. In line with this, the government passed race relations acts in 1965, 1968 and 1976 (Solomos 2003: see Chapter 4). Their aim was to combat discrimination on the basis of race, in other words skin colour and national or ethnic origin. The scope of the legal measures of anti-discrimination subsequently expanded from public transport and housing to cover public institutions and employment practices. The acts further installed quasi-governmental boards to monitor the progress of race relation policies and to work as mediators in relevant social realms. In relation to the second set of instruments concerning social policies, race relation policies of the 1960s and 1970s specifically targeted local processes, governments and actors. To this end, with the first Race Relations Act the National Committee for Commonwealth Immigrants (NCII) came into existence which integrated within the Commission for Racial Equality in 1976 (Messina 1987: 189, Solomos 2003: 81). Especially at the beginning, its main task was to provide support to local committees and associations and to pay the local Community Relations Councils the salary of community relations officers. These local councils were to identify ethnic leaders which in turn would mediate between the racial and ethnic minorities and the local authorities. Furthermore, the Local Governments Act through its section 11 gave financial support to local authorities with a certain share of immigrant population. These schemes addressed the 'special needs of immigrants' and supported local social services and education, especially English language teaching in order to support immigrants' adaptation (Soysal 1994:

58, Seifert 2000: 144). The Local Governments Grants (Social Need) Act of 1969 and the related urban programme, in contrast, targeted the deprived inner city areas and in principle did not specifically target ethnic and racial minority issues. Due to the concentration of these populations in the respective residential areas many of the subsidized projects did relate to immigrants, though. In the years 1968 to 1975 the urban programme benefited around 300 localities with 3,750 projects (Mahnig 1998: 14–23).

In the following years growing racial tensions gave way to violent 'race riots' in different urban areas in the early and mid-1980s. In this phase political responses are characterized by a number of different policy strategies: first, a generally more hesitant central government policy on race and discrimination; second, greater limits to local governments and a revision of urban policies; and third, the emergence of more proactive and multicultural policy initiatives in a number of (mostly Labour governed) localities (Vertovec 1996b, Solomos 2003: see Chapter 5). Scholars have virtually unanimously pointed to the great reluctance of the national government since the late 1970s to address racial inequality and race relations (Britain was governed by the conservative party from 1979 to 1997). The national course of this phase is rather characterized by a renewed emphasis on British culture, habits and language which had to be protected from being 'swamped' by other cultures (Solomos 2003: 66, see also Back et al. 2002). Although relevant bodies such as the Commission for Racial Equality (CRE) as well as Lord Scarman's report on the urban unrest of the early 1980s advocated for substantial reforms, the national government showed little interest in doing so. In fact, the latter's instruments included the further restriction of immigration through the British Nationality Act of 1981 and inner cities where riots had occurred came to be seen from a 'law and order' perspective based on the premise that observed problems were a matter of criminality rather than of social exclusion (Mahnig 1998: 21–3). In parallel, the CRE made use of its competences to further advance and extend anti-discrimination policies and developed codes of conduct to combat discrimination in the workplace (Solomos 2003: 88). In addition, the Commission provided considerable funding for local projects by non-state actors, including those of migrant organizations (Soysal 1994: 56; see below). In relation to local governance, the national government aimed at limiting the intervention of local authorities in social services, housing and education and further restricted the autonomy of local governments, especially where those deviated from the national course (Mahnig 1998: 21–3, Solomos 2003: 112–113). The revision of urban policies, which had already started in the mid-1970s, led to more direct intervention by the central government in certain urban areas supporting urban renewal and economic regeneration. These gave little concern to social policies which had been crucial within the urban programme and involved private enterprises to a greater degree. This also implied cutbacks on local authorities' funding. In addition, some of the central government's actions aimed at limiting local space for manoeuvre. One major issue in this respect was the limitation of the use of contract compliance through the Local Government Act of 1988. This was a reaction to the fact that a number of authorities, from London and Birmingham for example, had made use of such policies in order to make private enterprises comply with race relations policies using equal opportunity clauses on employment (Solomos 2003: 113). On a local level varying responses existed ranging from those of resisters rejecting the idea of specific policies for immigrants to pioneers with a multicultural agenda (Young, Connelly 1981). Among the latter, a number of authorities in and around London, as well as in Birmingham, Bradford, Manchester and Leicester and some others have become renowned for their proactive policies and more radical solutions to the problem of racism and discrimination (Rex, Samad 1996, Vertovec 1996b, Solomos 2003: 97, Moore 2004). Three important lines of activities characterize the local multicultural approaches (Mahnig 1998: 22). First, equal opportunity employment became institutionalized, including the introduction of minimum quotas for the municipalities' staff from ethnic and racial minority groups; second, the administration and its services were to adapt to migrants' needs and cultures, including race awareness training. Here 'ethnically sensitive' services came on the agenda and migrant organizations received economic support for their welfare services; as a third line, the combat of racism became a central objective. Among the instruments of the latter were anti-discrimination practices in relation to housing and the use of contract compliance in some localities defining standards for private companies working for the city. Many other initiatives focused on anti-racist and multicultural education. This also included financial support for mother tongue teaching through ethnic communities, but also through Muslim groups as in Birmingham or Manchester, for example (Soysal 1994: 103). In contrast, the national governments' Education Reform Act of 1988 showed a clear commitment to immigrants' adaptation and an assimilationist approach (Mahnig 1998: 22).

Since the second half of the 1990s, mainly after a change in government to New Labour in 1997, a new course on race relations can be observed. Racial discrimination and inequalities of migrants and racial minorities were now seen in the wider context of social exclusion and embedded in the broader framework of diversity policies. In this framework localized initiatives and community-based strategies were reinforced (Solomos 2003: 114). The most important developments on the national government level can be seen in the publication of the Macpherson Report on the murder of the black teenager Stephen Lawrence and the subsequent police investigation, the reform of the race relations act, and the announcement of the government to improve anti-discrimination in the public sector (Solomos 2003: 89). The Macpherson report from 1999 advocated broader changes in a variety of areas in order to combat racial inequality and multiple deprivations. The Race Relations (Amendment) Act's main innovation is that public authorities now have a statutory duty to promote racial equality. Both documents imply the need to mainstream race equality issues in public affairs. These and other documents specifically advocate to take into account the reality of urban governance and therefore to involve a broad range of local partners in advancing social justice in the different local areas (Smith, Stephenson 2003: 13). This newer course entails a focus on localized initiatives to deal with multiply deprived communities as well as a greater recognition of voluntary and community-based organizations, including the encouragement of particular communities to become involved in self-help and race policies (Solomos 2003: 13–15, Smith, Stephenson 2003, McLeod, Owen, Khamis 2001). After new riots in 2001, community cohesion became a main goal of national and local bodies in order to overcome separation and the lack of everyday contact within communities in the localities where riots had occurred. In particular, new urban policies are characterized by collaborations between national and local governmental agencies and community groups to improve public social service, revitalize deprived urban areas and deal with crime (Solomos 2003: 114).

The above-mentioned documents and new policies from the national government together with an increasing awareness of the limited outcomes of the existing local structures and frameworks for consultation also led to a move from multicultural approaches toward diversity in many of the proactive localities. For example, the city of Birmingham had developed racial equality and multicultural instruments in the 1980s. In 1996 the city reorganized its administrative structure in order to follow a new course. Its race relations unit merged together with the units on the disabled and the one on women into one single body, the Equality Division. As of 2001, the division is no longer the central coordinating body of equal opportunity measures. Equality Officers now operate in each of the municipal departments (Smith, Stephenson 2003). Similar developments can be observed in Manchester and some other localities across the UK (Antalovsky, Wolffhardt 2002: 90–103). The Local Government Act of 2000 strengthened this form of diversity management for all British localities. New local concepts generally entail the explicit recognition of the multiple identities held by persons and the multiple, interplaying forms of discrimination associated with it. As a consequence, responses are now issue- rather than (minority) group-based. The Birmingham Racial Action Programme (BRAP), set up in 1998, describes its approach on its website the following way:

> We work towards an inclusive and rights-based approach to equality, one that recognises that we are all different, and because of this cannot easily fit ourselves into the current equality picture, which tends to see us as belonging to a particular group. We avoid an approach to equality that relies on promoting one group's needs over another's, as we think that this more often restricts the progress of equality, rather than promotes it. Our approach, above all else, recognises the rights of people. (BRAP 2011)

These changes have also affected relationships with migrant organizations and their involvement with formal politics and services.

Before analysing these aspects in greater detail, the role of transnational engagements needs to be addressed since this aspect also came into the spotlight in the second half of the 1990s as part of the debate on the migration-development linkages. A 1997 White Paper urged the British development agency DfID to 'build on skills and talents of migrants and other members of ethnic minorities within the UK to promote the development of their countries of origin' (cited in De Haas 2006: 60). From this white paper followed a number of further initiatives as well as some newer funding schemes for the support of awareness raising and capacity building among migrant organizations and groups. These have also been consulted in setting up action plans for certain development regions. Migrants' transnational activities are now also an issue on the agenda of some of the proactive local authorities such as Bradford or Leicester within their community cohesion agendas (Thornton, Hext 2009: 24–5). So far, initiatives concentrate on workshops and conferences and no particular funding scheme seems to exist which supports migrant organizations in their cross-border projects on either national or local levels.

Local relationships with migrant organizations

Relationships between public authorities and migrant organizations in the UK are to a great degree focused on the local level, including the measures deriving from the national level of government. In the 1950s local groups emerged to assist newly arriving migrants and some first migrant organizations were among them. Over many years, these groups have assisted the arrival of new migrants, supported the migrants' claims and accompanied the development of anti-discrimination policies (Räthzel 1994: 242–3). These groups became the basis for the evolution of the more formally organized Voluntary Liaison Committees and Community Relations Councils (CRC) as they came to be known. Since 1965 national level agencies, today represented by the Commission for Racial Equality (CRE), have granted support in financial terms and advice to local organizations. This has included the salaries of fulltime community relations officers working for the local committees (Messina 1987: 180–81). Although not all local committees received funding, and many did only after several years after their founding, the environment was generally conducive to their existence. The number of these local committees grew from 15 which had been set up by 1964 to 50 in 1967 and to over 100 all over Britain by 1985 (Messina 1987: 180–81). The main task of the local committees was to contribute to harmonious community and race relations. To this end they were to identify black and ethnic leaders and their organizations serving as mediators to the respective ethnic and minority communities (Messina 1987: 189, Rex, Samad 1996, Vertovec 1996b). The local CRCs had different structures, but, as in the case of Birmingham, often 'included substantial white city council representation' (Rex, Samad 1996: 25) together with migrant organizations' representatives. They served as a mechanism of consultation and advisory services and issued reports on housing, education and social services, and worked as social welfare advisers, legal watchdogs and policy advocates (Vertovec 1996b: 52). National bodies also made attempts to control the local committees and to bring them under their guidelines, defining their working mechanisms and tasks more uniformly. To this end, the national-level Commission for Racial Equality has also made use of its financial pressure by withdrawing CRC grant aid (Messina 1987:

192). In the mid 1980s, the Commission supported local bodies with almost £4 million, of which £2.5 million went to the Community Relations Councils (Messina 1987: 187). In 1991, the Commission passed £5.3 million to local groups and projects offering social services to migrants and combating discrimination (Soysal 1994: 56). However, emerging migrant organizations received little support, if at all, and resources concentrated on the CRCs and these were generally also scarce (Cheetham 1988: 124).

In the course of local multiculturalism, more attention was paid to the support of the collective formation of racial and ethnic minorities. In Birmingham, after a number of different attempts, the search for new consultative structures finally led to the creation of minority umbrella groups. From the mid-1980s on, at least nine such groups were founded, such as the Pakistani Forum in 1988, the Midlands Vietnamese Refuge Association in 1989 or the African Caribbean People's Movement in 1991 (Rex, Samad 1996, Smith, Stephenson 2003). The umbrella organizations received a start-up grant and salaries for two officers. These, in turn, were represented in the Standing Consultative Forum (SFC), which became institutionalized in 1990. In this process many local networks came into existence since the umbrellas grouped a great number of smaller organizations from one 'minority group' together, who in turn elected the representatives of their umbrella group. The emergence of similar interlocking can be observed in other British localities with a multicultural agenda as well (Vertovec 1996b). In parallel, the growing concern for the social disadvantages of members of minority groups led to more specifically designed services focused on ethnic groups. In this situation, local authorities became important funders for migrant organizations (McLeod, Owen, Khamis 2001: 4). This has meant that some organizations acted as agencies of the local authorities such as the Handsworth Employment Centre or the Afro-Caribbean Resource Centre. Many others have received funding for their projects (Cheetham 1988, Rex, Samad 1996). In this vein, welfare funding was meant to support organizations that represent and serve 'the whole community' (Vertovec 1996b: 54). At the same time, this was accompanied by the emergence of the 'contract culture' during the 1980s which put emphasis on professionalism, evaluation and 'quality assurance' (McLeod, Owen, Khamis 2001: 5). It should also be noted, that this contracting-out of social services took place in the context of the British government's policy on the privatization of public services during the 1980s and 1990s.

In the mid-1990s, the general critique of multiculturalism also affected the mechanisms of consultation and dialogue. Local authorities now greatly criticized that (self-appointed) ethnic leaders with little support of 'their' community dominated the scenery, and that these were mainly middle-aged males of the first generation of immigrants (Smith, Stephenson 2003). As a consequence, the relationship between local authorities and migrant organizations developed two tendencies: on the one hand public authorities showed less interest in community representation while on the other hand the advocacy of individual (ethnic and minority groups) experts became increasingly appreciated. In Birmingham this led to the dissolution of the ethnically organized consultation structure of the SFC. Instead, with the BRAP a new structure came into place. BRAP's board represents key local institutions such as the Birmingham City Council, the health authority or the local voluntary service council. It works with the Race Action Forums in relevant areas such as health care, young adults' education or arts and culture. Twelve community advocates participate in each action group, a structure which now substitutes for collective consultation. These advocates are selected on the basis of skills and knowledge in order to step away from 'over-reliance on so-called community leaders' (BRAP 2002, cited in Smith, Stephenson 2003: 14). In this sense, this newer policy aims to encourage cross-community dialogue and collaborations.

On the other hand side the increasing emphasis on community involvement and the greater recognition of the voluntary sector in the UK has further enhanced legitimacy and resources for non-state actors' involvement into service delivery and community work. Although this is not new in British policies in general and also not in those on migrants, resources seem to expand rather than to diminish, reflected in the growth of migrant organizations' budgets and public funding in the 1990s (McLeod, Owen, Khamis 2001). Thus, race relations policies from the national level may be interpreted as focused on individuals rather than on groups, since they aim at providing equal opportunities to all (Soysal 1994: see Chapter 4). At the local level, though, multicultural policies relying on concepts of culture and ethnic and minority groups gained great momentum during the 1980s in the UK. Today, although group-based approaches have lost some legitimacy, a shift toward greater self-help and community engagement has also furnished migrant organizations with economic support.

Migrant organizations in British cities

'Following large scale migrations from the Indian subcontinent and the Caribbean in the late 1950s, immigrant associations emerged in every main centre of settlement, particularly in connection with the need to find work and accommodation – often in the face of racism and exclusion' (McLeod, Owen, Khamis 2001: 11). Among the early migrant organizations were also workers associations, often related to the trade unions as is the case of the Indian Workers Associations (IWA) (Rex, Josephides 1987). Whether organizations emerged from political or workers groups or out of cultural and religious communities, 'self-help (…) developed out of the necessity of meeting unmet needs' (McLeod, Owen, Khamis 2001: 11, see also Cheetham 1988: 121). Although most of these early migrants to the UK were citizens, access to the labour market remained difficult and state attendance to the specific needs of new arrivals was scarce. New commonwealth migrants in particular found it difficult to access mainstream services and existing facilities (Ouseley 1984: 133, McLeod, Owen, Khamis 2001: 11). Over the course of time, state authorities and actors, mainly at the local level, recognized the need to deal with this situation. Since the 1960s this has meant support to organizations offering practical help to migrants, from the central government level and through urban policies as well as from the local governments on their own behalf.

Around 2,000 migrant organizations existed in British localities at the end of the 1980s (Anwar 1991, cited in Soysal 1994: 102). A large-scale survey from 2001 on (black and other) minority organizations in England and Wales estimates that there are currently 5,500 of these organizations, with 85 per cent formally registered (McLeod, Owen, Khamis 2001). This would amount to around 4,700 formal migrant organizations. The study also documents great sustainability since over 60 per cent of the organizations of the smaller in-depth sample had existed for ten years or more. At the same time, this documents the many new formations which occurred during the decade of the 1990s.

The range of activities of local migrant organizations in the UK is broad, as in other European cities, but most are at least partly engaged in the delivery of welfare services. According to the CRE database, 70 per cent already reported giving advice and social services in the mid-1980s (Soysal 1994: 88, Table 6.1). Some organizations have even served as municipal agencies while many others receive local funding for their projects (Rex, Samad 1996). The most important service activities include advice and advocacy, health, welfare or income support, housing, education and employment. Other issues concern culture, sports and recreational activities as well as religion, with many Islamic organizations often also carrying out services to their constituency (McLeod, Owen, Khamis 2001: 27, Figure 5, see also Cheetham 1988, Rex, Samad 1996).

A majority of migrant organizations in British localities receive financial support from public authorities, and here especially local levels are important funders. In a study from the mid-1980s, of 29 investigated migrant organizations, half already received local public funding (Cheetham 1988). At that time, this was interpreted as little state support from the emerging multicultural policy point of view, but compared to other countries and cities investigated in this book it is considerable, when compared to Berlin for instance. Today the greater part of the income of migrant organizations stems from public authorities. This is specifically important for smaller organizations (with an income of less than £50,000), which receive 50 per cent of their budget from local authority grants (McLeod, Owen, Khamis 2001: 36–8, Figure 6). In addition, this income had been rising for almost half of the organizations investigated in that study. A recent survey on migrant organizations in London also reveals that on average 35 per cent of their financial resources comes from local grants, and another 23 from grants from other governmental levels (Devadason 2009). Thus, even though there are cutbacks in local authorities' budgets, including that of the voluntary sector, migrant organizations have received great economic support, at least in the 1990s.

Funding is available predominately for welfare services and educational activities while migrant organizations have received little support for cultural programmes (Cheetham 1988: 127). In some localities, specifically in those which had a clear multicultural approach in the 1980s, such as Birmingham or Manchester, migrant organizations also received support for mother language teaching, in Urdu or Hindi, for example (Soysal 1994: 103). Grants also support the gaining and maintaining of offices and community centres (Vertovec 1996b: 63).

Many indications exists that engagement in self-help and professional service provision has continuously extended since the emergence of the first migrant organizations in the 1950s. This is reflected in the growing number of migrant organizations of which most are engaged in some kind of welfare services (McLeod, Owen, Khamis 2001). Two dynamics have greatly contributed to this trend: first, the development of multicultural approaches in a number of localities, accompanied by the idea of ethnically targeted services, especially since 1980. Second, the fact that state–society relations are decentralized and social services provision relies more on private initiatives opened venues for migrant organizations at an early stage (Soysal 1994: Chapter 4). Further privatization and delegation of public services, paralleled by an emphasis on community self-help, has extended since the 1980s. Interestingly, the shift from mainstream to community and 'ethnically sensitive' services is also reflected in the perspectives of migrant organizations. In a study from the mid-1980s, public agencies and migrant organizations representatives agreed in their perspective that their shared aim was the improvement of mainstream services. Migrant organizations were to advise the adaptation of those services, but not offer the services to their communities (Cheetham 1988: 148). A decade later the perspective changed. In an interview in a study from the mid-1990s, a migrant organization representative asserted that: 'It is better for us to take care of our own problems in our own community' (Soysal 1994: 103).

Although comparatively few organizations report on 'advocacy and interest representation' among their activities (only 10 per according to the CRE database Soysal 1994: 88, Table 6.1), migrants have used their networks for collective mobilization. Since the 1950s migrant organizations have been connected to campaigns against racism and discrimination and protest in favour of cultural and social rights (Räthzel 1994: 233–5, Vertovec 1996b, Rex, Samad 1996, McLeod, Owen, Khamis 2001: 11–12). Furthermore, the share of migrants' claims in the public discourse on immigration and ethnic relations is greatly above the level encountered in other European countries and this also holds true when comparing different European cities. In the urban regions of Leeds, Bradford and Birmingham this share ranges between 40 and almost 50 per cent, whereas in German cities migrants' share in the discourse is generally below 15 per cent and sometimes less than 2 per cent (Koopmans 2004). The identified claims in Britain are also more proactive in favour of migrants' rights and their extension and refer to cultural rights, predominantly related to Islam, as well as to social and economic rights. This is in stark contrast to claims encountered in Germany where defensive demands and claims for protection against racial violence predominate (Koopmans, Statham 1999).

The focus on local minority communities since the second half of the 1980s has also contributed to local interconnectedness among the various groups of one racial, ethnic, or religious community. Umbrella organizations formed despite many differences in ideological or religious orientation, as in the case of the Council of Mosques in Bradford, for instance (Rex, Samad 1996: 21), or Leicester's Federation of Muslim Organizations (Vertovec 1996b: 63). The various groups within one community also have joined forces in campaigns against racist attacks or in favour of certain rights such as the introduction of halal meals in schools.

Concerning the relationship between the organizations and their members, professionalization and public funding seems to have brought about some similar features as those found in the Spanish case studies presented in Chapter 4 of this book. First, membership relations seem rather unclear and the meaning of it varies from organization to organization (Cheetham 1988: 125). While some organizations refer to a certain number of actively involved persons, others consider all those on their mailing lists members. The clientele to which services are offered is, in turn, not limited to members. Yet it seems that this is mainly limited to one ethnic or racial group, in contrast to migrant organizations in Spanish cities. The latter were found serving or claiming to serve a broader spectrum of persons among their clients beyond their own 'roots' (see Chapter 4). In addition, the category of staff plays an important role. A greater number of migrant organizations (an estimated 2,000 according to the England and Wales study, see McLeod, Owen, Khamis 2001) employ four or more workers. As a consequence the distribution of tasks should be a major issue. In the past, this had led to problems and questions of the legitimacy and representativeness of these organizations. For example, one main problem encountered in relation to the Birmingham Standing Consultative Council (SFC) was the delegation of policy work to the paid staff. The local authorities funded community development workers for each of the (ethnic and racial minority) umbrella organizations which were members of the SFC. This helped them to elaborate analysis of social policy issues and supported the interaction with the city council and the various municipal departments. At the same time, the representatives of the umbrella organizations, who were generally volunteers, chose to leave policy issues and attendance of the SFC meetings to the staff paid by the municipality. 'They thought that the [community] development worker could do the work' (Interview with a Birmingham public official, cited in Smith, Stephenson 2003: 10). Such practices were one of the reasons that eventually led to the dissolution of the SFC.

In addition, political activism also seems to encounter some external constraints. Organizations which are recognized with a charitable status, thus guaranteeing certain tax advantages, are not allowed to engage in political activities (Cheetham 1988: 128). This has been difficult for some organizations and puts them at odds with authorities over the interpretation of the definition of politics and its relationship with other activities on the agenda of individual organizations. Political engagement seems to be particularly problematic when it is related to the country of origin. There are examples showing that where organizations did not manage to disentangle themselves from what to them seemed closely related, namely assistance to migrants and refugees, cultural events, and interest and support to one of the political parties of their origin country, they were denied subsidies for any activity (Cheetham 1988: 128). Thus, even in times when race and ethnicity received recognition and were supported, authorities perceived migrants' engagement with the 'homeland' negatively.

In fact, in the media very few voices from migrant organizations concern the country of origin according to the already cited comparative city study (Koopmans 2004: 465, Table 4). In the urban region of Birmingham no references to the origin country were identified. In Greater London, Bradford and Leeds such claims ranged between 4.6 and 6.8 per cent of all claims that migrants had voiced in the public sphere. In contrast, voices referring to actors and institutions in the country of origin encountered in migrants' public discourse in German cities range between 31.4 (Berlin) and 77.8 per cent (Stuttgart). Still, not a few migrant organizations in British cities have been engaged in transnational activities and concerned with the political and socio-economic situation in the place of their origin. This applies for example to the Indian Workers Associations (IWA) which emerged to defend migrant workers' rights in the UK but nevertheless were concerned with India (Rex, Josephides 1987, Rex, Samad 1996). Although many organizations became more and more involved with the situation in Britain, not all cut 'homeland' ties. From research on former activist of the IWA, however, it was pointed out that '[d]evelopment belongs to the private kinship sphere of their lives, whereas their political activism is focused on the UK public sphere' (Lacroix 2010: 19). This seems to hold true for the more general picture since very few migrant organizations in the UK are formally involved in international development. Around 4 per cent of the activities on which migrant organizations report refer to development abroad (McLeod, Owen, Khamis 2001: 27, Figure 5; see also De Haas 2006: 61). Although there is considerable effort and attention on the side of relevant development agencies for the involvement of migrant organizations into development cooperation, few migrant organizations have been successful in grant applications within development schemes. However, very few have presented an application in the first place (De Haas 2006: 63). Different from the Spanish case presented earlier in this book, funded projects concern workshops and training in the UK and do not include cross-border development cooperation by migrants. Thus, transnational ties existed at the point of emergence of many migrant organizations and may partly still persist. The involvement with the place of reception seems greater, though, especially when contrasted to the situation of migrant organizations in Berlin or Amsterdam.

Chapter summary

This chapter has been interested in the processes of accommodation of migrant organizations in established immigration cities and localities in Germany, the Netherlands and the United Kingdom. Thereby, it has specifically shown how the political–institutional contexts in cities have shaped the processes of accommodation. The main findings of the chapter shall be summarized in the following, before the next and last chapter of this book contrasts these with each other and with the results from the analysis of the accommodation of migrant organizations in recent immigration cities.

Migrant organizations in Berlin have been shaped by changing and diverging contexts emerging from national and local governments. The German immigration regime, in other words the regulation of entry, stay and work of guest workers, accorded these migrants relatively stable and secure statuses as well as social rights almost equal to those of nationals. This was considered transitory, though, since the stay of guest workers was meant to be temporary as well. Return programmes and financial incentives for investment in places of origin have supported this and still in the 1980s new measures were set up in this respect. At the same time, although few policies developed specifically dealing with the more permanent stay or integration of migrants at the beginning, state and state-funded social attendance to guest workers and later also to their families existed. When integration entered the political debate in the late 1970s, policies from the national government followed a rather assimilationist approach demanding adaptation to the language and habits of German society. This also meant that access to citizenship and political participation remained difficult until 2000 even for the second generation born in Germany. Since the early 1980s, the city of Berlin has been more proactive. It has used its discretionary competences in relation to naturalization for instance, and has tended toward multiculturalism in its approach on migrants' integration. The city's approach is, however, better described by the (newer) term interculturality for its emphasis on dialogue and non-separation, not unlike the approach identified in Barcelona or Madrid. This has included the recognition of migrant organizations at a time when these were still seen as a form of ethnic retention and withdrawal from German society on the national level of government as well as in many other localities. Together with the changes in the local governance model characterized by greater recognition and economic support to self-help initiatives and voluntary civil society activities, this has opened venues for migrant organizations as well. A consultative council with the participation of migrant organizations came into existence only in 2003, but other forms of dialogue and exchange as well as formalized participation channels existed before this. In this context, migrant organizations in Berlin emerged as social clubs, religious and leisure organizations in the 1960s, many of which had close linkages to actors and places in the country of origin. The spectrum of organizations and the activities the organizations undertook diversified during the 1970s along with settlement and family reunification. The main activities have been related to culture, religion, and interest articulation. Compared to other German cities, political articulation by migrants in the public sphere is today also stronger in Berlin, although weaker than in cities in the Netherlands and the UK, including Amsterdam and Birmingham (Koopmans 2004). In the 1980s already more support and advisory activities came on the agendas, and social activities for youth and women emerged, partly responding to the changing context of Berlin's greater attention and financial support to local self-help initiatives.

Origin-country-related activities have remained or re-emerged on the agendas as some recent case studies show (Çağlar 2006, Yurdakul 2006), although these have often been underestimated in other research. During the 1980s social ties and economic investment in migrants' origin countries were still supported as part of Germany's return policies, but with the increasing emphasis put on integration, migrants' transnationalism is increasingly less welcomed as a feature among those who stay. This has obviously led to a situation where references pertaining to the country of origin in the public discourse exist to a high degree (Koopmans 2004) and organizations have relationships to actors in origin countries, but in general migrant organizations do not report on this as a major activity (Vermeulen 2006: 88–9). The degree and types of transnational involvement among migrant organizations in Berlin cannot be determined from the scarce available research. Where it exists, is seems to go along with settlement and integration related activities, though.

The newly forming migrant organizations in Amsterdam originally encountered similar contexts as those in Berlin in the 1960s and 1970s, while from 1980 onward 'ethnic minority policies' shaped a very different situation. The Dutch immigration regime and the early policies dealing with migrants' reception were also highly state-regulated, with inflows mainly composed of (post-)colonial citizens and recruited guest workers, most of whom were expected to return to their country of origin after temporary stay or refuge. Private organizations supported and assisted the arrival of the newcomers and since the 1960s they have received economic support from the public authorities for this task. In 1981 the approach shifted toward multiculturalism, both on the national and the local level of Amsterdam. Maintenance of ethnic identities was an integral element of these policies. This comprised generous subsidies and assistance to migrant organizations for their cultural and emancipatory activities. National and local consultative councils organized along ethnic lines. At the same time, administrative decentralization of the 1980s ended the role of private foundations in service delivery for the different migrants groups. These became integrated into local mainstream services and consultation with migrant organizations was meant to enable them to adapt to their new clientele. At least since the end of the 1990s a greater shift occurred away from a group-focused minority approach toward an approach on diversity and multiple identities and their potentially diverging forms of discrimination, accompanied by greater emphasis on intercultural dialogue and a new role of migrant organizations in policy implementation and social services. In the Amsterdam context, migration organizations thus emerged as social and leisure organizations, many of whom were oriented to the country of origin and the political and socio-economic development there. During the 1970s and 1980s settlement, family reunification and family formation contributed to a greater diversity of organizations and their numerical growth. The growth rate is greater than that among migrant organizations in Berlin and interest representation and socio-cultural activities score highest on their agendas. Welfare services were almost totally absent until the 1990s when a new generation of organizations started to emerge that is characterized by a focus on specific issues and the provision of services (Uitermark, Rossi, van Houtum 2005). At the same time, the role of migrant organizations in formal politics is decreasing. According to available studies, it seems that transnational activities also persist or re-emerge, but generally at a low level (Vermeulen 2005: 88–9). This, however, seems to be not necessarily an effect of progressive integration into Dutch society and a corresponding loosening of ties to the places of origin. At least for some migrant groups more restrictive immigration regulations and worsening living conditions have limited their resources to contribute to cross-border projects (Mazzucato, Kabki 2009: 240).

Migrant organizations in British localities such as Birmingham and Bradford have developed somewhat differently. Initially immigration consisted of citizens or British subjects with (almost) all the rights of nationals and who could naturalize fairly easily. But specific attendance to immigrants' arrival did not exist, and most migrants did not come with a job. In 1965, race relations policies started to combat discrimination and promote equal opportunities, while generally other social and employment-related training measures were scarcer when compared to the Netherlands or Germany. In parallel, urban programmes and local governments have played an important role, including local consultative councils with the participation of migrant organizations. This has also meant support for service delivery to private initiatives and self-help by non-state actors among which migrant organizations existed. In the 1980s, multiculturalism emerged as an approach, especially in some localities and it is on these that this chapter has concentrated. There, migrant organizations became more involved in consultation and the provision of ethnically targeted services. Today a newer approach on diversity has withdrawn the attention on migrant organizations and collective community representation, while voluntary sector and community involvement led to more services by migrant organizations. In this context, the evolution of local migrant organizations has been oriented toward welfare services since the 1950s. Scholars have also observed the many political activities and interest representation by migrants' groups and networks in British cities (Koopmans, Statham 1999, Koopmans 2004, Solomos 2003). These are hardly a function of migrant organizations (McLeod, Owen, Khamis 2001), though, and rather take place outside of the formal organizations, but frequently use their networks. Transnational activities are also generally low and for members of organizations seem to be located in the realm of their private initiatives rather than to be a function of migrant organizations.

Chapter 6
Conclusions

Migrant organizations are today recognized actors in European cities and receive great attention from policy makers, public authorities as well as academics. Their role in politics and social welfare, in the realms of cultural and religion as well as their transnational activities for political and socio-economic change in countries of origin are currently revealed by a growing body of literature. This book has presented primary empirical case study evidence from migrant organizations in the recent immigration cities of Barcelona and Madrid, and it has drawn on existing studies on migrant organizations in established immigration cities, namely Berlin, Amsterdam and some of UK's localities renown for their multicultural approaches. The analysis has been interested in the formation of migrant organizations in these cities and the changes they have undergone over time, and it has looked into the activities and claims these organizations pursue. Thereby the aim was show how the particular city context shapes the accommodation processes of migrant organizations.

While research on migrant organizations is often concerned with their contributions to migrants' political and social integration, this study has taken a partly different perspective, drawing on the concept of accommodation. This has meant looking at processes and not at outcomes, considering activities oriented toward the side of reception as well as that of origin, and placing the processes within their city context. It is thus fair to say that in this book migrant organizations are considered actors in their own right. This is also to say that migrant organizations not necessarily, and in fact very seldom, represent broader collectives in the stricter sense. Membership relations within migrant organizations are frequently weak and often few members are active. Nevertheless, migrant organizations fulfil relevant functions in that they provide welfare services to members and broader publics, give support to cultural identification and religious orientation, engage in politics to advance the rights of migrants and improve their living conditions, and work for change and development in migrants' places of origin through transnational activities. Policy responses to migrant organizations have variously assessed the latter's role as well as the question of membership and representativeness. They have inhibited, ignored, recognized or promoted the different functions of these organizations. The diverging assessments have affected the processes of accommodation, which are characterized by variation over time and across space. Hence, in this book migrant organizations are considered one important element in the understanding of the process of international migration and the ways societies deal with it. Whether their formation, existence, activities or claims have further effects for the broader migrant community, groups or individual migrants, defined in ethnic, national or racial categories or other terms, is a question the analysis presented here has not investigated.

The chapters of this book have given more space to the recent immigration city cases since little is known about either migrant organizations or the shaping factors influencing them in these locales; to date most knowledge in this field rests on studies from the more established places. Thereby new empirical insights on new cases specifically and on the accommodation processes of migrant organizations more generally can be gained. To this end, different from existing research, this book has proposed to systematically take into account the interplay of various key elements in order to understand the accommodation of migrant organizations. Further, a transnational perspective is employed which avoids establishing a conceptual dichotomy between activities oriented toward integration into the receiving society and transnational engagements with places of origin. This has included looking at activities in both directions, albeit for migrant organizations in the more established immigration cities this was possible only in limited ways, since existing literature has often ignored migrants' transnationalism.

The book has suggested an analytical framework that accounts for the interplay of four key elements: a) the approach and attitude of powerful actors and especially the government towards migrants and their integration into society and the role accorded to migrant organizations. Approaches and attitudes, however, do not translate into a uniform set of policies. Migrants' individual reception and integration may also be addressed differently than the organizations of migrants. Therefore, the second element which has been taken into account consists of b) the existing and changing state–society relations, in particular those between state and non-state actors. Here, the changing models of local governance have opened, closed and shaped the venues for migrant organizations. The third element of this framework reflects the fact that c) in the city, influences from multiple political–institutional levels play out, and here the analysis has concentrated on national- and local-level approaches and policies. Finally, d) it is a main argument of this book to also include the immigration regime into the framework of political institutions relevant for the accommodation of migrant organizations. Existing studies on migrant organizations have not systematically included the immigration regime as a relevant influence for the formation and activities of migrant organizations. The analyses of this book, however, show that the conditions of entry, stay and work which migrants encounter in a specific place also influence the processes of accommodation. Together these elements shape the ways in which migrant organizations have developed in European cities. The elements and their combined effects have emerged from the dialogue of existing theoretical approaches and the empirical research on the Spanish city case studies. To date, explanatory approaches and their application on migrant organizations in established immigration destinations have generally used one of these elements or referred to various elements without systematically distinguishing them. The immigration regime is an exception here because it has been vastly neglected by the major part of existing studies altogether. Moreover, most frequently studies on migrant organizations have looked at their subject at one given point in time without acknowledging that these elements and therefore city contexts have changed over the decades. Against this background, comparative research has revealed differences in the accommodation of migrant organizations, especially across countries. Migrant organizations located in different places, however, also share some features and differ in other respects, and this, too, varies over time. It is the argument here that accounting for the above-mentioned key elements and their specific combinations helps to unravel and explain theses features and their changes. Thus, the first aim of this conclusion is to illustrate the benefit of this perspective by contrasting city cases along some of the combined effects. The data and knowledge on which Chapter 5 has drawn for the migrant organizations' accommodation in established immigration cities has come out of research with different theoretical approaches. Therefore, at this stage, comparison from the perspective of the proposed framework is only possible to a limited degree. The following exercise of contrasting migrant organizations in different cities nevertheless exemplifies the insights to be gained from this framework.

The second aim of this conclusion is to discuss whether there is a 'transnational paradox', or in other words, to scrutinize the assumption that migrant organizations emerge from strong links to the culture and country of origin but progressively become engaged with their situation in and the institutions of the receiving society. Many authors have sustained that in those places where migrants and their organizations encounter opportunities to participate in the relevant (local) institutions on the side of the receiving society, transnational orientations would lessen with progressive integration, and some authors conclude from their research that only in unfavourable settings which are non-conducive to migrants' integration or aim to force them into assimilationist adaptation would transnational orientations and cross-border activities remain (Layton-Henry 1990b, Koopmans, Statham 2003). Other authors have countered that a multicultural approach may also favour transnational engagement since it supports the maintenance of cultural distinctiveness and origin-country identification (Faist 2000: see expl. 214). In that case, rather than a move from 'home' to 'host' engagements, dual agendas should be more likely given the opportunities for both local integration and cross-border transnationalism. Still, these arguments are premised upon one element only, namely the approach on integration especially on the national level. This seems too narrow from the perspective of this book. Taking into account the different elements of the proposed framework thus reveals a somewhat more complex picture.

Contrasting recent and established city contexts

When contrasting the accommodation processes of migrant organizations in recent and established cities of immigration, one aspect is particularly striking. The migrant organizations investigated in the recent immigration cities of Barcelona and Madrid formed in a context of an immigration regime in which irregularity plays a major role. The existence, persistence and possible change of illegal statuses, including regularization but also the potential fall-back into irregularity, is one major aspect with which migrant organizations have dealt here. This has meant that upon the emergence of these organizations, social protection, legal issues and access to regular statuses were central to their agendas and have remained important. Advice and information about current existing social rights and services available to (irregular) migrants are now additional aspects of this work.

State institutions, both from national and local levels have recognized this function of migrant organizations, along with other non-state actors. This has also included financial state support for these organizations, although selectively and differently from place to place. National funds in the realm of immigrant reception and integration concentrated predominantly on Madrid-based organizations, and funding from the city of Madrid has benefited some of these same organizations, while in Barcelona few subsidies existed for these tasks. At the same time, state/non-state actors' relationships in Barcelona seem more favourable to migrant organizations and they have been afforded a participatory channel since the mid-1990s, in other words, at a relatively early stage of international migration. In this positive environment in Barcelona many, often small migrant organizations came into existence. In contrast, in Madrid the number of migrant organizations is smaller (although the foreign migrant population is double there), but some of these organizations have a large number of members in the several thousands, are well subsided and represented on different levels of government. The greater majority of organizations in Madrid seem rather marginalized from public attention and funding.

In the established immigration cities and localities considered in this book, immigrants arrived as guest-workers or (post-)colonial citizens and thus were equipped with secure statuses and access to social rights and services to a high degree, often comparable to those of (other) nationals. Specifically in the German and Dutch cases, state-funded welfare organizations catered to the needs of migrants and later to their families. At same time, return perspectives played an important role for both migrants and state authorities. In these contexts, migrant organizations which emerged among migrant communities in Berlin and Amsterdam were often leisure and cultural clubs. Based on a comparison of one national group, namely the Turks, in the two cities this similarity has been attributed to group factors such as cultural characteristics or the size of the immigrant group (Vermeulen 2006). However, the immigration regime, the legal and social security it granted, its transitory nature, and the existence of state and state-funded social assistance have shaped the formation of migrant organizations in both cities as well. As a consequence, other national groups show similar features, as studies from Berlin and other German cities reveal (Fijalkowski, Gillmeister 1997, Hunger 2002). Thus, rather their condition as guest-workers than the national origin can explain the similar characteristics of the organizations formed by these migrants. This situation was partly different in British localities where many immigrants were

British subjects or citizens, but did not have a workplace or a home when they arrived. Particular state attendance was absent, and access to mainstream services has often been difficult due to different kinds of barriers including discrimination and racism (McLeod, Owen, Khamis 2001: 11, Ouseley 1984: 133). In this situation, 'self-help [organizations] ... developed out of the necessity of meeting unmet needs' (McLeod, Owen, Khamis 2001: 13). These first organizations served as informal credit systems since access to housing was difficult, as an interface with mainstream services, and as providers of services on their own account. From the mid-1960s on this function was recognized by the authorities from the home office as well as from local government, which supported the organizations in their offers for practical help. These functions have expanded over time, driven both by existing state/non-state actors' relationship as well as by multiculturalism which became an important approach in the 1980s in some British cities such as Birmingham, Bradford and Leicester.

Over time, the social and political activities and roles of migrant organizations have also changed along with the changes in, first, the immigration regimes, which restricted further immigration to a considerable degree, but allowed for family reunification and contributed to more permanent settlement; second, the developing approaches on migrants' integration; and third, the reconfiguration of state/non-state actors' relationships in the last two or three decades in many places. Although with partly different contents, migrant organizations in the British and Spanish cities in focus in this book engage extensively in support and social services for migrants. The role of non-state actors and that of social initiatives in the provision of services is traditionally relatively strong in the two countries, and decentralization and new forms of local governance have further strengthened this (Soysal 1994: see Chapter 4, Rodríguez Cabrero, Codorniú 1997, Navarro Yáñez 2001). Here, existing subsidies and newly established funds to confront migration have been opened to migrant organizations, together with other non-state actors. This concerns more organizations in British localities which receive a greater part of their budget from local and other authorities (McLeod, Owen, Khamis 2001, Devadason 2009), while in the Spanish cities only a smaller number of organizations receive the same treatment (see Chapter 4 of this book). In addition, multicultural approaches that emerged specifically in some British cities in the 1980s have also led to services which aim at particular (ethnic or racial) groups, exemplified by the Afro-Caribbean Resource Centre in Brimingham (Rex, Samad 1996). Migrant organizations in the Spanish cases show a tendency toward greater openness as regards their potential membership or clientele, following the Spanish intercultural approach. Here, some migrant organizations have changed their names as is the case with Vomade, originally denominating the Dominican origin, which today is called Vomade-Vincit in order to refer to all international migrant workers. Interviewees from migrant organizations employ a distinction between (ethnic/national) 'roots' and (client) 'services' when explaining their diverging functions for those joining them seeking cultural closeness and others in search of judicial advice which is 'the same to everybody' (Interview transcript, no. 21) independent of origin.

In contrast to local migrant organizations in British and Spanish cities, in Amsterdam and Berlin welfare services were not very prominent on the agendas of migrant organizations during the first decades, given the role of the state and the existence of state-funded welfare services. In that phase migrant organizations generally received little or no attention or support from the authorities. The evolution of multicultural approaches in the 1980s brought some changes in this respect. These contributed to more differences in the accommodation of migrant organizations in the two cities. On the one hand multiculturalism was more pronounced in Amsterdam and also stemmed from the national level, while in Berlin such an approach was less prominently reflected in fewer measures which are also closer to an intercultural approach with its greater emphasis on dialogue and non-separation of groups. One the other hand, decentralization in the Netherlands in the 1980s brought more competences and funds to the municipalities and integrated the so far existing ethnically separate service provision by private foundations into local public mainstream services. In the same period, in Berlin new actors became involved in welfare services and these included migrant organizations. Case studies show that project-based activities and welfare for youth, women or other particular issues emerged among migrant organizations in Berlin in the 1980s with the city's focus on self-help initiatives, while this was hardly the case in Amsterdam before the 1990s (Schwarz 1992, Kraal 2001, Uitermark, Rossi, van Houtum 2005). The situation of Afro-Surinamese organizations in Amsterdam was different since these had been accorded a special role and were funded by the city as part of their welfare services to that community. As a consequence, welfare provision was an important activity among these organizations in the 1970s and 1980s, while it was absent on the agenda of Turkish migrant organizations before 2000 (Vermeulen 2005). At the same time, comparison between Turkish organizations in the two cities shows that in the period of extended multicultural policies and support to migrant organizations in Amsterdam during the 1980s, the growth rate of those organizations was greater there than in Berlin, taking into account the size of the immigrant population. In addition, organizations in the Dutch city were also more oriented toward interest representation and socio-cultural activities, in line with the city's approach (Vermeulen 2006: 88, Table 4.1).

Changing political–institutional settings have also influenced migrant organizations' political activities. Involvement in formal politics and interest representation is relatively strong among migrant organizations in Amsterdam. It also exists on the agendas among organizations in Berlin, although to a somewhat lesser extent (Vermeulen 2006: see Chapter 4). Here they have also participated in formal consultation at least since the 1990s (Fijalkowski, Gillmeister 1997), notwithstanding the fact that a consultative council on the level of the city(–state) was only formed in 2003. Protest action and mobilization, in turn, are hardly reported from these two cities and the participation of migrants in the public discourse is greater in Amsterdam, where interest representation is a recognized function, and more limited in Berlin (Koopmans 2004). There, migrant organizations' interest representation and network formation was in principal also welcomed, but sometimes seen with greater reservation and limited by concerns of voluntary self-separation and withdrawal from mainstream society (Schwarz 2001). Data from local migrant organizations in the UK, in turn, suggests that notwithstanding a broad variety of activities and strong involvement in the delivery of services, politics is generally not among the main activities of migrant organizations (Soysal 1994: see Chapter 6, McLeod, Owen, Khamis 2001). Nevertheless, the mobilization of migrants, their organizations and their claims in public discourse are more prevalent and seem particularly strong in those cities and urban regions where multicultural policies have played an important role (Koopmans 2004). Already in the 1950s migrant organizations used their networks to mobilize collectively, and many organizations have participated in the campaigns against racisms and discrimination (McLeod, Owen, Khamis 2001). In the cities pursuing multicultural policies, mobilizations in favour of migrants' social, cultural and religious rights, often through migrant organizations' networks, are greatly documented (Rex, Samad 1996, Vertovec 1996b, Koopmans 2004). Thus, migrant organizations here seem to use the resources and networks of migrant organizations for mobilization, but politics is not considered a function of these organizations.

From the Spanish cases a different picture emerges. The delivery of services to migrants and the participation in formal and informal politics go hand in hand. This feature is particularly strong among the investigated Madrid-based migrant organizations which participate in the national and sometimes also in the local consultative councils for migrants' integration, the membership criteria for which include the delivery of services and the successful handling of subsidies. In Barcelona, where there are no such membership requirements, smaller organizations which do not receive funding also participate in the local integration council. Since 2005 there has been central governmental funding for local migrant organizations' work in the reception and integration of migrants, channelled through the municipality. The result is that more organizations in Barcelona now receive funding and most of them have been members of the integration council. Thus a linkage between services and formal politics here now also emerges to some degree. In addition, protest mobilization for regularization and the rights of irregulars as well as for voting rights for migrants exist. Here, some of the actors in Barcelona have engaged in more contentious action while those in Madrid did so when they emerged around 1990, but since they have become more established and connected to different political levels today they are less inclined to participate in radical actions such as occupations of public buildings.

The identified key elements help one to understand the processes of accommodation of migrant organizations in European cities. They combine in specific contexts and thereby influence specific ways of accommodation. Systematic city comparison across and within countries is likely to reveal more clear-cut patterns than what can be seen from the city contrasts of this study. Still, this illustration shows the importance of the dynamic interplay of the elements for accommodation processes.

A transnational paradox?

Research so far has generally supported the idea of the ethnic as well as the transnational 'paradox'. The 'ethnic paradox' assumes that migrant organizations undergo an evolution from ethno-cultural identity formation toward greater openness and progressive integration into the society of reception (Park, Miller 1969, Faist 1996, see Chapter 2 of this book). In parallel it is also expected that while migrant organizations are at first more inclined toward the places of origin upon formation, they gradually move toward orientations and activities related to the place of reception (Miller 1981, Layton-Henry 1990). Today, the major part of migration scholars as well as policy-makers and society more generally seem to accept that migrants form their own organizations and public authorities often support these organizations along with the recognition of ethnic and cultural pluralism, whether from a multicultural or intercultural approach. Transnational orientations, in turn, are still seen with greater reservation if not rejection.

Although the majority of the available studies on migrant organizations in established immigration localities show that an evolution from origin-country toward reception-side orientation has occurred in many cases, this has not meant that origin-country relations disappear. Some organizations have maintained dual agendas, an aspect which only more recently receives greater attention in migration scholarship. In addition, dynamics and processes of accommodation in recent immigration places question this observation as a generalized assumption. Migrant organizations there rather evolve from reception-side orientated actors into transnational (development) actors, in general without lessening prior activities. Here again, the degree to which this is the case and the specific activities organizations undertake in this framework are locally different, since the political–institutional contexts that influence them also vary from place to place.

In Berlin and Amsterdam, initial migrant organizations since the 1960s often were related to actors and institutions in the origin country, and parts of their activities concerned political and socio-economic changes and development in that country. This was promoted by immigration regimes organized around temporary stay and timely return. To a certain degree this idea persisted in Berlin where authorities and politicians on national and local levels continued to articulate an 'integration or return' option (Meier-Braun 1988) in the 1980s. It has also led to some ambivalence in the acceptance of origin-country orientations and a certain tolerance as long as German society and citizenship are not concerned. In parallel, migrant organizations were encouraged to participate in local politics and welfare in Berlin. In this context, claims and standpoints referring to actors and situations in the country of origin exist in the local public discourse by migrants and their organizations. Compared to other German cities such transnational references are lower in Berlin, though, but higher than in other European cities, including Amsterdam (Koopmans 2004). Taking the example of two Turkish umbrella organizations in Berlin – both which emerged in the early 1980s – recent research shows that one type of organization focuses exclusively on Germany, while a second type maintains the idea of transnational politics, since ties and political regulations of the origin country influence the lives of the local migrant community (Yurdakul 2006). In addition, new (Turkish) hometown associations emerge in Berlin, but these address integration issues as well (Çağlar 2006). From the available studies it is very difficult to assess the degree and different forms of transnationalism among migrant organizations in Berlin. Still, these show that existing transnational orientations and activities are today often not a result of return expectations, but may go along with settlement and integration efforts. The combination of the long-held return perspective in Germany's and Berlin's policies on migrants, the more assimilationist approach on the national level and the intercultural policies of Berlin seem to have contributed to the overall mixed picture. While the previously mentioned Turkish umbrella organizations were approached in similar ways by the local authorities and the foreigners' commissioner in the 1980s and 1990s, this may be changing today. Considering the financial resources allocated to the two organizations by public authorities, the first type, which receives around 1 million euros in subsidies, seems more welcomed than the second, which has a budget of only 27,000 Euros. The future course of both national and local political–institutional developments will further shape the accommodation processes and influence their outlook in the long run (Yurdakul 2006: 449).

Different from the situation in Berlin, ethnic minority policies from Dutch national and local levels in Amsterdam since the 1980s rejected the maintenance of home-country return options as a governmental policy and intended to make minority cultures part of local society. In line with this, recent migration–development initiatives do not intend to support migrant organizations, but rather focus on more private, individual efforts (De Haas 2006). Migrant organizations in that Dutch city have transnational activities on their agenda but to a lower degree, and their share has declined over the decades. Recent research on hometown associations from African migrants in Amsterdam furthermore sustains that an increasingly restrictive immigration regime and more difficult living conditions for these migrants have made it more difficult to engage in transnational activities (Mazzucato, Kabki 2009). Contrasting this with the British localities, some differences become visible. Return did not form part of British immigration regulations and although emerging organizations were sometimes related to political developments in the origin country, they were more concerned with the situation in the places where they lived. Here, cultural identity as well as 'home-country development' are often seen as part of the private realm (Rex 1987, Lacroix 2010). Where transnational engagements continue to exist or re-emerge they have often changed their character from personal hometown engagements toward a more philanthropic motivation of relatively well-established migrants (Lacroix 2010). The recent migration–development efforts of development agencies and some integration departments have so far not been taken up by many localities, local actors or migrant organizations in these three countries (De Haas 2006). Whether this changes and brings more attention to the transnational activities of migrant organization will further shape their trajectories.

The investigated migrant organizations in the Spanish localities, in turn, were concerned with the situation in the place of arrival and reception when they emerged, leaving little room for collective hometown engagements. Only over time did they start to add 'home' development to their agendas, although this was an objective at the point of formation for many of them, reflected in founding documents and statutes. The more established organizations in particular, with more resources, many of which are located in Madrid, engage in transnational development activities now. These activities receive great recognition and economic support in the framework of the newer migration-development and co-development policies which either stem from or involve local governments. They specifically aim to support migrants' collective engagements in their places of origin. Here, the city of Madrid has played an important role since the late 1990s. Moreover, co-development forms part of local, and today also national, approaches on integration into local society premised on the recognition of migrants' transnational engagement with their places of origin and their involvement in the local networks in the realm of development cooperation, as well as that of integration. Here, migrant organizations working in transnational cooperation maintain their work for integration. So far, fewer organizations in Barcelona seem to be involved in those activities. This can be explained by the fact that the city has not had a proactive policy in this respect, and organizations have also not received greater support for many other activities, and are therefore generally less established as compared to some of Madrid's migrant organizations.

Hence, some city contexts have worked as an actively encouraging environment for transnational activities of migrant organizations. In the case of Madrid this is explicitly connected to the approach on integration. In other cities, political-institutional contexts in the realms of both immigration and integration rather promoted transnationalism as an alternative to long-term settlement and integration. This is exemplified by the case of Berlin where migrants' return and investment in the country of origin still received symbolic and financial support from local and national levels in the 1980s. Today existing transnational activities of migrant organizations in Berlin, however, form part of the agenda of political and social integration in the receiving society and are hardly linked to return perspectives, in particular not among such established groups as the Turks. Cities where multicultural policies were stronger, where return policies were non-existent or not very prominent in the last decades and where transnational activities were not encouraged by other means, have obviously contributed to lower levels of transnationalism among migrant organizations. However, at this stage, the picture emerging from existing research is very mixed. Some studies exclusively concentrate on transnationalism while others ignore this possibility and pay attention to activities related to the situation and rights in the reception country only. So far this does not allow for a systematic comparison of the degree and forms of transnational activities among migrant organizations in European cities. Still, rather than a paradoxical situation which dissolves over time, along with integration, migrants' transnationalism forms part of the accommodation of migrant organizations in European cities. It does so to different degrees and in different ways, though. It is not necessarily linked to return perspectives, but may also go along with settlement and integration into local society. Among some organizations, transnational activities in origin countries also refer to integration either by activating political institutions there to act on their behalf before receiving side institutions and governments (see also Østergaard-Nielsen 2003) or by providing information services for future migrants as exemplified by the cases from the Madrid sample. For others transnationalism is a philanthropic activity expressing closeness to the places of origin of migrants and their descendants.

Future accommodation processes of migrant organizations in European cities will be further shaped by changing political–institutional contexts. The now global migrant and development debate has already led to some new perspectives and instruments in the promotion of migrant communities and organizations as agents of development in their origin places (De Haas 2006, Faist, Fauser 2011). So far these are still relatively limited in most localities. Nevertheless, some cities, not only in Spain, but also in Germany and the UK have already started to set up initiatives. Whether and how these will be continued and expanded will influence new formations, transformation and activities of migrant organizations. Further, the role of non-state actors and self-help initiatives are gaining importance all over Europe. New forms of local governance emerge and these involve locally specific forms of the incorporation of new actors in implementation, consultation and decision-making. This has already opened venues for migrant organizations' recognition and funding in the last decades and currently seems to be expanding. The ways in which this affects migrant organizations greatly depend on the approach to integration in place. Various trends point toward more intercultural and diversity-oriented approaches. While the former put more emphasis on dialogue among different (ethnic or racial) minority and majority groups, the latter concentrates on the individual and issue-specific solutions to social problems. In cities that currently follow diversity approaches in particular, such as Amsterdam and Birmingham, representation of ethnic and racial groups has been deactivated while organizations that offer particular services and display greater openness toward other local groups and individuals receive greater attention and resources (Uitermark, Rossi, van Houtum 2005). Lastly, immigration regimes have become more heterogeneous in the last decades than at the beginning of post-war immigration. Today, many different categories of migrants exist which differ in their conditions of entry, stay and work, and the migrant populations in European cities are therefore characterized by greater diversity concerning their status, resources and needs. The analysis on migrant organizations in the more established immigration cities has mainly concentrated on those formed form the guest-worker and (post-)colonial groups which were the most important types of inflows for many decades. It is likely that today's more heterogeneous types of immigration will bring about more varied forms of accommodation processes among organizations emerging from these different types of migrants.

Appendix 1
Methodology for the Spanish City Cases

The empirical research to the Spanish city cases, as any other studies, started with the revision of existent studies, in the realm of migrant organizations' formation, mobilization and participation in that specific case. Not only is there not one single theory, insights are based upon different types of data and methods, including often more descriptive quantitative surveys, media-content analysis and qualitative case studies both concentrating on single cases and comparative approaches focusing on various national or ethnic groups, countries and also, although to a smaller degree, cities. An important stream in current research tells us whether political institutions have an influence on migrant collective formation and what the outcomes of particular institutional features are as compared to others. Very little insight is provided in these studies on how exactly these institutional contexts and their different elements issue their influence on migrant organizations. Moreover, studies following an institutionalist perspective, whether these are constructed upon sociological neo-institutionalism or political-opportunity structure approaches, generally start with a strong concept of which institutional structures matter for migrants' agency. Different from that, research for this book started with a more inductive approach where the research field and the elements taken into account emerge through the ongoing research (Flick, von Kardorff, Steinke 2005: 17, Amann, Hirschauer 1997). In that sense, grounded theory provided an appropriate framework for a research design which is open, flexible and procedural in nature (Glaser, Strauss 1967, Strauss, Corbin 1996). This seemed especially adequate for the study of migrant organizations in recent immigration cities where little research has been done so far on these organizations and where migration research focusing on other aspects, such as national level policies or inflows has pointed to the many differences as compared to older destinations of post-war migration in Europe (King, Black 1997, Baldwin-Edwards, Arango 1999, Danese 2001). This proceeding did, however, not imply to ignore existent research in the field which is also not required from a research strategy following grounded theory (Strauss, Corbin 1996: in particular Chapter 4, Strübing 2008: 57–8). This research strategy had two main implications. At the beginning of research, the interest for accommodation processes in cities neither expected to go beyond local institutions nor to include transnationalism. Both seemed crucial after first data collection, analysis and consultation of existing research and theoretical concepts which helped sharpening the research question in the course of the research process (Flick 2005: 258). This has brought about new insights on the processes of accommodation which differ from existing knowledge.

The strategy of sampling is purposeful and follows the theoretical interest (Kuzel 1992, Strauss, Corbin 1996: 148–50, Patton 2005: 169–70). This research distinguishes two strategies which were pursued in the two stages of the field research. First sampling concentrated on the two Spanish major cities with almost the same percentage of migrant population. These were chosen in order to potentially contrast the driving forces and factors provided by different local contexts. Subsequently five migrant organizations in each of the cities were selected for in-depth investigation. This sample was meant to reflect different national groups since the interest was on the role of the institutional contexts. Thereby variation included covering organizations from migrant groups with different duration of their presence in the cities as reflected in statistical data on inflows and growth of migrant populations. The second strategy of sampling is based on a first stage of data gathering and analysis; against this background three particular phenomena, here called 'fields of action and contention' were identified for further in-depth investigation. These three fields embrace protest on regularization, struggles for local voting rights, and transnational action and development cooperation. Whereas the selection of the cities and the migrant organizations served as an entrance to the field and allowed for answering questions related to the emergence, existence and changes of the organizations, the selection of the three fields of action and contention emerged out of the research process and concern the activities, struggles and positions of migrant organizations. The two strategies of sampling can also be seen part of the triangulation employed in this research strategy (see below).

Data, methods and triangulation: Interviews in context

Field research constitutes the most important source for data collection for this research and was carried out in two main stages. The first stage of field research took place between February and March 2006 and the second from September to October of the same year. Before, in between and after these stages, data collection continued, especially in the gathering of additional documents and contents of web-pages. A short field trip in September 2007 served to complement the primary data, but also to gather some specific documents and studies carried out by a number of institutes in Spain.

Interviews constitute the core material of the study. Interview material shall not be considered 'pure' information, and is rather to be seen 'in context', this is to say in the context of the overall interview situation and in the context of other data, hence triangulation. Further data consists of written documents and other 'naturally' existent material from the selected migrant organizations, but also from others when available, as well as from the public authorities at different levels of government, including written concepts, reports, self-descriptions, flyers, contents of webpages, journals, year books, DVDs, calls for tender, legal texts and press articles. In addition, participant observation at a few public events as well as before, during and after interviews was possible.

The forms of interviews in qualitative research range from more to less standardized and from considering them from 'giving answers to questions' to 'negotiated texts' (Fontana, Frey 2000, Silvermann 2001: 87). In this present research, interviews are meant to constitute a source of information in relation to the perspectives and meanings articulated by the interviewee. The interview was generally unstructured, although in the second stage of field research interviews were focused more strictly on the three fields already mentioned. Interview material is thus one part of the data used to reveal aspects and shaping forces concerning the accommodation of migrant organizations, gained by comparing codes of interviews and other documents, complemented by literature review and further data gathering and analysis.

This entails consideration of triangulation in various respects: first, through the two stages of field research and two sampling strategies; second, by collecting different types of data, including different categories of 'producers' of these data, that is public authorities, migrant organizations' representatives, NGOs, trade unions, as well as other researchers. In addition, persons with different relations to the respective migrant organization were encountered for the interview. Some of the interviewees are founding members, some of them currently act as the president, some of them were representing the organization in the public and participatory platforms; others rather take care of the day to day work, or can rather be considered as staff of relatively professional non-state agencies. In other instances these are (non-paid) engaged persons working for solidarity with migrants. Repeated interviewing with most of the organization meant talking to different persons in the two stages of field research. This allows accounting for different perspectives on the role and working of migrant organizations not only across, but also within individual organizations. Thereby triangulation intends to contribute to complementary perspective and a comprehensive understanding of the phenomenon of interest (Denzin, Lincoln 2000, Flick 2004), namely the process of accommodation.

Field access

Identifying migrant organizations followed a definition of a voluntary association composed of a majority of migrants (Moya 2005). In addition, these should be formally registered. Field access was not without problems, however. Discovering an organization, knowing whether it complies with the criteria, contacting the organization, and eventually locating it was not always an easy task. To find migrant organizations, different sources were used: accessible public registries, various webpages, press-articles reporting on organizations' activities and claims, existing lists of member organizations of consultative bodies, lists provided by embassies, online databases offered by research and networking projects, as well as suggestions by other researchers. Nonetheless, the organizations were difficult to find and correspondence with the definitions could often only be made after collecting some information on an organization. While an organization may appear to be a migrant organization, it is sometimes led by native Spanish people. The field also proved relatively volatile where organizations emerge and disappear; they often have no locale or move frequently form one place to another. Three of the ten organizations investigated in-depth in the course of this study had moved in the period from the first stage of field research (spring) to the second stage (autumn) of the same year. Three others had just moved into new office spaces shortly before the first interview.

Data analysis

At the beginning, the first interviews were fully transcribed, and first coding and comparison of codes of individual interviews led to further sampling of additional migrant organizations as well as later on of the fields of action and contention for more in-depth analysis. Later interviews were more selectively transcribed, in relation to previously identified codes. In addition, particular paragraphs or parts of documents were also coded, as a number of flyers and publications from migrant organizations or from the municipal integration plans for instance. This procedure also includes going back and forth to many of the audio files, and progressively transcribing additional fragments as new codes emerged or became more precise.

Appendix 2
Visited Institutions

ACCD –Agència Catalana de Cooperació al Desenvolupament.
ACRS – Associació Catalana de Residents Senegalesos.
ACULCO – Asociación Cultural pro Colombia e Iberoamérica.
AECUATORIE – Asociación Ecuatoriana de Inmigrantes Radicados
  en España.
AESCO – América-España, solidaridad y cooperación.
Ajuntament de Barcelona, Gabinete Técnic d' Immigració.
Ajuntament de Barcelona, Regidoria delegada per al Pla Municipal
  d´Immigració.
Ajuntament de Barcelona, Sector Serveis Socials, Direcció de Serveis de
  Dona i Drets Civils.
AMAYA – Asociación de Asesoramiento y de Rumania.
AMIC – Associació d´ajuda mútua d´Immigrants a Catalunya.
ATIMCA – Asociación de Trabajadores y Inmigrantes Marroquíes de
  Cataluña.
ATIME – Asociación de Trabajadores e Inmigrantes Marroquíes en España.
Ayuntamiento de Madrid, Codesarollo y Emergencias, Departamento
  de Cooperación, Dirección General de Inmigración, Cooperación y
  Voluntariado.
Ayuntamiento de Madrid, Cooperación al Desarollo, Departamento de
  Cooperación.
Ayuntamiento de Madrid, Departamento de Estudios y Desarollo de
  Buenas Prácticas, Dirección General de Participación Ciudadano,
  Dirección General de Inmigración, Cooperación y Voluntariado.
Ayuntamiento de Madrid, Dirección General de Inmigración, Cooperación
  y Voluntariado.
Casal Argentí de Barcelona.
CITE – Comisiones Obreras.
CPB – Centro Peruano de Barcelona.
Delegación del Gobierno en Barcelona.
Diputació de Barcelona, Servei de Polítiques de Diversitat I Ciutadania.
Ecuador Llactacarú, Asociación de Inmigrantes Ecuatorianos en Catalunya
  para la Solidaridad y la Cooperación.
Fedelatina – Federación de entidades Latinoamericanas de Cataluña.
Fons Català de Cooperació al Desenvolupament.

Grupo Parlamentario PSOE.

MDLP – Movimiento para la Paz, el Desarme y la Libertad.

Ministerio de Trabajo y Asuntos Sociales, Subdirección General de Relaciones
Institucionales.

Observatorio de las Migraciones y de la Convivencia Intercultural de la
Ciudad de Madrid.

REMCODE – Red Euromediterranea de Cooperación al Desarollo.

VOMADE-Vicint – Asociación Voluntariado de Madres Dominicanas-
Voluntariado Integración Internacional de Trabajadores.

Appendix 3
Evolution of Migrant Population in Barcelona and Madrid

Table A3.1   Top ten of non-communitarian migrants in the City of Barcelona

Evolution 1996–2008				
Nationality	**1996**	**2000**	**2004**	**2008**
Ecuador	202	2,703	32,946	22,943
Bolivia	110	268	4,810	18,759
Pakistan	614	2,129	10,198	15,966
Peru	2,094	5,669	13,163	15,240
Morocco	3,196	6,074	13,594	13,998
Colombia	703	2,288	13,307	13,032
China	804	1,929	7,195	12,938
Argentina	1,871	1,750	11,437	9,922
Brazil	492	1,034	3,557	9,006
Dom. Republic	1,066	3,349	6,777	7,101

Source: Ajuntament de Barcelona, Departament d'Estadística, padró municipal d'habitants (various years), data as of 1 January.

Table A3.2   Top ten of non-communitarian migrants in the City of Madrid

Evolution 2002–2008					
Nationality	1996	2000	2002	2004	2008
Ecuador	1,044	30,398	107,346	140,435	97,852
Bolivia	332	1,383	5,616	14,578	44,760
Peru	6,387	11,624	17,933	26,886	38,930
Colombia	1,952	12,951	42,692	44,089	37,085
China	1,384	4,551	8,926	16,157	26,506
Morocco	6,823	13,613	19,853	24,236	26,465
Dom. Republic	3,850	9,114	13,283	16,496	23,008
Paraguay	93	128	344	2,007	18,929
Brazil	754	1,741	3,616	6,070	17,188
Argentina	2,009	2,583	7,482	11,163	10,123

Source: Ayuntamiento de Madrid, Dirección General de Estadística, Padrón de habitantes (various years); 1996 as of 1 May, 2000 as of 1 January, 2002, 2004, 2008, as of 1 July.

Primary Sources

Chapters 3 and 4

List of statistical references

OPI 2004. Anuario de Extranjería, Ministerio de Trabajo y Asuntos Sociales, Observatorio Permanente de la Inmigración, Madrid.

OPI 2008. Anuario Estadístico de Inmigración, Ministerio de Trabajo y Inmigración, Observatorio Permanente de la Inmigración, Madrid.

INE 2008. INEbase. Censos de Población. Instituto Nacional de Estadística.

MTAS 2003. Anuario de Migraciones. Ministerio de Trabajo y Asuntos Sociales, Madrid.

List of legal documents

LO 7/1985, Ley Orgánica 7/1985 sobre derechos y libertades de los extranjeros en España, BOE núm. 158 de 3 de julio de 1985.

LO 4/2000, Ley Orgánica 4/2000 sobre derechos y libertades de los extranjeros en España y su integración social, BOE núm. 10 de 12 de enero de 2000.

LO 8/2000, Ley Orgánica 8/2000, de reforma de la Ley Orgánica 4/2000, de 11 enero, sobre derechos y libertades de los extranjeros en España y su integración social, BOE núm. 307 de 23 de diciembre de 2000.

LO 11/2003, Ley Orgánica 11/2003, de medidas concretas en materia de seguridad ciudadana, violencia doméstica e integración social de los extranjeros, BOE núm. 234 de 30 de septiembre de 2003.

LO 14/2003, Ley Orgánica 14/2003, reforma de LO 8/2000, mod. 4/2000 y LO 11/2003, BOE núm. 279 de 21 de noviembre de 2003.

Tribunal Constitucional, 2007, STC 265/2007, de 20 de diciembre de 2007

Orden TAS/1783/2006, de 2 de junio.

RD 367/2001 por el que se regula la composición, competencias y régimen de funcionamiento del Foro para la Integración Social de los Inmigrantes, BOE núm. 83 de 8 de abril de 2001.

RD 3/2006 2001 por el que se regula la composición, competencias y régimen de funcionamiento del Foro para la Integración Social de los Inmigrantes, BOE núm. 14 de enero de 2006.

Others

Foro 2002. Memoria de las actividades realizadas por Foro para la Integración Social durante 2002.

Foro 2003. Memoria de las actividades realizadas por Foro para la Integración Social durante 2002.

Foro 2007. Dictamen del Foro para Foro para la Integración Social sobre el Proyecto de Plan Estratégico de Ciudadanía e Integración 2007–2010.

MAS 1994. Plan Integración, *Plan* para la *Integración* Social de los *Inmigrantes*, aprobado por Acuerdo del Consejo de Ministros de 2 de diciembre de *1994,* Ministerio de Asuntos Sociales (MAS), Madrid.

MIN 2001. Programa Global de Regulación y Coordinación de la Extranjería y la Inmigración en España (Programa GRECO), Resolución de 17 de abril 2001, aprobado por el Acuerdo del Consejo de Ministros, BOE núm. 101, of 27 april 2001, Ministerio del Interior (MIN), Madrid.

MTAS 2007. Plan Estratégico Ciudadanía e Integración 2007–2010, aprobado por Acuerdo del Consejo de Ministros de 16 de febrero de 2007, Ministerio de Trabajo y Asuntos Sociales (MTAS), Madrid.

MTIN 2009. Fondo de Apoyo. BOE Núm. 80, 2.04.2009 and BOE Núm.157 Martes 30.06.2009.

Documents, City of Barcelona

Ajuntament de Barcelona 2006. Mèmoria 2005, Gabinet Tècnic d´Immigració, Ajuntament de Barcelona, Barcelona.

Ajuntament de Barcelona 2002. Pla Municipal d´Immigració, Barcelona.

Ajuntament de Barcelona 2004. Informe sobre 'El dret a vot per als immigrants'. Regiodoria Delegada per al Pla Municipal d`Immigració.

Ajuntament de Barcelona 2008. Plan de trabajo immigración 2008–2011.

Ajuntament de Barcelona. Municipal registry of associations.

Ajuntament de Barcelona. Departament d´Estadistics, Padró municipal d´habitants (various years).

Ajuntament de Barcelona. Subvencions (various years).

Ajuntament de Barcelona-OND 2006. Memòria 2005. Oficina de la No Discriminació, Regidora de Dona i Drets Civils.

Ajuntament de Barcelona 1997. Consell Municipal d`Immigració. Normes Reguladores.

Ajuntament de Barcelona 1998. Carta Municipal de Barcelona, Llei 22/1998, de 30 de desembre, DOGC no. 2801.

Documents, City of Madrid

Ayuntamiento de Madrid 2003. Memoria Anual del Area de Gobierno de Empleo y Servicios al Ciudadano.

Ayuntamiento de Madrid 2004. Reglamento Orgánico de Participación Ciudadana.
Ayuntamiento de Madrid 2005a. Plan Madrid de Convivencia Social e Intercultural.
Ayuntamiento de Madrid 2005b. Plan General de Cooperación 2005–2008.
Ayuntamiento de Madrid, Dirección General de Estadística (various years).
Ayuntamiento de Madrid. Muncipal registry of associations.
Ayuntamiento de Madrid. Programa Cooperación al Desarollo. Memoria de Actividades and Subvenciones (various years).
Observatorio Madrid. 2005. *Sinopsis Proceso Consulta Social: Plan de Acción para el impulso y creación de las Mesas de Diálogo y Convivencia de la Ciudad de Madrid.* Madrid: Madrid Convive. Observatorio de las Migraciones y de la Convivencia Intercultural de la Ciudad de Madrid.

Other sources

ACRS website. Available at: www.senegalesos.org [accessed 19 September 2008].
ATIME 2002. Informe de gestión, 4. Congreso de ATIME, Madrid.
Cinco Días from 18./19. June 2005.
Coordinadora 2004. Press release from 7 June 2004. Available at: www.rebelion. org [accessed 31 August 2006].
El País, 15 January 2000.
El País, 16 November 2004.
El Mundo, 6 June 2004.
Europa Press, 20 March 2003.
Europa Press, 27 October 2004.
Europa Press, 18 March 2005.
FAVB 2001, Press note from 22.01.2001: Més de 300 immigrants continuen en vaga de fam a l´església del Pí. Available at: www.canal-h.net [accessed 2 March 2009].
Fons Català 2006. Co-développement Catalogne- Sénégal: leçons de 10 ans d'expérience. Évaluation du projet Migration et Développement Local (MIDEL) et des actions préalables. Fons Català de Cooperació al Desenvolupament: Barcelona.
Fons Català website. Available at: www.fonscatala.org [accessed 10 May 2007].
LIA 1999. LIA/Eurocities Thematic Sub-Report. Promoting the participation of migrants and ethnic minorities in the local political life, Brussels.
Llactacarú website. www.llacta.org [accessed 10 May 2007].
Red Ciudadana 2002. Press Release 2002. Available at: www.ania.urcm.net/ noticia, [accessed 9 December 2002].
VOMADE 2003. Primer Congreso de Asociaciones Dominicanas en el Mundo. Madrid: Betania.
VOMADE 2005. Memoria de actividades 2005.

Chapter 5

Berlin 2006. Pressemitteilung der Stadt Berlin vom 26.04.2006, Beauftragter für Integration und Migration.

Berlin 2009. Senatsverwaltung für Integration, Arbeit und Soziales 'Berlin gemeinsam gestalten. Der Berliner Landesbeirat für Integrations- und Migrationsfragen'.

Berlin 2011. Available at: www.berlin.de/lb/intmig/publikationen/index.htm [accessed 15 March 2011].

Berliner Zeitung 1997.

BRAP 2011. Birmingham Race Action Programme, available at: www.brap.org.uk [accessed 15 March 2011].

Bundesregierung 2011. Pressemitteilung vom 13.01.2011.

Amsterdam 2011. Advisory Council Integration and Diversity, available at: www. adviesraaddiversiteit.amsterdam.nl [accessed 15 March 2011].

Der Spiegel 1983.

Deutscher Bundestag 2010. Pressemitteilung des Unterausschuss Bürgerschaftliches Engagement vom 21.10.2010.

TBB 2011. Türkischer Bund Berlin Brandenburg, available at: www.tbb-berlin.de [accessed 15 March 2011].

TGB 2011. Türkische Gemeinde zu Berlin, available at: www.tgb-berlin.de [accessed 15 March 2011].

Interview with public officials, Integration Department Berlin, 2010.

Bibliography

Agrela, B. and Dietz, G. 2006. Nongovernmental versus Governmental Actors? Multilevel Governance and Immigrant Integration Policy in Spain, in *Local Citizenship in Recent Countries of Immigration: Japan in Comparative Perspective*, edited by T. Tsuda. Lanham, MD: Lexington Books, 205–33.

Aja, E. 2006. La evolución de la normativa sobre inmigración, in *Veinte Años de Inmigración en España: Perspectivas Juridícas y Sociológicas (1985–2004)*, edited by E. Aja and J. Arango. Barcelona: Fundació CIDOB, 17–44.

Aja, E. and Díez, L. 2005. La participación política de los inmigrantes. *Puntos de Vista*, 2, 7–20.

Alba, R. and Nee, V. 2003. *Remaking the American Mainstream: Assimilation and Contemporary Immigration*. Cambridge, MA: Harvard University Press.

Alexander, M. 2003. Local policies toward migrants as an expansion of host-stranger relations: A proposed typology. *Journal of Ethnic and Migration Studies*, 29(3), 411–30.

Alexander, M. 2004. Comparing Local Policies toward Migrants: An Analytical Framework, a Typology and Preliminary Survey Results, in *Citizenship in European Cities: Immigrants, Local Politics and Integration Policies*, edited by R. Penninx, K. Kraal, M. Martiniello and S. Vertovec. Aldershot: Ashgate, 57–84.

Amann, K. and Hirschauer, S. 1997. *Die Befremdung der eigenen Kultur: Ein Programm*. Frankfurt am Main: Suhrkamp.

Ancin, D. 2004. El asociacionismo de los inmigrantes marroquíes y senegaleses en la ciudad de Granada. *Actes del IV Congrés sobre la immigració a Espanya: Ciutadania i Participació, Girona*.

Andersen, U. 1990. Consulative Institutions for Migrant Workers, in *The Political Rights of Migrant Workers in Western Europe*, edited by Z. Layton-Henry. London: Sage Publications, 113–26.

Andreotti, A., García, M., Gomez, A., Hespanha, P., Kazepov, Y. and Mingione, E. 2001. Does a Southern European Model Exist? *Journal of European Area Studies*, 9(1), 43–62.

Andrew, C. and Goldsmith, M. 1998. From Local Government to Local Governance – and Beyond? *International Political Science Review*, 19(2), 101–17.

Antalovsky, E. and Wolffhardt, A. 2002. *Migration und Integration: Teil 3. Kontext Staat und Kommune*. Wien: Europaforum Wien.

Aparicio, R. and Tornos, A. 2003. Towards an Analysis of Spanish Integration Policy, in *The Integration of Immigrants in European Societies. National*

Differences and Trends of Convergence, edited by F. Heckmann and D. Schnapper. Stuttgart: Lucius & Lucius, 213–52.

Aragón Medina, J., Artiaga Leiras, A., Haidour, M.A., Martínez Poza, A. and Rocha Sánchez, F. 2009. *Las políticas locales para la integración de los inmigrantes y la participación de los agentes sociales.* Madrid: Catarata.

Arango, J. 2000. Becoming a country of immigration at the end of the twentieth century: The case of Spain, in *Eldorado or Fortress? Migration in Southern Europe*, edited by R. King, G. Lazaridis and C.G. Tsardanidēs. Basingstoke: Macmillan Press, 253–76.

Auriat, N. and Rochet, L. 2001. Preface, in *Multicultural Policies and Modes of Citizenship in European Cities*, edited by A. Rogers and J. Tillie. Aldershot: Ashgate, ix–xiii.

Back, L., Keith, M., Khan, A., Shukra, K. and Solomos, J. 2002. New Labour's White Heart: Politics, Multiculturalism, and the Return of Assimilation. *The Political Quarterly*, 73(4), 445–54.

Baldwin-Edwards, M. 1999. Where Free Markets Reign: Aliens in the Twilight Zone, in *Immigrants and the Informal Economy in Southern Europe*, edited by M. Baldwin-Edwards and J. Arango. London: Frank Cass Publishers, 1–15.

Baldwin-Edwards, M. and J. Arango. (eds). 1999. *Immigrants and the Informal Economy in Southern Europe*. London: Frank Cass Publishers

Ballis Lal, B. 1990. *The Romance of Culture in an Urban Civilization: Robert E. Park on Race and Ethnic Relations in Cities.* London: Routledge.

Bauböck, R. 2003. Reinventing Urban Citizenship. *Citizenship Studies*, 7(2), 139–60.

Blanco Fernández de Valderrama, C. 2001. La integración de los inmigrantes. Fundamentos para abordar una política global de intervención. *Migraciones*, 10, 207–48.

Blaschke, J. 1996. *Förderung von Selbsthilfegruppen und Selbsthilfeorganisationen in Immigrantenmilieus - Erfahrungen aus der Berliner Praxis.* Berlin: Edition Parabolis.

Bloemraad, I. 2005. The Limits of de Tocqueville: How Government Facilitates Organisational Capacity in Newcomer Communities. *Journal of Ethnic and Migration Studies*, 31(5), 865–87.

Bousetta, H. 1997. Citizenship and political participation in France and the Netherlands: Reflections on two local cases. *New Community*, 23(2), 215–31.

Brenner, N. 1999. Globalisation as reterritorialisation: The re-scaling of urban governance in the European Union. *Urban Studies*, 36(3), 431–51.

Breton, R. 1964. Institutional Completeness of Ethnic Communities and the Personal Relations of Immigrants. *The American Journal of Sociology*, 70(2), 193–205.

Brubaker, R. 1994. *Citizenship and Nationhood in France and Germany.* Cambridge, MA: Harvard University Press.

Brugué, Q., Goma, R. and Subirats, J. 2001. Multilevel Governance and Europeanization: The Case of Catalonia, in *Europeanization and the Southern*

Periphery, edited by K. Featherstone and G. Kazamias. London: Frank Cass Publishers, 95–118.

Bruquetas Callejo, M., Fuentes Moreno, J.F. and Walliser Martinez, A. 2000. Bottom-up? Grassroot initiatives and urban governance in Madrid and Barcelona, in *On the Origins of Urban Development Programmes in Nine European Countries*, edited by P. de Decker, J. Vranken and I. van Nieuwenhuyze. Antwerpen: University of Antwerpen, 139–63.

Bundesamt für Migration und Flüchtlinge. 2007. *Migrationsbericht 2007*. Berlin.

Bundesamt für Migration und Flüchtlinge. 2009. *Migrationsbericht 2009*. Berlin.

Cabellos Espiérrez, M.À. and Roig Molés, E. 2006. El tratamiento jurídico del extranjero en situación regular, in *Veinte Años de Inmigración en España: Perspectivas Juridícas y Sociológicas (1985–2004)*, edited by E. Aja and J. Arango. Barcelona: Fundació CIDOB, 113–27.

Çağlar, A.S. 2006. Hometown Associations and Grassroots Transnationalism. *Global Networks*, 6(1), 1–22.

Calavita, K. 1998. Immigration, Law, and Marginalization in a Global Economy: Notes from Spain. *Law and Society Review*, 32(3), 529–66.

Caponio, T. 2005. Policy Networks and Immigrants' Associations in Italy: The Case of Milan, Bologna and Naples. *Journal of Ethnic and Migration Studies*, 31(5), 931–50.

Carrillo, E. and Delgado, L. 1998. *El Entorno, los Instrumentos y la Evolución de la Política de Inmigración en España (1985–1996)*. Madrid: Instituto Universitario Ortega y Gasset.

Casas Álvarez, F-J. 2000. Emigración, Codesarrollo y Cooperación para el Desarollo. Reflexiones desde una Óptica Española. *Migraciones*, 8, 101–26.

Casey, J. 1998. *Non-Government Organizations as Political Actors: The Case of Immigration Policies in Spain: Doctoral Thesis*. Barcelona: Departament de Ciéncia Política i de Dret Públic, Universitat Autónoma de Barcelona.

Castles, S. 1995. How nation-states respond to immigration and ethnic diversity. *New Community*, 21(3), 291–308.

Cheetham, J. 1988. Ethnic Associations in Britain, in *Ethnic Associations and the Welfare State: Services to Immigrants in Five Countries*, edited by S. Jenkins. New York: Columbia University Press, 107–54.

Comisiones Obreras. 2003. Vías de acceso al empleo de los trabajadores extranjeros. *Cuadernos de información sindical*, 46, 30–37.

Cordero-Guzmán, H. 2005. Community-Based Organisations and Migration in New York City. *Journal of Ethnic and Migration Studies*, 31(5), 889–910.

Cornelius, W.A. 1994. Spain: The Uneasy Transition from Labor Exporter to Labor Importer, in *Controlling Immigration. A Global Perspective*, edited by W.A. Cornelius, P.L. Martin and J.F. Hollifield. Stanford: Stanford University Press, 331–69.

Cornelius, W.A. 2004. Spain: The Uneasy Transition from Labor Exporter to Labor Importer, in *Controlling Immigration*, edited by W.A. Cornelius, T. Tsuda, P.L. Martin and J.F. Hollifield. Stanford: Stanford University Press, 389–436.

Danese, G. 2001. Participation beyond citizenship: Migrants' associations in Italy and Spain. *Patterns of Prejudice*, 35(1), 69–89.

De Graaf, H., Penninx, R. and Stoové, E.F. 1988. Miniorities Policies, Social Services, and Ethnic Organizations in the Netherlands. Historical Background, in *Ethnic Associations and the Welfare State: Services to Immigrants in Five Countries*, edited by S. Jenkins. New York: Columbia University Press, 203–39.

De Haas, H. 2006. *Engaging Diasporas. How Governments and Development Agencies Can Support Diaspora Involvement in the Development of Origin Countries. A Study for Oxfam Novib.* Oxford: International Migration Institute. University of Oxford.

Denzin, N.K. and Lincoln, Y.S. 2000. Introduction: The Discipline and Practice of Qualitative Research, in *Handbook of Qualitative Research*, edited by N.K. Denzin. Thousand Oaks, CA: Sage, 1–28.

Devadason, R. 2009. London city report, in *Localmultidem. Deliverable 10: City Reports on the Organisational Survey*, edited by L. Morales, 22–36.

Diehl, C. 2002. *Die Partizipation von Migranten in Deutschland. Rückzug oder Mobilisierung?* Opladen: Leske + Budrich.

Díez Nicolás, J. and Ramírez Latifa, M.J. 2001. *La voz de los inmigrantes.* Madrid: Ministerio de Trabajo y Asuntos Sociales.

Duyvené de Wit, T. and Koopmans, R. 2001. Die politisch-kulturelle Integration ethnischer Minderheiten in den Niederlanden und Deutschland. *Forschungsjournal Neue Soziale Bewegungen*, 14(1), 26–41.

Entzinger, H. 1994. Niederlande, in *Zuwanderungspolitik in Europa. Nationale Politiken - Gemeinsamkeiten und Unterschiede*, edited by H. Heinelt. Opladen: Leske + Budrich, 195–219.

Entzinger, H. 2003. The Rise and Fall of Multiculturalism: The Case of the Netherlands, in *Toward Assimilation and Citizenship: Immigrants in Liberal Nation-States*, edited by C. Joppke and E. Morawska. Basingstoke: Palgrave Macmillan, 59–86.

Ette, A. and Fauser, M. 2005. Die Externalisierung der britischen und spanischen Migrationskontrolle. *Materialien zur Bevölkerungswissenschaft*, 115, 7–27.

European Council. 2004. *Common Basic Principles. Council Document 14615/04 of 19 November 2004.*

Faist, T. 1996. Das ethnische Paradox und die Integration von Immigranten: Zur Bedeutung von sozialen und symbolischen Kapital in vergleichender Perspektive. *Peripherie*, 64(16), 70–95.

Faist, T. 2000. *The Volume and Dynamics of International Migration and Transnational Social Spaces.* Oxford: Oxford University Press.

Faist, T. 2009. Diversity – a new mode of incorporation? in *Ethnic & Racial Studies*, 32(1), 171–90.

Faist, T. and Fauser, M. 2011. The Migration-Development Nexus: Toward a Transnational Perspective, in *The Migration-Development Nexus. A Transnational Perspective*, edited by T. Faist, M. Fauser and P. Kivisto. Basingstoke: Palgrave Macmillan, 1–26.

Fauser, M. 2007. Selective Europeanization: Europe's Impact on Spanish Migration Control, in *The Europeanization of National Policies and Politics of Immigration: Between Autonomy and the European Union*, edited by T. Faist and A. Ette. Basingstoke: Palgrave Macmillan, 136–56.

Fauser, M. 2008. Autoridades locales e integración política en ciudades de nueva inmigración. Los casos de Madrid y Barcelona, in *Los gestores del proceso de inmigración. Actores y redes de actores en España y en Europa*, edited by R. Zapata-Barrero and G. Pinyol. Barcelona: Fundació CIDOB, 131–48.

Fauser, M. 2011. How receiving cities contribute to simultaneous engagements for incorporation and development, in *The Migration-Development Nexus. A Transnational Perspective*, edited by T. Faist, M. Fauser and P. Kivisto. Basingstoke: Palgrave Macmillan, 134–58.

Favell, A. 2001. Integration Policy and Integration Research in Europe: A Review and Critique, in *Citizenship Today: Global Perspectives and Practices*, edited by T.A. Aleinikoff. Washington, DC: Carnegie Endowment for International Peace, 249–399.

FEMP. 1995. *Los municipios y la integración social de los inmigrantes: Análisis y Propuestas de Actuación*. Madrid: Federacion Española de Municipios y Provincias.

Fennema, M. and Tillie, J. 1999. Political participation and political trust in Amsterdam: Civic communities and ethnic networks. *Journal of Ethnic and Migration Studies*, 25(4), 703–26.

Fijalkowski, J. and Gillmeister, H. 1997. *Ausländervereine - ein Forschungsbericht über die Funktion von Eigenorganisation für die Integration von Zuwanderern in eine Aufnahmegesellschaft- am Beispiel Berlin*. Berlin: Hitit Verlag.

Finotelli, C. 2008. Regularisierung illegaler Migranten in Spanien und Italien: Planlose Steuerung oder effektive ex-post Regulierung?, in *Migrations- und Integrationsprozesse in Europa: Vergemeinschaftung oder nationalstaatliche Lösungswege?*, edited by U. Hunger, C.M. Aybek, A. Ette and I. Michalowski. Wiesbaden: VS Verlag für Sozialwissenschaften, 75–100.

Flick, U. 2004. *Triangulation*. Wiesbaden: VS Verlag für Sozialwissenschaften.

Flick, U. 2005. Design und Prozess qualitativer Forschung, in *Qualitative Forschung - Ein Handbuch*, edited by U. Flick, E. von Kardorff and I. Steinke. Reinbeck: rowohlts enzyklopädie, 252–64.

Flick, U., Kardorff, E. von and Steinke, I. 2005. Was ist qualitative Forschung? Einleitung und Überblick, in *Qualitative Forschung - Ein Handbuch*, edited by U. Flick, E. von Kardorff and I. Steinke. Reinbeck: rowohlts enzyklopädie, 13–29.

Fontana, A. and Frey, J.H. 2000. The Interview. From structured questions to negotiated text, in *Handbook of Qualitative Research*, edited by N.K. Denzin. Thousand Oaks, CA: Sage, 645–72.

Freeman, G. 1994. Commentary, in *Controlling Immigration. A Global Perspective*, edited by W. Cornelius, P. Martin and J.F. Hollifield. Stanford: Stanford University Press, 297–303.

Friedmann, J. and Wolff, G. 1982. World city formation: An agenda for research and action. *International Journal of Urban and Regional Research*, 17(6), 309–44.

Garbaye, R. 2000. *Ethnic Minorities, Cities, and Institutions: A Comparison of the Modes of Management of Ethnic Diversity of a French and a British City.* Florence: European University Institute.

García, M. 2006. Citizenship Practices and Urban Governance in European Cities. *Urban Studies*, 43(4), 745–65.

Gerdes, J., Rieple, B. and Faist, T. 2007. We are all "Republican" Now: The Politics of Dual Citizenship in Germany, in *Dual Citizenship in Europe. From Nationhood to Societal Integration*, edited by T. Faist. Aldershot: Ashgate, 45–76.

Gesemann, F. 2001. Einleitung: Migration und Integration in Berlin, in *Migration und Integration in Berlin: Wissenschaftliche Analysen und politische Perspektiven*, edited by F. Gesemann. Opladen: Leske + Budrich, 11–31.

Gil, A. 1998. Proyecto de Integración Participativa de la Población Inmigrante en la Zona Centro de Madrid. *Migraciones*, 3, 195–210.

Giménez Romero, C., Martínez Martínez, J.L., Fernández García, M. and Cortés Maisonave, A. 2006. *El Codesarollo en España. Protagonistas, Discursos y Experiencias.* Madrid: Catarata.

Gitmez, A. and Wilpert, C. 1987. A Micro-Society or an Ethnic Community? Social Organization and Ethnicity amongst Turkish Migrants in Berlin, in *Immigrant Associations in Europe*, edited by J. Rex, D. Joly and C. Wilpert. Aldershot: Gower, 86–126.

Giugni, M. and Passy, F. 2004. Migration Mobilization between political institutions and citizenship regimes: A comparison of France and Switzerland. *European Journal of Political Research*, 43(1), 51–82.

Glaser, B. and Strauss, A. 1967. *The Discovery of Grounded Theory: Strategies for Qualitative Research.* Chicago: Aldine.

Glick Schiller, N. and Çağlar, A.S. 2009. Toward a Comparative Theory of Locality in Migration Studies: Migrant Incorporation and City Scale. *Journal of Ethnic and Migration Studies*, 35(2), 177–202.

Glick Schiller, N., Basch, L. and Blanc-Szanton, C. 1994. *Nations Unbound: Transnational Projects, Postcolonial Predicaments, and Deterritorialized Nation-States.* Amsterdam: Gordon and Breach Publishers.

Goldring, L. 2002. The Mexican State and Transmigrant Organizations: Negotiating the Boundaries of Membership and Participation. *Latin American Research Review*, 37(3), 55–99.

Goldsmith, M. 1992. Local Government. *Urban Studies*, 29(3–4), 393–410.

González-Enríquez, C. 2009. *Country Report Spain. Report of the Research Project Clandestino. Undocumented Migration. Counting the Uncountable. Data and Trends across Europe.*

Gortázar, C. 2002. Spain: Two Immigration Acts at the End of the Millennium. *European Journal of Migration and Law*, 4(1), 1–21.

Green, N.L. 1991. The Comparative Method and Poststructural Structuralism: New Perspectives for Migration Studies, in *Migration, Migration History, History: Old Paradigms and New Perspectives*, edited by J. Lucassen and L. Lucassen. Amsterdam: Peter Lang, 57–72.

Guarnizo, L.E., Portes, A. and Haller, W. 2003. Assimilation and Transnationalism: Determinants of Transnational Political Action among Contemporary Migrants. *American Journal of Sociology*, 108(6), 1211–48.

Guiraudon, V. 1998. Citizenship Rights for Non-Citizens: France, Germany, and the Netherlands, in *Challenge to the Nation-State: Immigration in Western Europe and the United States*, edited by C. Joppke. Oxford: Oxford University Press, 272–318.

Guiraudon, V. and Lahav, G. 2000. A reappraisal of the state sovereignty debate: The case of migration control. *Comparative Political Studies*, 33(2), 163–95.

Hammar, T. 1985. *European Immigration Policy: A Comparative Study.* Cambridge: Cambridge University Press.

Hunger, U. 2002. *Von der Betreuung zur Eigenverantwortung. Neuere Entwicklungstendenzen bei Migrantenvereinen in Deutschland.* Münster: Münsteraner Diskussionspapiere zum Nonprofit-Sektor No. 22, Arbeitsstelle Aktive Bürgerschaft. Universität Münster.

Hunger, U. and Thränhardt, D. 2001. Die Berliner Integrationspolitk im Vergleich der Bundesländer, in *Migration und Integration in Berlin: Wissenschaftliche Analysen und politische Perspektiven*, edited by F. Gesemann. Opladen: Leske + Budrich, 109–27.

International Migration Review. 1985. Introduction. Political and Civil Rights of Immigrants. A Research Agenda. *International Migration Review*, 19(3), 400–414.

Ireland, P.R. 1994. *The Policy Challenge of Ethnic Diversity. Immigrant Politics in France and Switzerland.* Cambridge, MA: Harvard University Press.

Itzigsohn, J. 2000. Immigration and the Boundaries of Citizenship: The Institutions of Immigrants Political Transnationalism. *International Migration Review*, 34(4), 1126–54.

Izquierdo Escribano, A. 1996. *La Inmigración inesperada de la Población Extranjera en España (1991–1995).* Madrid: Editorial Trotta.

Jahn, G. and Sen, F. 1984. Ausländische Selbstorganisationen in der Bundesrepublik Deutschland. *ZAR- Zeitschrift für Ausländerrecht und Ausländerpolitik*, (3), 135–41.

Jenkins, S. (ed.). 1988. *Ethnic Associations and the Welfare State: Services to Immigrants in Five Countries.* New York: Columbia University Press.

King, R. and Black, R. (eds). 1997. *Southern European and the New Immigrations.* Brighton: Sussex Academic Press.

King, R., Lazaridis, G. and Tsardanidēs, C. (eds) 2000. *Eldorado or Fortress? Migration in Southern Europe.* Houndmills and London: Macmillan Press.

Kivisto, P. 2005. Social Spaces, Transnational Immigrant Communities, and the Politics of Incorporation, in *Incorporating Diversity: Rethinking Assimilation in a Multicultural Age*, edited by P. Kivisto. Boulder, CO: Paradigm Publishers, 299–320.

Kivisto, P. 2005. The Revival of Assimilation in Historical Perspective, in *Incorporating Diversity: Rethinking Assimilation in a Multicultural Age*, edited by P. Kivisto. Boulder, CO: Paradigm Publishers, 3–29.

Koff, H. 2006. Does Hospitality Translate into Integration? Subnational Variations of Italian Responses to Immigration, in *Local Citizenship in Recent Countries of Immigration: Japan in Comparative Perspective*, edited by T. Tsuda. Lanham, MD: Lexington Books, 173–203.

Koopmans, R. 2004. Migrant Mobilisation and Political Opportunities: Variation among German Cities and a Comparison with the United Kingdom and the Netherlands. *Journal of Ethnic and Migration Studies*, 30(3), 449–70.

Koopmans, R. and Berger, M. 2004. Bürgerschaft, ethnische Netzwerke und die politische Integration von Türken in Amsterdam und Berlin. *Forschungsjournal Neue Soziale Bewegungen*, 17(1), 70–79.

Koopmans, R. and Statham, P. 1999. Challenging the Liberal Nation-State? Postnationalism, Multiculturalism, and the Collective Claims-Making of Migrants and Ethnic Minorities in Britain and Germany. *The American Journal of Sociology*, 105(3), 652–96.

Koopmans, R. and Statham, P. 2000. Migration and Ethnic Relations as a Field of Political Contention: An Opportunity Structure Approach, in *Challenging Immigration and Ethnic Relations Politics: Comparative European Perspectives*, edited by R. Koopmans and P. Statham. Oxford: Oxford University Press, 13–56.

Koopmans, R. and Statham, P. 2003. How National Citizenship Shapes Transnationalism: Migrant and Minority Claims-making in Germany, Great Britain and the Netherlands, in *Toward Assimilation and Citizenship: Immigrants in Liberal Nation-States*, edited by C. Joppke and E. Morawska. Basingstoke: Palgrave Macmillan, 195–238.

Koopmans, R., Statham, P., Giugni, M. and Passy, F. 2005. *Contested Citizenship. Immigration and Cultural Diversity in Europe*. Minneapolis, MN: University of Minnesota Press.

Kraal, K. 2001. Amsterdam: From group- specific to problem- oriented policy, in *Multicultural Policies and Modes of Citizenship in European Cities*, edited by A. Rogers and J. Tillie. Aldershot: Ashgate, 15–40.

Kreienbrink, A. 2004. *Einwanderungsland Spanien: Migrationspolitik zwischen Europäisierung und nationalen Interessen*. Frankfurt am Main: IKO-Verlag für Interkulturelle Kommunikation.

Kuzel, A.J. 1992. Sampling in Qualitative Inquiry, in *Doing Qualitative Research*, edited by B.F. Crabtree and W.L. Miller. Newbury Park, London, New Delhi: Sage, 31–45.

Lacroix, T. 2010. *Hometown Organisations and Development Practices*. Oxford: IMI Working Paper No. 28. University of Oxford.

Lahav, G. 1998. Immigration and the State: The Devolution and Privatisation of Immigration Control in the EU. *Journal of Ethnic and Migration Studies*, 24(4), 675–94.

Lahav, G. and Guiraudon, V. 2000. Comparative Perspectives on Border Control: Away from the Border and Outside the State, in *The Wall around the West*, edited by P. Andreas and T. Snyder. Lanham, MD: Rowman & Littlefield, 55–80.

Landolt, P. 2008. The Transnational Geographies of Immigrant Politics: Insights from a Comparative Study of Migrant Grassroots Organizing. *The Sociological Quarterly*, 49(1), 53–77.

Laubenthal, B. 2007. *Der Kampf um Legalisierung: Soziale Bewegungen illegaler Migranten in Frankreich, Spanien und der Schweiz*. Frankfurt/New York: Campus Verlag.

Layton-Henry, Z. (ed.). 1990a. *The Political Rights of Migrant Workers in Western Europe*. London: Sage Publications.

Layton-Henry, Z. 1990b. Immigrant Associations, in *The Political Rights of Migrant Workers in Western Europe*, edited by Z. Layton-Henry. London: Sage Publications, 94–112.

Layton-Henry, Z. 1994. Britain: The Would-be Zero-Immigration Country, in *Controlling Immigration. A Global Perspective*, edited by W. Cornelius, P. Martin and J.F. Hollifield. Stanford: Stanford University Press, 273–96.

Layton-Henry, Z. 2004. Britain: From Immigration Control to Migration Management, in *Controlling Immigration*, edited by W.A. Cornelius, T. Tsuda, P.L. Martin and J.F. Hollifield. Stanford: Stanford University Press, 297–342.

Levitt, P. 2001. *The Transnational Villagers*. Berkeley: University of California Press.

Linz, J.J. and Miguel, A. de. 1966. Within-Nation Differences and Comparisons: The Eight Spains, in *Comparing Nations: The Use of Quantitative Data in Cross-national Research*, edited by R.L. Merritt and S. Rokkan. New Haven, CT: Yale University Press, 267–320.

López Sala, A.M. 2005. *Inmigrantes y estados: La respuesta política ante la cuestión migratoria: Tesis Doctoral*. Madrid: Universidad Complutense de Madrid, Facultad de Ciencias Políticas y Sociología.

MacLeod, G. and M. Goodwin. 1999. Space, scale and state strategy: Rethinking urban and regional governance, in *Progress in Human Geography*, 23(4), 503–27.

Mahnig, H. 1998. *Integrationspolitik in Grossbritannien, Frankreich, Deutschland und den Niederlanden: Eine vergleichende Analyse*. Neuchâtel: Schweizerisches Forum für Migrationsstudien.

Mahnig, H. 2004. The politics of minority–majority relations: How immigrant policies developed in Paris, Berlin and Zurich, in *Citizenship in European Cities: Immigrants, Local Politics and Integration Policies*, edited by R. Penninx, K. Kraal, M. Martiniello and S. Vertovec. Aldershot: Ashgate, 17–37.

Marques, M.M. and Santos, R. 2001. Politics, Welfare and the Rise of Immigrant Participation in a Portuguese Suburban Context: Oeiras during the 1990s, in *Multicultural Policies and Modes of Citizenship in European Cities*, edited by A. Rogers and J. Tillie. Aldershot: Ashgate, 143–72.

Marques, M.M. and Santos, R. 2004. Top Down and Bottom Up Reconsidered: The Dynamics of Immigrants' Participation in Local Civil Society, in *Citizenship in European Cities: Immigrants, Local Politics and Integration Policies*, edited by R. Penninx, K. Kraal, M. Martiniello and S. Vertovec. Aldershot: Ashgate, 107–26.

Martín Pérez, A. 2004a. Associations d'immigrés et politiques publiques en Espagne. Revendications, prestations de services et participation politique limitée. *Migrations Société*, 95(16), 15–28.

Martín Pérez, A. 2004b. Las asociaciones de inmigrantes en el debate sobre las nuevas formas de participación política y de ciudadanía: Reflexiones sobre algunas experiencias en España. *Migraciones*, 15, 113–43.

Martin, P.L. 2004. Germany: Managing Migration in the Twenty-First Century, in *Controlling Immigration*, edited by W.A. Cornelius, T. Tsuda, P.L. Martin and J.F. Hollifield. Stanford: Stanford University Press, 221–53.

Martínez Veiga, U. 1999. Immigrants in the Spanish Labour Market, in *Immigrants and the Informal Economy in Southern Europe*, edited by M. Baldwin-Edwards and J. Arango. London: Frank Cass Publishers, 105–28.

Mazzucato, V. and Kabki, M. 2009. Small is beautiful: The micro-politics of transnational relationships between Ghanaian hometown associations and communities back home. *Global Networks*, 9(2), 227–51.

McAdam, D., McCarthy, J.D. and Zald, M.N. (eds). 1996. *Comparative Perspectives on Social Movements: Political Opportunities, Mobilizing Structures, and Cultural Framings.* Cambridge: Cambridge University Press.

McLeod, M., Owen, D. and Khamis, C. 2001. *Black and Minority Ethnic Voluntary and Community Organisations: The Role and Future Development in England and Wales.* York: Joseph Rowntree Foundation.

Meier-Braun, K-H. 1988. *Integration und Rückkehr?: Zur Ausländerpolitik des Bundes und der Länder, insbesondere Baden-Württemberg.* Mainz: Grünewald.

Méndez, M. 2005. Los Derechos Políticos de los Inmigrantes, in *La condición inmigrante: Exploraciones e investigaciones desde la Región de Murcia*, edited by A. Pedreño and M. Hernández. Murcia: Universidad de Murcia, 25–139.

Messina, A.M. 1987. Mediating race relations: British Community Relations Councils revisited. *Ethnic and Racial Studies*, 10(2), 186–202.

Miller, M.J. 1981. *Foreign Workers in Western Europe: An Emerging Political Force.* Portsmouth, NH: Praeger Publishers.

Moore, D. 2001. *Ethnicité et politique de la ville en France et en Grande Bretagne.* Paris: L'Harmattan.

Moore, D. 2004. Migrants as Mediators in a Comparative Perspective, in *Citizenship in European Cities: Immigrants, Local Politics and Integration*

Policies, edited by R. Penninx, K. Kraal, M. Martiniello and S. Vertovec. Aldershot: Ashgate, 127–38.

Morales, L. and Jorba, L. 2010. The transnational links and practices of migrants' organisations in Spain, in *Transnationalism and Diaspora. Concepts, Theories and Methods*, edited by R. Bauböck and T. Faist. Amsterdam: Amsterdam University Press.

Morales, L., González, A. and Sánchez, G. 2004. La integración política de los inmigrantes: Un estudio sobre las asociaciones de immigrantes en Madrid y Múrcia. *Actes del IV Congrés sobre la immigració a Espanya: Ciutadania i Participació, Girona.*

Morawska, E. 2003. Immigrant Transnationalism and Assimilation: A Variety of Combinations and the Analytic Strategy it Suggests, in *Toward Assimilation and Citizenship: Immigrants in Liberal Nation-States*, edited by C. Joppke and E. Morawska. Basingstoke: Palgrave Macmillan, 133–76.

Morell Blanch, A. 2005. El papel de las asociaciones de inmigrantes en la sociedad de acogida: Cuestiones teóricas y evidencia empírica. *Migraciones*, 17, 111–42.

Morén-Alegret, R. 1997. *Template Barcelona: Report According to the Grid for City Templates of MPMC-Project* [Online]. Available at: www.unesco.org/most/p97barc.doc [accessed 17 February 2009].

Morén-Alegret, R. 2001. Tuning the Channels: Local Government Policies and Immigrants' Participation in Barcelona, in *Multicultural Policies and Modes of Citizenship in European Cities*, edited by A. Rogers and J. Tillie. Aldershot: Ashgate, 61–85.

Morén-Alegret, R. 2002a. Gobierno local e inmigración extranjera. Aproximación a los casos de Barcelona y Lisboa durante los años 90. *Migraciones*, 11, 25–81.

Morén-Alegret, R. 2002b. *Integration and Resistance: The Relation of Social Organisations, Global Capital, Governments and International Immigration in Spain and Portugal.* Aldershot: Ashgate.

Moya, J.C. 2005. Immigrants and Associations: A Global and Historical Perspective. *Journal of Ethnic and Migration Studies*, 31(5), 833–64.

Muus, P. 2004. The Netherlands: A pragmatic approach to economic needs and humanitarian considerations, in *Controlling Immigration*, edited by W.A. Cornelius, T. Tsuda, P.L. Martin and J.F. Hollifield. Stanford: Stanford University Press, 263–88.

Nadal, M., Oliveres, R. and Àngel Alegre, M. 2002. *Les actuacions municipals a Catalunya en l'ámbit de la immigració.* Barcelona: Fundació Jaume Bofill.

Navarro Yáñez, C.J. 2001. Límites y contingencia de la democracia asociativa. Gobierno municipal y asociaciones cívicas en Italia y España (1960–1995), in *Ciudadanos y decisiones públicas*, edited by J. Font. Barcelona: Ariel, S.A., 95–110.

Navarro Yáñez, C.J. 2004. Participatory Democracy and Political Opportunism: Municipal Experience in Italy and Spain (1960–93). *International Journal of Urban and Regional Research*, 28(4), 819–38.

Observatorio Madrid. 2005. *El proceso de normalización de trabajadores extranjeros: Impacto en la ciudad de Madrid.* Madrid: Madrid Convive. Observatorio de las Migraciones y de la Convivencia Intercultural de la Ciudad de Madrid.

Ohliger, R. and Raiser, U. 2005. *Integration und Migration in Berlin. Zahlen – Daten – Fakten.* Berlin: Der Beauftragte des Senats von Berlin für Integration und Migration.

Orozco, M. and Lapointe, M. 2004. Mexican Hometown Associations and Development Opportunities. *Journal of International Affairs*, 57(2), 1–21.

Østergaard-Nielsen, E.K. 2011. Codevelopment and citizenship: The nexus between policies on local migrant incorporation and migrant transnational practices in Spain. *Ethnic and Racial Studies*, 34(1), 20–39.

Østergaard-Nielsen, E.K. 2003. *Transnational Politics. Turks and Kurds in Germany.* London: Routledge.

Ouseley, H. 1984. Local authority race initiatives, in *Local Socialism? Labour Councils and New Left Alternatives*, edited by M. Boddy and C. Fudge. Basingstoke: Macmillan Press, 133–59.

Özcan, E. 1989. *Türkische Immigrantenorganisationen in der Bundesrepublik Deutschland.* Berlin (West): Hitit Verlag.

Pacheco Medrano, K. 2003. El Codesarrollo en España: Posibilidades y Desafíos. *Migraciones*, 13, 185–207.

Pájares, M. 2004. *Inmigración irregular en Cataluña: análisis y propuestas.* Barcelona: Centre d'estudis i recera sindicals (Ceres).

Pájares, M. 2006. Las políticas locales en el ámbito de la inmigración, in *Veinte Años de Inmigración en España. Perspectivas Jurídicas y Sociológicas (1985–2004)*, edited by E. Aja and J. Arango. Barcelona: Fundació CIDOB, 369–92.

Park, R.E. 1914. Racial Assimilation in Secondary Groups with Particular Reference to the Negro. *American Journal of Sociology*, 19(5), 606–23.

Park, R.E. 1964. Our Racial Frontier on the Pacific, in *Race and Culture: Essays in the Sociology of Contemporary Man*, edited by R.E. Park. London: The Free Press of Glencoe, 138–51.

Park, R.E. and Burgess, E.W. 1969. [1921] *Introduction to the Science of Sociology.* 3rd Edition. Chicago: University of Chicago Press.

Park, R.E. and Miller, H.A. 1969. [1921] *Old World Traits Transplanted.* New York: Arno Press and the New York Times.

Park, R.E., Burgess, E.W. and McKenzie, R.D. 1968. [1925] *The City.* Chicago: University of Chicago Press.

Patton, M.Q. 2005. *Qualitative Evaluation and Research Methods.* 3rd Edition. Thousand Oaks, CA: Sage.

Penninx, R. and Martiniello, M. 2004. Integration Processes and Policies: State of the Art and Lessons, in *Citizenship in European Cities: Immigrants, Local Politics and Integration Policies*, edited by R. Penninx, K. Kraal, M. Martiniello and S. Vertovec. Aldershot: Ashgate, 139–64.

Penninx, R., Kraal, K., Martiniello, M. and Vertovec, S. (eds). 2004a. *Citizenship in European Cities: Immigrants, Local Politics and Integration Policies.* Aldershot: Ashgate.

Penninx, R., Kraal, K., Martiniello, M. and Vertovec, S. 2004b. Introduction: European Cities and Their New Residents, in *Citizenship in European Cities: Immigrants, Local Politics and Integration Policies*, edited by R. Penninx, K. Kraal, M. Martiniello and S. Vertovec. Aldershot: Ashgate, 1–16.

Penninx, R., Schoorl, J. and van Praag, C. 1993. *The Impact of International Migration on Receiving Countries: The Case of the Netherlands.* Den Haag: Netherlands Interdisciplinary Demographic Institute, NIDI CBGS Publications.

Però, D. 2007. Migrants and the politics of governance. The case of Barcelona. *Social Anthropology*, 15(3), 271–86.

Petronoti, M. 2001. Ethnic Mobilisation in Athens: Steps and Initiatives towards Integration, in *Multicultural Policies and Modes of Citizenship in European Cities*, edited by A. Rogers and J. Tillie. Aldershot: Ashgate, 41–60.

Portes, A. 1999. Conclusion: Towards a new world – the origins and effects of transnational activities. *Ethnic and Racial Studies*, 22(2), 463–74.

Portes, A. 2000. Immigration and the Metropolis: Reflections on Urban History. *Journal of International Migration and Integration*, 2(1), 153–75.

Portes, A. 2001. Introduction: The debates and significance of immigrant transnationalism. *Global Networks*, 1(3), 181–93.

Portes, A. and Böröcz, J. 1989. Contemporary Immigration. Theoretical Perspectives on its Determinants and Modes of Incorporation. *International Migration Review*, 23(3), 606–30.

Portes, A., Escobar, C. and Arana, R. 2008. Bridging the gap: Transnational and ethnic organizations in the political incorporation of immigrants in the United States. *Ethnic and Racial Studies*, 31(6), 1025–55.

Portes, A., Escobar, C. and Walton Radford, A. 2007. Immigrant Transnational Organizations and Development: A Comparative Study. *International Migration Review*, 41(1), 242–81.

Pries, L. and Sezgin, Z. (eds). 2010. *Jenseits von 'Identität oder Integration' - Grenzen überspannende Migrantenorganisationen.* Wiesbaden: VS Verlag für Sozialwissenschaften.

Pumares Fernández, P., Fernández Prados, J.S., Rojas, A.J. and Asensio Hita, À. 2001. La gestión de los flujos inmigratorios y su influencia en el sistema productivo, in *El Ejido: la ciudad - Cortijo: Claves socioeconómicaos del conflicto étnico*, edited by F. Checa. Barcelona: Icaria editorial, 99–125.

Pumares, P. 2003. L'immigration subsaharienne et la politique migratoire de l'Espagne. *Cahier de Migrations Internationales*, 54, 52–94.

Puskeppeleit, J. and Thränhardt, D. 1990. *Vom betreuten Ausländer zum gleichberechtigten Bürger: Perspektiven der Beratung und Sozialarbeit, der Selbsthilfe und Artikulation und der Organisation und Integration der eingewanderten Ausländer aus den Anwerbestaaten in der Bundesrepublik Deutschland.* Freiburg i.B.: Lambertus-Verlag.

Ramos, J.A., Bazaga, I., Delgado, L. and del Pino, E. 1998. *La política para la integración social de los inmigrantes: Una perspectiva intergubernamental.* Madrid: Fundación Ortega y Gasset.

Rath, J. 2009. The Netherlands: A reluctant country of immigration. *Tijdschrift voor Economische en Sociale Geografie*, 100(5), 674–81.

Räthzel, N. 1994. Vereinigtes Königreich, in *Zuwanderungspolitik in Europa. Nationale Politiken - Gemeinsamkeiten und Unterschiede*, edited by H. Heinelt. Opladen: Leske + Budrich, 220–54.

Registro Nacional de Asociaciones. 2008.

Rex, J. 1987. Introduction: The Scope of a Comparative Study, in *Immigrant Associations in Europe*, edited by J. Rex, D. Joly and C. Wilpert. Aldershot: Gower, 1–10.

Rex, J. and Josephides, S. 1987. Asian and Greek Cypriot Associations and Identity, in *Immigrant Associations in Europe*, edited by J. Rex, D. Joly and C. Wilpert. Aldershot: Gower, 11–41.

Rex, J. and Samad, Y. 1996. Multiculturalism and Political Integration in Birmingham and Bradford. *International Migration Review*, 9(1), 11–31.

Rex, J., Joly, D. and Wilpert, C. (eds). 1987. *Immigrant Associations in Europe.* Aldershot: Gower.

Reyneri, E. 2001. *Migrants' Involvement in Irregular Employment in the Mediterranean Countries of the European Union.* Geneva: International Migration Papers. International Labour Organization (ILO), (41).

Rodríguez Cabrero, G. 2003. Protección social de los inmigrantes extranjeros, in *Inmigración: Mercado de trabajo y protección social en España*, edited by A. Izquierdo Escribano. Madrid: CES, 249–99.

Rodríguez Cabrero, G. and Codorniú, J.M. 1997. *Las Entidades Voluntarias en España. Institucionalización, estructura económica y desarollo asociativo.* 2nd Edition. Madrid: Ministerio de Trabajo y Asuntos Sociales.

Rodríguez i Villaescusa, E. 2003. La inmigración: Contexto general y población en Barcelona y su región metropolitana, in *Inmigración y política urbana en la Región Metropolitana de Barcelona*, edited by E. Rodríguez i Villaescusa. Barcelona: Fundació Carles Pi i Sunyer, 49–64.

Rogers, A. and Tillie, J. (eds). 2001. *Multicultural Policies and Modes of Citizenship in European Cities.* Aldershot: Ashgate.

Rubio-Marin, R. 2006. The evolution of nationality law in Spain 2006, in *Acquisition and Loss of Nationality: Policies and Trends in 15 European States*, edited by R. Bauböck, K. Groenendijk, E. Ersboll and H. Waldrauch. Amsterdam: Amsterdam University Press.

Ruiz Jiménez, L. 2006. *Información Coordinada. Cooperación Efectiva. Un proyecto Informativo sobre la Cooperación de España y Portugal con América Latina.* Madrid.

Ruiz, I. 2003. *Estratègies Associatives dels Col.lectius Marroquins a Barcelona: Informe de recera.* Barcelona: Centre d'Estudis Africans de Barcelona.

Santolaya, P. 2006. Los inmigrantes en situación irregular: Derechos, expulsión y regularización (1990–2004), in *Veinte Años de Inmigración en España. Perspectivas Jurídicas y Sociológicas (1985–2004)*, edited by E. Aja and J. Arango. Barcelona: Fundació CIDOB, 129–41.

Sarasa, S. and Guiu, J. 2001. El Consejo Municipal de Bienestar Social de Barcelona, in *Ciudadanos y decisiones públicas*, edited by J. Font. Barcelona: Ariel, S.A., 125–37.

Sassen, S. 1991. *The Global City: New York, London, Tokyo*. Princeton, NJ: Princeton University Press.

Schöneberg, U. 1985. Participation in Ethnic Associations: The Case of Immigrants in West Germany. *International Migration Review*, 19(3), 416–37.

Schönwälder, K. 2001. *Einwanderung und ethnische Pluralität: Politische Entscheidungen und öffentliche Debatten in Grossbritannien und der Bundesrepublik von den 1950er bis zu den 1970er Jahren*. Essen: Klartext-Verlag.

Schrover, M. and Vermeulen, F. 2005a. Special Issue on Immigrant Organisations. *Journal of Ethnic and Migration Studies*, 31(5).

Schrover, M. and Vermeulen, F. 2005b. Immigrant Organisations. *Journal of Ethnic and Migration Studies*, 31(5), 823–32.

Schwarz, T. 1992. *Zuwanderer im Netz des Wohlfahrtsstaats: Türkische Jugendliche und die Berliner Kommunalpolitik*. Berlin: Edition Parabolis.

Schwarz, T. 2001. Integrationspolitik als Beauftragtenpolitik: Die Ausländerbeauftragte des Berliner Senats, in *Migration und Integration in Berlin: Wissenschaftliche Analysen und politische Perspektiven*, edited by F. Gesemann. Opladen: Leske + Budrich, 127–45.

Seifert, W. 2000. *Geschlossene Grenzen - offene Gesellschaften? Migrations- und Integrationsprozesse in westlichen Industrienationen*. Frankfurt am Main: Campus.

Sezgin, Z. 2010. Türkische Migrantenorganisationen in Deutschland - Zwischen Mitgliederinteressen und institutioneller Umwelt, in *Jenseits von 'Identität oder Integration' - Grenzen überspannende Migrantenorganisationen*, edited by L. Pries and Z. Sezgin. Wiesbaden: VS Verlag für Sozialwissenschaften, 201–32.

Silvermann, D. 2001. *Interpreting Qualitative Data – Methods for Analysing Talk, Text and Interaction*. 2nd Edition. London, Thousand Oaks, CA and New Delhi: Sage.

Simmel, G. 1995. [1903] Die Großstädte und das Geistesleben, in *Gesamtausgabe: Aufsätze und Abhandlungen 1901–1908*, edited by R. Kramme, A. Rammstedt and O. Rammstedt. Frankfurt am Main: Suhrkamp, 116–31.

Smith, G. and Stephenson, S. 2003. *The Theory and Practice of Group Representation: Reflections on the Politics of Race Equality in Birmingham*. Edinburgh: Paper presented at ECPR joint sessions.

Smith, M.P. 2001. *Transnational Urbanism – Locating Globalisation*. Malden and Oxford: Blackwell Publisher.

Smith, M.P. 2003. Transnationalism, the State, and the Extraterritorial Citizen. *Politics and Society*, 31(4), 467–502.

Smith, M.P. 2007. The two faces of transnational citizenship. *Ethnic and Racial Studies*, 30(6), 1096–116.

Smith, M.P. and Bakker, M. 2005. The transnational politics of the Tomato King: Meaning and impact. *Global Networks*, 5(2), 129–46.

Smith, M.P. and Guarnizo, L.E. (eds). 1999. *Transnationalism from Below*. New Brunswick, NJ: Transaction Publishers.

Solé, C. 1997. La irregularidad laboral de la inmigración extracomunitaria. *Migraciones*, 1, 7–40.

Solomos, J. 2003. *Race and Racism in Britain*. Basingstoke: Palgrave Macmillan.

Soysal, Y.N. 1994. *Limits of Citizenship. Migrants and Postnational Membership in Europe*. Chicago, IL: University of Chicago Press.

Strauss, A. and Corbin, J. 1996. *Grundlagen Qualitativer Sozialforschung*. Weinheim: Beltz Psychologischer Verlag Union.

Strübing, J. 2008. *Grounded Theory - Zur sozialtheoretischen und epistemologischen Fundierung des Verfahrens der empirisch begründeten Theoriebildung*. 2nd Edition. Wiesbaden: VS Verlag für Sozialwissenschaften.

Synder, R. 2001. Scaling Down: The Subnational Comparative Method. *Studies in Comparative International Development*, 36(1), 93–110.

Tarrow, S. 1996. States and opportunities: The political structuring of social movements, in *Comparative Perspectives on Social Movements: Political Opportunities, Mobilizing Structures, and Cultural Framings*, edited by D. McAdam, J.D. McCarthy and M.N. Zald. Cambridge: Cambridge University Press, 41–61.

Thornton, P. and Hext, S. 2009. *Review of DFID's Work to Build Support for Development through Work with Businesses, Trades Unions, Faith Communities, Black and Minority Ethnic Communities, and Diaspora Groups: Final Report*. Verulam Associates Ltd.

Thränhardt, D. 1995. Germany: An undeclared immigration country. *New Community*, 21(1), 19–36.

Thränhardt, D. 1999. Germany's Immigration Policies and Politics, in *Mechanisms of Immigration Control: A Comparative Analysis of European Regulation Policies*, edited by G. Brochmann and T. Hammar. Oxford and New York: Berg, 29–57.

Thränhardt, D. 2008. *Einbürgerung. Rahmenbedingungen, Motive und Perspektiven des Erwerbs der deutschen Staatsangehörigkeit. Friedrich Ebert Stiftung: Gutachten für die Friedrich-Ebert-Stiftung*. Bonn.

Thränhardt, D. and Dieregsweiler, R. 1999. Bestandsaufnahme der Potentiale und Strukturen von Selbstorganisationen von Migrantinnen und Migranten mit Ausnahme der Selbstorganisationen türkischer, kurdischer, bosnischer und maghrebinischer Herkunft in Nordrhein-Westfalen, in *Ministerium für Arbeit, Soziales und Stadtentwicklung Kultur und Sport des Landes Nordrhein-Westfalen (Hg.) – Selbstorganistionen von Migrantinnen und Migranten*, 11–74.

Tsuda, T. (ed.). 2006. *Local Citizenship in Recent Countries of Immigration: Japan in Comparative Perspective.* Lanham, MD: Lexington Books.

Tsuda, T. 2006. Localities and the Struggle for Immigrant Rights: The Significance of Local Citizenship in Recent Countries of Immigration, in *Local Citizenship in Recent Countries of Immigration: Japan in Comparative Perspective*, edited by T. Tsuda. Lanham: Lexington Books, 3–36.

Uitermark, J., Rossi, U. and Van Houtum, H. 2005. Reinventing multiculturalism: Urban citizenship and the negotiation of ethnic diversity in Amsterdam. *International Journal of Urban and Regional Research*, 29(3), 622–40.

Van Amersfoort, H. 1999. Migration control and minority policy: The case of the Netherlands, in *Mechanisms of Immigration Control: A Comparative Analysis of European Regulation Policies*, edited by G. Brochmann and T. Hammar. Oxford and New York: Berg, 135–68.

Van Amersfoort, H. and van Heelsum, A. 2007. Moroccan Berber immigrants in the Netherlands, their associations and transnational ties: A quest for identity and recognition. *Immigrants and Minorities*, 25(3), 234–62.

Veredas Muñoz, S. 1998. *Las asociaciones de inmigrantes marroquíes y peruanos en la Comunidad de Madrid: Tesis Doctoral.* Madrid: Universidad Complutense de Madrid.

Veredas Muñoz, S. 2001. Spain, in *Voices of Change: European Minority Organisations in Civil Dialogue*, edited by A. Rudiger. Berlin: Regionale Arbeitsstelle für Ausländerfragen, Jugendarbeit und Schule, 15–24.

Veredas Muñoz, S. 2003. Las asociaciones de inmigrantes en España. Práctica clientar y cooptación política. *Revista Internacional de Sociología*, 36, 207–25.

Vermeulen, F. 2005. Organisational Patterns: Surinamese and Turkish Associations in Amsterdam, 1960–1990. *Journal of Ethnic and Migration Studies*, 31(5), 951–73.

Vermeulen, F. 2006. *The Immigrant Organising Process. The Emergence and persistence of Turkish Immigrant Organisations in Amsterdam and Berlin and Surinamese Organisations in Amsterdam, 1960–2000.* Amsterdam: Amsterdam University Press.

Vertovec, S. 1996a. Berlin Multikulti: Germany, 'foreigners' and 'world-openness'. *New Community*, 22(3), 381–99.

Vertovec, S. 1996b. Multiculturalism, culturalism and public incorporation. *Ethnic and Racial Studies*, 19(1), 49–69.

Vertovec, S. 2006. *The Emergence of Super-Diversity in Britain.* Oxford: Compas Working Paper No. 25. University of Oxford.

Vogel, D. 2003. Illegaler Aufenthalt: Konzepte, Forschungszugänge, Realitäten, Optionen, in *Migration im Spannungsfeld von Globalisierung und Nationalstaat*, edited by D. Thränhardt and U. Hunger: Leviathan Sonderheft 22, 161–79.

Waldrauch, H. and Sohler, K. 2004. *Migrantenorganisationen in der Großstadt. Entstehung, Strukturen und Aktivitäten am Beispiel Wien.* Frankfurt and New York: Campus Verlag.

Waldrauch, H. *Electoral Rights for Foreign Nationals: A Comparative Overview of Regulations in 36 Countries: National Europe Centre Paper No. 73.* Canberra: Australian National University.

Walliser, A. 2001. Decentralization and Urban Governance in Barcelona, in *Governing European Cities – Social Fragmentation, Social Exclusion and Urban Governance*, edited by H.T. Andersen and R. Van Kempen. Aldershot: Ashgate, 297–320.

Warner, W.L. and Srole, L. 1947. *The Social Systems of American Ethnic Groups.* New Haven: Yale University Press.

Wimmer, A. and Glick Schiller, N. 2002. Methodological nationalism and beyond: Nation-state building, migration and the social sciences. *Global Networks*, 2(4), 301–34.

Young, K. and Connelly, N. 1981. *Policy and Practice in the Multi-racial City.* London: Policy Studies Institute PSI.

Yurdakul, G. 2006. State, political parties and immigrant elites: Turkish immigrant associations in Berlin. *Journal of Ethnic and Migration Studies*, 32(3), 435–53.

Zapata-Barrero, R. 2002. *El turno de los inmigrantes. Esferas de justicia y políticas de acomodación.* Madrid: Instituto de Migraciones y Servicios Sociales (IMSERSO).

Zapata-Barrero, R. 2004. *Inmigración, innovación política y cultura de acomodación en España: Un análisis comparativo entre Andalucía, Cataluña, la comunidad de Madrid y el gobierno central.* Barcelona: Fundació CIDOB.

Zapata-Barrero, R., Adamuz García, C. and Martínez Luna, I. 2002. Estructuras institucionales y redes de actores en las políticas de acomodación de los inmigrantes en España: Cultura de acomodación y cambio estructural, in *La inmigración en España: Contextos y alternativas*, edited by M.L. García Castaño. Granada, 83–110.

Index

RESEARCH IN MIGRATION AND ETHNIC RELATIONS SERIES

Full series list

9 781138 268524